Welcome
to the
Hotel California

Leroy F. Bennett

PAGE PUBLISHING, INC.
New York, NY

First originally published by Page Publishing, Inc. 2017

ISBN 978-1-64082-299-3 (Paperback)
ISBN 978-1-64082-888-9 (Hard Cover)
ISBN 978-1-64082-300-6 (Digital)

Printed in the United States of America

DEDICATION

I want to take the time to thank my family and friends who supported my Go Fund Me campaign efforts in producing this book. I want to dedicate this book to the only young lady who loves me unconditionally, from the moment she first laid her eyes on me until this very day. While my mother was the absolute first woman, my granddaughter Shay'lee Prophet loves me unconditionally and I would like to present her with special dedication. Shay'lee, I remembered the first day that your mom bought you over to the house. I asked her if I could hold you, she agreed and even insisted. I never experienced picking up a child without them crying until I picked you up. In your own simple infantile way you were telling me than that if I picked you up, that we were stuck together for the rest of our lives. That was a little more than a week after you were born. You and I experienced your first Christmas, and your first mani/pedi together. When I shared with you that I was homeless when you were 12 years old, you've taken it upon yourself to volunteer to help others homeless people in your community. I know that you've done this because you were thinking of me. May you continue to keep the compassionate character and spirit that has been instilled in you by your parents, grandparents and family. May you also continue to be a vessel in giving of yourself to other those who are less fortunate than you. I love you and God bless you.

MR. WENDELL
by TW Santoro

No one ever knew his name/ 'Cause he's a no one/ Never thought twice 'bout spendin' on an old bum/ Till I had the chance to really get to know one.

—Arrested Development, 1992

How do they get there? Why sleep under the overpass? How do they ever stay warm and survive? Aren't there shelters they can go to? Why don't they just get a job?

Obvious questions, but not so obvious answers. It's something I've seen first-hand growing up and personally, but not for the reasons you might think. As a kid, I always had a pillow to lay my head on at night, which was always warm in the winter, cool in the summer. My parents always had plenty of food and water provided for my siblings and me. My parents never once used alcohol or drugs. Two of the three of us kids graduated from private high school and attended a private university. I was provided for and given every "head start" in the book for what "they say" is needed for kids to grow up into successful adults.

But I am an exception. I attended and graduated public high school and attended a state university. I have always been the odd duck in the family. Unlike every family member I have, I'm the only one who's homeless. And the perception of most people is that the homeless are all uneducated dropouts who have alcohol or drug addiction issues. Sure, those problems do contribute to the chronic homelessness many of us face. But the reality is that you can't paint that broad of a brush stroke.

My homelessness problems began when I lost my son to suicide. I have written before that he was "too little to see the big picture" and that he "didn't see how his suicide would paralyze me even to this day." Everyone has a story, and everyone is fighting different battles we have no understanding of. And for me to be able to get out from my current situation and into a better place, many things have to happen.

You'd think that all it takes to not be considered homeless is to have a place to sleep, bathe, and eat. First, though, you've got to find employment somewhere and have money coming in. Then, you need someone willing to rent or lease to you. How many lease or job applications have you seen that haven't wanted either your last three residences and your last three job references, which many of us do not have? And maybe employers are reluctant to hire those either on the streets or those fortunate enough to be in shelters because people don't want to spend time and resources in hiring and training us for the job when we could very possibly be here one day and gone the next.

I know several guys who have chosen to live life "outside." I have repeatedly tried yet consistently failed to convince one friend of mine to come back to the shelter. He said he prefers it this way. He was tired of all the rules, the people, the mandatory chapels, and an early curfew, or not having a later curfew.

You name it as far as excuses go. And when I talk to him, alcohol's on the breath between us. He doesn't see it. He doesn't get it. I've told him, "Here you have everything you need: shelter from the elements, food, showers to use at any time and free soap, free laundry facilities and detergent. Here you'll never be hungry, never be in fear of being jumped on, beaten up, or robbed of the valuables you have."

He sees his life outside as freedom and has deluded himself that he is, in a convoluted way, free. Whether it's a mixture of chemicals or just hopelessness, he's given up on being anything greater in his life. It's too deep a hole for him to climb out of.

They say that in order for someone to love and care for you, you must first love and care for yourself. That, sadly, is the mindset of those least affected by homelessness. Why should I donate, help out, or volunteer if they won't even help themselves become independent and reputable members of society? Well, I hope the following pages will give you some insight into the world of the homeless population, the struggles, temptations, and mindset that some of us have. And I trust your heart will be warmed, enlightened, and motivated to help.

Very truly yours,
TW Santoro

CONTENTS

CHAPTER I

An Unknown Frontier

In February 2010, I was living in the middle of the great recession. This came about because of the biggest bank collapse since the Great Depression. It is only the second year of the Obama administration, and my mother, who was alive then, never thought that she would see the day when an African American would be elected to the highest office in the nation. Her health was getting progressively worse before she was to leave to have back surgery. She was suffering with vertigo and wasn't able to drive her car over the past several months. Mom had six children from her first husband, which included five boys and a girl, and a stepdaughter and stepson from her current marriage. This woman had countless number of back surgeries since 1972 that included having four disc removed from her back after a fall down the stairs when they collapsed off a portable trailer used for a classroom when she was teaching summer school.

Doctors had told her that she was going to need to have this surgery or risk the chance of losing her ability to walk again. Mom didn't want to do it again after having nine surgeries on her back, rotator cuff, and both knees replaced. She was very adamant about going under the knife again. She told me, "Leroy, I really don't want to have this surgery, and I don't think I'm going to do it." I told her that if she didn't want to do it, then she shouldn't. I didn't care if I had to work eight jobs. If she needed a mobile chair, then I'd do that, but she shouldn't do it if she wasn't comfortable about it. She replied, "I'm not going to get in that thing, but I just want this pain to end."

Just a couple of days before she was to go into the hospital, my sister came to visit and care for her. She made all her favorite dishes, cleaned for her, and talk to her closest confidant as they always have been as adults. The day before she went in, my sister rented some movies for her to view. The last movies that she viewed were *The Blind Side* and *Precious*. The next day was going to be Mom's last time leaving her home. She went to the hospital to have the procedure to alleviate the pain she had in her back, but it was still there. The procedure that normally would've taken a day had a longer-than-expected recovery time.

This poor woman had to feel like a human pincushion by being poked, prodded, and sliced open from 1973 to 2010. Mom had the surgery earlier that day. I came to the hospital after work when all the family members were gone to their houses. After the doctor gave Mom a sedative so that she could rest comfortably, I entered into her hospital room and sat in the recliner that was in her room. I was in there for about two hours just sitting there in the dark with no lights, radio, or television on. Almost two hours later, she woke up and asked me why was I there after hours. I told her that I spoke with the nurses and I wasn't going to go until I knew that she was all right. I wanted Mom to see that I was there, because I was working a lot of long hours for my job. She told me to go home and that she would see me the next day.

When the next evening came around, I returned to the hospital where my younger brother stayed with her. Mom was talking about me coming in the other night. She told us that she had a dream that she saw her father whom all his grandchildren affectionately called Pop. He had driven by in his Buick to pick her up. She said that Pop asked her, "Dorothy, are ready to come home?" She answered, "Yeah, but we're going to have to leave Leroy, because he's not ready to come yet." I had a feeling that after she made a joke about seeing Pop, the family and I didn't have much time left to be with Mom. Mom went into the hospital to have the surgical procedure on February 22 and still wasn't feeling much better than the time that she went in.

I delayed staying with her for the night as long as I could, until Mom requested me to stay for the evening of the second of March, which was ironically her first mother in-law's birthday. I came to stay with her that evening after I got off work and left the gym from my workout. When I arrived to her room, I had a sandwich from Subway that I picked up along the way there. When I arrived, my stepfather was there waiting on me before I came. I had a change of clothes in my car, because the gym that I was working out in was located at my job. My stepdad was saying his good night to her in an apologetic way, but he told her that he loved her. As he was leaving, he told me if anything in her condition changed to let him know.

Now it was just she and I in the room together overnight. She told me that the doctors said that her condition was improving and that they were going to move her out from intensive care to a normal bed the next day. That was great news, and I told her that I was going to forego working overtime to come and see her early for the next day. We were watching one of her favorite shows that I can remember from the days of my childhood. *Jeopardy* was on and she used to be a pretty sharp sofa-playing contestant. Now I was having a pretty good evening of getting the correct answers. She told me that I was good and that I should try to audition as a contestant. I was flattered that she thought enough of me to encourage me to do that. As the program proceeded, Mom fell asleep, and I hoped that she was resting comfortably. I stayed with her until six that following morning, and in true maternal fashion, she woke up at five thirty to make sure that I wouldn't be late for work. I gave her a kiss on her forehead and told her I loved her. I reminded her that I'll be back in the evening to check on her.

The following evening I stopped in to see her, but all chaos broke out. When they moved her to a new room, she wasn't happy because the room was small and didn't have an outdoor view. The window only showed a wall with a fire escape. Then the complications from the surgery happened, and the orderlies moved Mom back into intensive care. She was very hot, and we had the hospital staff set the room temperature to a cool setting. She told me to take off my hat to fan her, and I did. The doctors and his staff came in to give her a treatment to make her feel better. Once that happened and she was comfortable, my oldest brother did their part to stay with her overnight. I told her that I was going to stay too, but she told me to go home so that I could get ready for work. I told her no, but she said, "Leroy, put on your hat that you look good in and I'll be all right." I told my brother who I share an apartment with, "If there's any change in Mom's condition, call me and I'll be there." When I went home I sat on the sofa for a minute before I dropped to my knees. I had a little talk with God, and I told him that I've always asked him if it was his will to give me another year with my mother. I told him if it was his will to take her home to be with him, then please take her. I didn't want her to suffer any longer. I got the call late that evening, and I went to the hospital. By the following afternoon, God had granted me my request to stop her suffering and took Mom home to be with Pop, Nanna, and him.

At the time of my mother's death, I was staying in a two-bedroom apartment in Columbia, South Carolina, with my oldest brother. With the both of us working in 2009–2010, we both were just barely able to support ourselves in a nice apartment. When Mommy died, the family agreed to let my stepfather have the house and some of the possessions that my mom had acquired over the years. My brother decided to move out of the apartment to start over in Charlotte. That was going to leave me to support myself in the apartment with the circumstances that I was confronted with. My cousin, who I practically grew up with as a child, had offered me an opportunity to put my past life in Columbia behind me and to start a new one in Salisbury, North Carolina.

Mom was gone, and the only thing that I had going for me was a job and the love of my granddaughter to keep me there. After two months of my cousin and her husband persuading me to move to Salisbury, I checked with my employer to see if there was any way that I could transfer my position to the Charlotte area. Originally, my job told me that it was possible for me to work from home as long as my residence was less than thirty-five miles from the office. It was but a couple of weeks before I was scheduled to leave when they retracted that offer and told me no. I informed my cousin and her spouse what transpired and that I didn't know how long it would take me to get a job. They assured me that everything would work out and to come on.

Nine months after moving to Salisbury, I hadn't secured a job. In that process, I had lost my car along with my driving privileges, because I was driving without insurance. Shortly thereafter, I was asked to leave their residence. Looking back, my mother would always say that hindsight is always 20/20 vision. With that being said, I found myself having to move into the local shelter. The only place for me to go was just off the main strip in downtown Salisbury. I found myself at the Rowan Helping Ministries. There, I was able to get a place where I got a cot for the evening, got a hot breakfast in the morning, and got a meal at night. I found myself at a point in my life where I never would've pictured myself. Here I was a college graduate with a degree in child and family Development, graduated at the top third of my class and unable to secure a job. I was going to use this time to try to reinvent myself.

While living at the shelter, I knew that I had to find a way to get out and become that person I knew that I wanted to be. My downfall in moving to Salisbury was the fact that the support network that I thought I had wasn't there. I found myself turning to the foundation that was instilled in me by my parents. I would have to rely on my faith that God will get me through this storm. As a child, I was too ignorant to think that my parents and family was well off. Both of my parents were teachers when I was growing up on 35 Eaton Place in East Orange, New Jersey. Every Saturday evening, we would have to take our baths after dinner, get our Sunday's best out so that Mom would press them out for church. All the children would have to shine their shoes that evening so that we would look immaculately dressed for service the next morning. After Sunday morning breakfast, we would all be getting dressed. Dad would play records on the stereo while we were prepping for service. He would normally play a mix of gospel music by Mahalia Jackson, the Gospel Clefs, and throw in some jazz to the mix as well with the music of Horace Silver, Donald Byrd, and John Coltrane. I realized soon after being checked into the shelter that those memories would be that—a very distant memory.

As the late Leo Gorcey used to say when he wanted to signal the Bowery Boys that there was trouble ahead, "School's out." I was going to have to do this on my own or have to rely on my cunning wit and whatever resources that I had. I'd checked myself and things into the shelter, and at that time, I knew it was time for me to grow up. I would be living by someone else's rules. I met with the person who would be my caseworker, David Holston. He explained to me what was expected of me when I was admitted as a guest of the shelter. I was expected to abide by the rules that the administration had set for the residents of the shelter. I needed to check myself in by nine o'clock, do a chore when my name fell into the rotation, no profanity or disrespecting the aides or the volunteers who worked at the shelter, and no violence. I was also subject to blowing into a breath detector for alcohol consumption and have to take random drug test. That was the easy part. I hadn't used any drugs since the week that I buried my mother when I smoked a joint of weed.

Going into the shelter you would realize that you have reached the lowest depth of the social ladder, besides being classified as an ex-convict. Once a month, on the first Thursday, the administration would conduct a shelter meeting conducted by Rodney, the shelter director. This was his opportunity to let the residents know if there were going to be any changes to the rules and regulations of the shelter. This would happen at 9:00 p. m. after dinner was served. The discussion would center on several different things, normally the conduct of the shelter guests. Rodney would remind people that we needed to check into the shelter by 9:30 p. m. or we wouldn't be allowed to stay in for the evening. If there was an emergency that caused for us to come in after that time, we should call our case manager to notify them of the emergency. Space in the shelter was at a premium. If you had to compare it to something, it would be like that of the real estate value in midtown Manhattan. If you resided there for a spell, guest would receive a cubby hole where the staff would leave you a towel and a set of pajamas to get when you arrived there in the evenings. Residents were asked to keep one large heavy-duty trash bag on top of the cot that they were assigned and given a storage bin to put their personal items in, which was stored in the closet. People were extremely territorial when it came down to the space in the closet. You would see fights over someone putting their things on top of another person's stuff that was in the closet. Shelter aides, caseworker, and the shelter director would have to go in there once or twice a month to clean out the stuff that may have been left by a previous guest who may have moved out and left their belongings there.

Guests are required to take a shower when they arrived for the evening before eating dinner. Guests would go to the window by the laundry room to get a laundry bag, soap, shampoo, washcloth, toothbrush, toothpaste, and shower shoes if they had any left. Personally, I preferred to take a shower in the morning before I went out to meet the world, but it wasn't a big deal to me. I was easy to adapt to taking my shower at night, because some of the people who came in had worked at jobs that was hard back-breaking labor. The odor that some of the people who were working those jobs permeated strongly. I was happy to oblige to this rule. When you came out of the shower, guest would go to the window of the laundry room to give them your laundry. Guest would enter the facility at 6:00 p. m. and would have to get this done before they served dinner at 7:00 p. m. Anyone coming in after that would also have to shower before eating and do this before the shelter volunteers stop serving at 8:30 p. m.

The meals were served and prepared by the volunteers from various churches, civic, and other non-profit organizations. Some of the meals that were served were pretty good, but when they were prepared them, they didn't consider the fact that there were some people who needed to be aware of their own dietary needs. I couldn't put a number to it, but there were quite a few residents who were diabetic and another high percentage of the people there who suffer with hypertension. I had to be cognizant of what I was eating. I had to remember that this was the south, and the pork was king when it came down to the kind of meat that was mostly consumed by the people. I hadn't added pork into my diet since 1994. I chose not to do it because of personal and not religious reasons. One of the first things that people think of when you tell them that you don't eat pork is that you're doing it because of religious reasons. Jews, Muslims, Rastafarians, and other religious groups don't eat it because their doctrines dictate that they're not supposed to. I chose not to because, when I was younger, my blood pressure was elevated, and I didn't want to take the chance of being put on blood pressure medication like my younger brother who was on it before he was thirty. I also chose not to eat a lot of the canned vegetables too. Some of the canned veggies have a high-sodium content that the manufacturer used to preserve the food. I am cognizant of that, because of the fact that diabetes and high blood pressure run in my family. Recently there is now three generations of diabetes from my father's parents, my father, and just in 2012, my oldest brother. I noticed that living on the diet of the shelter, it would be very easy for me to contract diabetes. If you were a guest, this was what a dinner would look like: fried chicken, rice with gravy, macaroni and cheese, bread and canned vegetables, normally corn and green beans, with cake or pie for dessert. Corn, rice, macaroni, and bread are all starches, and starches turn into sugar that is the cause of diabetes. The cakes and pies are all loaded with sugar from the jump. So trying to eat well is just as important to me as trying to land a good job that will allow me to get out of the shelter. When I noticed that my pants were starting to fit tighter than they did before, that's when I took my diet seriously. I went from 185 to 210 pounds in less than six months.

Entering into the shelter I saw that it was like another world, far from what I was accustomed to. I was enlightened about the policy by one of the residents. Joe was one of the people who's been in the shelter for an extended time to the point that he'd moved most of his personal possessions in and had taken up the majority of the space in the storage closet. Joe was an artist, and a damn good one at that. He would have a hustle when there was a merchant festival that would take place on the first Friday downtown. He would be out there in the evening with his pencils and pad doing sketches of people and getting paid from the people who wanted him to draw them. Joe was the person who people often mistaken me for, because we were both tall with thin build and wore wire-framed glasses. The difference between he and I was that he had a close fade haircut and I wore my hair in locs. Many times when I walked down the streets in town, the people who thought that I was him would call me Joe the artist. I would politely tell them that I wasn't him, and that he didn't look as good as me or dress as well as I do. He was the person who stayed in the shelter who would tell everyone how to do their chores when they first came to place. He was probably the most outstanding personality that I met when I first moved into the shelter. The other was a brother named Forbes. He, from my understanding, had been in and out of jail, and he was fine with you as long as you didn't do anything to upset him when he was off his medication. My first night there, Forbes saw to it that I was provided with a blanket and a pillow. The shelter didn't provide those for you, but it was the volunteers who would bring in those supplies if they had them. Forbes was also a recovering crack addict who was looking at jail time for a previous offense that he had done when he was down in Charlotte. I noticed after talking to him for a few days that he also was suffering from some mental health issues that wasn't addressed by the caseworker who was assigned to him. There was also a con artist by the name of CW. He was a country white man who was from one of these counties that was located in between the major cities of Charlotte and Winston-Salem. He was one-third liar, one-third thief, and one-third addict. This man was so good at running game that he could steal your stuff when we had to clean out the storage closet at the end of the month. That if your stuff was about to get thrown out, he would grab it for himself. If you came back and couldn't find it, he would act as if he found it for you and then sell it back to you to help support his addiction. His drug of choice was cocaine and prescription drugs. He would crush up the prescription pills and snort them up his nose as if he was doing cocaine.

There were others who had their unique personality traits, but those were just a few of the guys who stood out from the others. The women were a different story altogether. One who stood out from most of the others was a quiet woman named Isabel. She claimed to be a graduate who held a couple of degrees from an Ivy League school. She was a very intelligent African American woman who, once I gotten a chance to know her, showed me some pictures of her when she'd visited the mother continent of Africa. Isabel was always reading, and a good majority of the books that she read happened to be written by President Obama. If you did something to upset her, she would just cut you off socially without speaking to you while she lived at the shelter. Then there was Judy, an Italian woman who was from Philadelphia, Pennsylvania. She was a large woman of stature who was fixated on only dating men of color. She was married to a Mexican man and lived in California before moving to Salisbury. She had two children who lived in Washington state with her mother before she moved to North Carolina. It wasn't unusual for her to flirt with someone who was new coming into the shelter as a guest. Janice, a white woman, was another case study if you want to call her that. She was married to a former military man, but she had issues with alcohol and drug addiction, which led to their separation. She was a woman who loved dipping tobacco and always accompanied with an empty soda bottle so that she can always spit out the excess in it. Janice also had a fixation with African American males. She was an older woman, or appeared to be, because of the wrinkles in her face. There were more wrinkles in her face than there was in a road-map of the Rowan County. I guess from the looks of things that life must've been pretty hard for her, because she would say things a lot of the times that didn't seem to make much sense. Looking at how things may have been, the cause of getting people who had to move into the shelter, not many things would've made sense to me when I started living there.

When I first came to the shelter, my caseworker told me that they were here to assist me in getting back on my feet and that they would be working on a case plan so that I could re-enter the working class to become self-sufficient. The staff was something less to be desired for the most part. When I entered, I was informed that they would do everything in their part to help me achieve these goals. There were shelter aides, the workers who worked a rotation shift—two from 12:30 a. m. to 9:00 a. m., two in the second shift from 9:00 a. m. to 5:00 p. m., and the third shift that worked the 5:00 p. m. to 12:30 a. m. When I first came there, the morning shift worker was a brother named Dennis. A short bald-headed brother who loved the Pittsburgh Squealers pro-football team and had a Napoleonic complex, always talking shit because he had the authority to dismiss a shelter guest if he felt they were being unruly. He worked that shift with a black woman named Julia. She's an older woman who you could tell was a cutie back in her day. Still was very nice looking for her age and didn't mind flirting. At one time I thought that she and Dennis may have had a thing going on, but really it wasn't any of my concern. My main concern was trying to find a way out of what I knew was a hellhole. The evening staff included Will and Willie—these two I referred to as slow and slower. When it came to getting the shelter residents entry into the facility for the evening, they would have to screen and search the guest. The screening process included having the guest blow into a breathalyzer to screen for alcohol usage, and check their carry-on bags for drug and weapons. You would also have to be wanded with a portable electronic metal device to guarantee that you weren't carrying any concealed weapons. Not abiding by these rules would mean that you wouldn't be granted entrance into the facility for the evening.

Will was the younger of the two, and he had more of an allegiance to the policies of the administration, when it came down to things that weren't allowed to be used once you entered— candy, soda, potato chips, tobacco, and cellphones. Those items had to be stored away for the evening and not used or consumed once you entered inside the shelter. If they caught you with these items, they were considered as contraband. The shelter aides would confiscate them and return them to you in the morning. You would get written up for breaking the rules, and too many write-ups would lead to the consequences of getting a night out. Will was a true company man and would do everything by the book. If there was something in the manual that anyone—workers, administrators, or shelter guests had a question about, he would be the person who people would ask to quote the regulation. Being an African American with very fair skin, it was always easy to tell when Will was kissing someone's ass because he'd get an instant suntan.

Willie was figuratively the polar opposite of Will. Willie was a retired military man who went to work in the mills when they were thriving in Salisbury before the recession hit in 2008 and forced the last of them to either shut down or move. Once that happened, Willie started working at the shelter. Willie was the kind of brother who would ease off the rules. If the Olympics, a football or basketball game were playing on the TV and would run after the 10:00 p. m. time to shut the TV and lights off, he'd let you see it as long as you didn't get crazy. Willie once worked the morning shift, and when he did, he gave the weather forecast before the shelter had a TV. That was a courtesy that only he had extended to the shelter guests. Right off the bat, Willie won my respect, because he showed me that he had some compassion for the people who had to live at the shelter.

The evening staff would be responsible for delegating the duties of chores of the residents. If there was a person who wouldn't show up, it would be required that the staff should add the next person on the list to do the chore. Willie would ask for a volunteer before he would go to the list of the next person to do it. If you were given a duty and started complaining about it, his favorite quote was "work with me, work with me." Barry was the other staffer at the shelter who had my respect. He was a man who had been a product of the shelter and had moved out to become a shelter aide staff member. He knew what it was like from the inside to live in the shelter as a resident, and he was also sympathetic to the needs of guest who lived in the shelter. Barry was a person who had lived in the shelter as a resident and had eventually worked his way up to move into the transitional housing unit called the Eagle's Nest. It was provided by the shelter for the residents who became employed with them and the residents who were disabled or retired from the military. Barry was a pretty easygoing and had a free-flowing disposition when it came down to anything that was borderline about abiding by the rules. He was a person who remembered how it was when he was on the other side of working for the shelter.

Outside of the usual morning and evening shelter aid workers, there were also the weekend aid workers. There was Austin, a young man in his early twenties who was enrolled at the local community college for social work. He had the unique knack for asking you your name when he first met you and wouldn't forget it during your duration of your stay there. He was originally from the Philadelphia area before moving to Salisbury and was a 76ers fan. The one thing that he and I had in common was our ardent disdain for the Boston Celtics and the Chicago Bulls. Then there was his partner Janice. She was a cutie with some of the prettiest eyes that could captivate you. Like many things that I wanted in my life, I couldn't have her for two reasons. The first reason was that the policy of the shelter prohibited fraternizing between the staff and the residents. The second reason was because she was married. Janice was a sweet person and loved to attempt to pick up a person's spirit by singing songs of inspiration. It may have helped if she could sing, but she couldn't hold a note, let alone water that was in a cup. Those two would be the weekend evening support aides who would be responsible for doing the laundry of the shelter residents, assigning beds or cots, and doing intake of new residents. During the morning, we had two others who would be there to do the morning duties of the shelter. The first one was a pre-law student, a young black man named Ashton. He was quite subdued and conservative. He would be the reason why you were told not to judge a book by its cover. When you first met him, you would probably think that he was a lot more radical and outgoing. He wore his hair in locs and dressed like the typical college student in blue jeans, flannel shirt, and sneakers. Ashton wasn't a person of many words, but if he had something on his mind, he wouldn't mind letting you know what it was that he was thinking. The other was the glamour girl of the staff. Sarah was her name, and she had a few problems that I found out shortly after admitting myself into the shelter. She was the other reason "not to judge a book by its cover," the type of person who, when you first view her, looked as if she belonged on the cover of *Seventeen*, *Glamour*, or *Vogue* magazine. She was a woman in her early thirties who had five children, but you'd never know it by looking at her. I kid you not when I tell you that this woman was truly gorgeous. She was in the middle of a bitter divorce battle with her soon-to-be ex-husband who was a city cop here in Salisbury. It's been said that he had stalked her when she was working, because he was so insecure. Not much more was known about her because she would leave within a couple of months after I became a resident.

Everything that I stated about the staff to this point had to take directions from someone who was in control of supervising them. This direction would come from the director of the shelter, the former chief of police for the city of Salisbury. Rodney had the shelter running the facility like a boot camp, mandating that passes were inspected on a daily basis and issued out on a weekly one. He would want to know how the guest would be spending their days and that their case plans had to include looking for employment or going to the shelter's adult day care facility, New Tomorrow. He would work with the director of the food bank to get guests who were just goofing off at the facility to put them to work by having them work at the warehouses gathering food and other supplies for the public who would come to the building for assistance with food, financial, and clothing from the crisis assistance network. People came to the Rowan Helping Ministries every weekday asking for assistance to help with the rent, keeping the lights on, heat in their homes, and using the food bank facility. People could ask for food and clothing assistance once every thirty days. Rodney made it very convenient for Nate, the manager of the food bank, to get the help he needed when he needed it most. There was something about him that I didn't trust. Maybe it's due to the fact that my godfather who was a former highly decorated cop of the NYPD himself told me never to trust a cop. It was just something about him that just didn't jive right with me.

Next there were the case workers. When I arrived at the shelter, I spoke with David Holston. I came into his office that was divided into a cubicle, and on his side of the cubicle was where he proudly displayed his degrees from Appalachian State and Wake Forest universities. He was there to explain the rules and regulations of the shelter and told me that I needed to do a work search to show that I'm actively looking for work. I told him that I was a college graduate that had achieved my degree in child and family development from Benedict College in Columbia, South Carolina. I let him know that I was looking for his assistance in securing a position with the degree that I have. The one thing that I noticed about David was that he had the perfect poker face. No matter what I was talking about, no matter what had been said, the expression on his face never changed. If I had farted and if it had stunk so bad that most people would've had no other choice but to make a change in their expression, David was true to himself, and nothing was going to change that. I mean absolutely nothing was going to make him lose himself out of character. David's responsibility was to do the intake procedures and the paperwork of the new people during the daytime hours.

The evening hours they had another part-time case worker on duty. Linda worked in the evening hours at the shelter. She worked at Livingstone College during the daytime, but during the evening, she worked part-time as a caseworker at the shelter. Rumor had it that she had an experience as a guest in a shelter prior to becoming a member of the staff. Linda gave the impression that she was unsympathetic to those who stayed there. She was a woman who did everything by the book as if she was the author of it. It must've been something that was written in the employee manual, because she was a lot like David. Neither one of them seemed to have any kind of compassion for the resident who stayed there, and never smiled.

The one thing that I've been blessed with growing up was having parents who were teachers. If I never remember another thing that my father, who was a retired teacher, say that has stuck with me for the rest of my life, he told me that the only person outside of God and my parents to trust is nobody but myself. That lesson was also reinstated to me by my godfather and uncle, the retired decorated New York City police officer. He told me not to trust a cop, because they're dirty. This brings me back to Nate. He was an ex-military and retired county sheriff's deputy. He was responsible for stocking the food pantry and running the soup kitchen. The one thing that I can say for Nate is that he did have a personality, if not a pulse, about what's going on in the community around the shelter area. I didn't know how to take him personally, but I did know that the longer that I'd stay here, the more I'd get to know him whether I wanted to or not. I also knew that I didn't want to get to know too many people. The more people that I got to know, the longer and harder it would be to get out of this situation. It would make me think of that song by the Eagles, "Welcome to the Hotel California. You can check out anytime you like, but you can never leave."

CHAPTER 2

Check Your Bags at the Door

Several days after moving into the shelter, I was given my duty on the chore list. This is a routine that all the guest have to perform for the duration of their stay at the shelter. The chores are divided into two parts. The first part is the evening chores that included wiping down the dining tables at the end of dinner and taking out the trash. Once you checked into the shelter, you weren't allowed to go back out of the doors unless you wanted to stay out of there for the evening. Asking if you could go outside those doors to take a smoke break wasn't an option, a moot point. Most of the guys who were put on the chore list were happy to take the trash out, because this way they were able to request to get their cigarettes or cigars and take a puff if they had them. The other part of the chore duties happened in the morning. Just like the night before, you had to make sure that the tables were cleaned, and the garbage was taken out as well as the other duties that included cleaning the kitchen that the volunteers use in the morning. The shelter staff would clean it up in the evening after the volunteers. Both the men's and women's dormitories and bathrooms had to be swept and mopped as well as the dining area. All of this had to be done before you were allowed to leave the facility.

In the morning either Julia or Dennis would turn on the lights at five twenty, saying, "Five twenty wake-up call. Five twenty, wake up." They would repeat this chant at five-minute intervals all the way up until five thirty. If you weren't sitting up with your feet on the side of the cot, then you would be written up for not doing this and subjected to being kicked out the shelter for not abiding by the rules. If there was an excess of new people who checked into the shelter who needed a place to stay, the dining area would have to be used so that it could accommodate the new guest. The first meal wouldn't be served until about five forty-five, and getting yourself ready was the equivalent of working the floor at Wall Street for the opening bell. The bathrooms would be packed to capacity with a urinal, two commodes, three sinks, and three showers. Going to use the bathroom reminded me of going into the elevators of the projects in New Jersey and New York where it always smelled of strong urine and funk. The showers could only be used in the evenings before you could come to the table for dinner. Pajamas were provided for the shelter guest by the staff, and had to be returned in the morning so that they could wash them so you could wear them when you returned in the evening. When I first arrived at the shelter, volunteers would donate pajamas for the guest to wear. Men and women would have to change into their clothes in restrooms. In most of the cases, after the guest got up getting themselves ready, one of the shelter aides would turn on the television. This was extremely helpful to the residents, because we needed to know how to dress for the elements that the day had in stored for us. Now, if a guest would piss off a staff member, they would punish the guest by delaying the opportunity to watch the news, more important than that, the weather report. Julia was very good at this. She would flirt with one of the guest one minute, and if you did something that didn't jive right with her, then she would flip on you and then she would put you on her shit list. The bad thing about it was that if it caused her any embarrassment, the whole shelter would suffer.

When the day got started, the artist Joe would always wake up in a bad mood. He felt it was his duty to restate who had chores to do on the list, and more importantly to tell others how to do their assigned chores. Never was this more evident when it came down to cleaning the bathroom. When I was assigned to do the bathroom,

Joe felt compelled to make sure he addressed me on how to clean the bathroom. What tickled me was the fact that he asked if I had all of the cleaning utensils and supplies. I thought to myself, "Is this guy for real?" When I was given that duty, I checked in with the staff to ask them to give me whatever it was that I needed. Joe had this Felix Unger mentality, a complete and total neat freak. It wouldn't be so bad if he didn't have most of his personal things and art supplies monopolizing the storage closet. In the three sides of a fifteen-by-fifteen square foot closet with three shelves on each of the walls, Joe had two shelves on one side of the closet with his clothes and mostly art supplies. When it came to cleaning the shower, he wanted to make sure that everyone used the long-handle scrubbing brush to clean the tile. After I finished cleaning the sinks, urinals, and toilets, I was about to clean the shower area followed by sweeping and mopping the floors. At that time, Joe just happened to walk in as I was about to start that part of the cleaning detail. He asked me if I was going to use the scrubber. By that time, I had enough of his mouth and commanding ways, and I told him that I didn't know how to do it. I asked him if he would be so kind enough to show me what I needed to do. Much to my surprise, he was happy to do it and explain what he was doing, how, and why he was doing it. I thought to myself, "Man, this is too easy!" So I played along with this stupid ass act as if I didn't know any better and conned him into finishing the cleaning detail. I asked if he would show me what else I needed to do, and if he would inspect the work that I've done and show me how to do the job right. Once again, he would complete the job for me, talking to me about how to do the cleaning duty correctly. This wasn't supposed to happen this easy for me. Joe claimed to be from Queens, New York. I never ran across a New Yorker who played himself as a sucker as easily as he did.

I found out that one reason why it was easy to play him the way he allowed me to was because he had some sort of street sense, little common sense, and practically no book sense. Joe was enrolled at the Rowan Cabarrus Community College (RCCC). He was there studying to receive his GED diploma. When he was off the campus, Joe could be seen at the Rowan Public Library, downtown at the

Robertson Eastern Gateway Park, or in front of a merchant's storefront doing someone's portrait for much less than what it was truly worth. People who would ask him to produce a pencil-sketched portraits knew that they would be getting over on him by only paying him fifteen to forty bucks for the beautiful work that he did. They took advantage of him due to the fact that they knew that he was homeless. They took advantage of that and played on the kindness of him doing the project and used that as a weakness of him. I told Joe that he was giving away his artwork and that he needed to charge more for the work that he was doing.

When I first moved to Salisbury, I noticed that it was an up-and-coming arts community in the North Carolina-Piedmont region. If you travel around the downtown area, you'll notice that there are several beautifully sculpted pieces of artwork around the original courthouse that was turned into the Rowan County Museum. There were other works of art at the library, county building, banks, and other locations around town. Just one block away from the location of the shelter is an area that they called the Railway Arts District. In that area is the former home of the National Sportswriter Sportscasters Association Hall of Fame and also houses two avant-garde non-traditional theatres for live stage performances in that area. On the main strip of South Main Street is the Meroney Theatre. This is a landmark theatre that holds the distinction of having the great Sarah Bernhardt and Lillian Gist grace the stage there. The building was an old structure, but was well restored and maintained by the Piedmont Player Theatre Company. Just around the corner, on North Fisher Street, was a newer theatre that once was a pool hall called the Norvell Theatre, also managed by the Piedmont Player Theatre Company. This was one of my dreams—to continue to do some acting, but also, in the process, to secure a position that would allow me to regain my quality of life that I lost when I moved to Salisbury.

Salisbury is a small community that hasn't grown much socially since the days of the civil war. It is the halfway point between the cities of Charlotte and Winston-Salem in North Carolina. When my cousin had rented a shop in the business district, she caught hell. Not because she was a black woman who was running a women's bou-tique on the ground floor of her shop. The residents there thought that part of the business was acceptable, but on the weekends, she hosted spoken word and live jazz parties in the upstairs of the estab-lishment for adults aged thirty and older. If you had a business in the city of Salisbury, you were allowed to host a party, but you could not serve alcohol. The law did make allowances for the patrons to bring a brown bag with either beer or wine. She prohibited the consumption of liquor when she hosted parties. When she did host parties where liquor was allowed to be consumed, she always went through the proper channels by putting in temporary applications with the state Alcohol Beverage Commission in Raleigh, and the city would have to get the approval from that agency before allowing the business to serve. When she applied for a full-time license to serve for the week-ends only, the city council initially approved it, but had recanted it when the *Salisbury Post*, the local newspaper, deliberately printed an article saying that she was illegally serving alcoholic beverages. So the hell that she caught was the fact that she was a black woman who was about to serve alcohol. What her business was about to do was going to cut into the profit margins of the local downtown establishments that served alcohol.

My routine was that I would leave the shelter in the morn-ing, heading out to the Goodwill Career Connections. It was located right across the street from the local unemployment office. Once there, I had access to the computers so that I could look for jobs and put in applications for them online. Many things have changed since the last time that I had to apply for a position back in 2008. Putting in applications for jobs was the main focus that consumed me more than anything. In 2008, I applied for quite a few jobs. Many of them were done through agencies in person. Some of them were to go into the firm, company, or organization in person, and about a third of the applications that I had to apply with was done online through the Internet. That would change a lot over the next couple of years. It happened to be the opposite when I was looking for jobs. This time, I saw that more of the jobs that I was qualified to do, I had to apply for them online. No more paper trail, because the planet and the country were starting to go green, meaning, it was trying to be more ecologically friendly, trying to cut back on using any products that were produced by trees. I would go to the career connections job center in the morning and would stay there from nine in the morning until three o'clock in the afternoon. From there, I would go to the library and, depending on the day, I would stay there until almost closing.

The library was the sanctuary for many people living at the shelter. There weren't too many places that you would be able to go to if you didn't have a job. If friends or relatives wouldn't allow you to go their place to visit when the library isn't open, then you would be stuck like Chuck. Rowan County in general didn't have much to offer since the recession hit, and the mills that used to be the heart and soul that generated the economic boom have either shut down or moved out from the county into another state or country. Most of the residents who didn't have a job would go to the library if they weren't hanging around the shelter. It was a place for resources, but not the kind for just the books, newspapers, and current magazines of the times. The library was the meeting place for the locals to discuss what was happening with individuals around town. They would mainly talk about the people who either lived in the shelter or those who would like to hang out there.

I remembered coming back to the shelter at the end of the day and waiting to come in for the evening. There was the usual long line to gain entrance into the building. Some days gaining entrance into the shelter was almost as bad as trying to get into Studio 54 during its heyday. The only thing that they didn't have was the velvet rope treatment, but the lines were long still the same. When there was nothing else to do but play the waiting game, I would be amazed by the other people who were living in the shelter. While we were all standing in line, we'd be exchanging stories of how we're trying to get out of the shelter and the steps that we're taking to try to get there.

CW was always one of the leaders sparking up a conversation about how he was working this hustle at a construction site. Now CW wasn't the brightest light bulb on the billboard, but still he had a light that could produce some rays of brilliance. Looking at him, he would remind you of "Larry the Cable Guy," but only younger. He was without a doubt the hustler of the shelter guests. CW liked to live life on the edge, because he didn't have any fear when it came to doing drugs. There were a lot of drugs being used at the shelter mainly prescribed for the disabled veterans and other people with disabilities, but the drugs weren't consumed by those for whom the medications were prescribed for. They would be available for any-one who wanted them for the black market of the streets. Nothing was off limits as far as purchasing Hydrocodone, Oxycodone, Xanax, Trazodone, Seroquel, and other narcotics drugs. These drugs were up for sale, and they could bring in a pretty nice windfall for the person who possessed them.

If you didn't have any prescription drugs for sale to the addicts, then CW and Joe the artist knew of another hustle that would help assure you of having a few dollars in your pocket. A local merchant that relocated from Winston-Salem would accept your food stamps. He was paying cash anyone who wanted to sell them. He had a con-venient store downtown and was purchasing food stamps by anyone who needed to put some cash in their pockets. He was generous in his purchase of the stamps by giving the seller sixty cents on the dol-lar. This was a great price, because if you received food stamps and if you sold them to your family or friends, the standard price that anyone will pay for the stamps is only fifty cents on the dollar. This was convenient for the residents of the shelter, because if you weren't working and had no source of income including receiving disability or unemployment checks, this was your only source of income that you had for the month. In order to survive, you had to learn how to be resourceful so there were certain things that may have brought you to the brink of questioning your own moral fiber.

Waiting in line to enter into the shelter, you would see the nor-mal cast of people who would be there. I would often wonder to myself how long have some of them been living here. What is their story and circumstances that caused them to move, and would I be here as long as or longer than most of them? When I first move in, there weren't many women who lived there. The women who come to mind when I first moved there was a mixed group who had diverse backgrounds.

Judy, the woman who I mentioned earlier, was a nice woman. She just loved flirting with black men and was very open about wanting to date them and only men of color. Flirting for her was viewed more as a sport, and if she liked you, she would try to see just how far she could go to get you. She was very proficient and fluent in speaking and reading Spanish. Judy would talk circles around anyone who thought that they knew Spanish. Her ex-husband was a Mexican, and when she moved to the West Coast, she spent a lot of time with his family and friends. She claimed to be an excellent cook and was always talking about making exotic Mexican dishes. When she wasn't talking about making these delicacies, she was usually on the make to try and find a man of color. She often gave me the impression that she was the kind of woman who didn't feel complete until she had a man in her life to validate her. Judy was helpful when we entered into the shelter. If there was a person who came into the shelter and they didn't speak English only Spanish, then she was the translator for the employees at the shelter. When the males who weren't assigned a cot had to wait to receive one, she would normally be the woman responsible for handing out the cots to the guys. She gave out the cots for the men, because the excess cots were located in the women's quarters of the shelter. All of this work would be assigned to her while she was staying at the shelter without the administration consider hiring her to work there as a bilingual caseworker, intake manager, or in another capacity to assist some of the people of the community who may need the help for the crisis center or the shelter.

After dinner, the guests would watch television, play cards or board games. Judy would play a game of spades while Janice would eat then converse with someone for a minute and hit the hay for the evening. Janice was pretty simpleminded for the most part. She would spend the good part of her day at the shelter sitting on the patio slab passing the majority of the day away. Occasionally, Janice would leave to go to the mall, or to the stores locally like Family Dollar, Kmart, or Wal-Mart since these stores were within walking distance. There was a pretty good bet that you could normally find her sitting on the concrete slab outside the shelter or inside at the crisis assistance area of the building. The things that kept her content was that she had her dipping tobacco, some nose candy, and the prescription drugs she had. If she needed a few dollars, she was one of the people who lived in the shelter who legally had prescription drugs that she would sell for some quick cash.

Drugs are something that were easy to get and very accessible for the people who lived at the shelter. Every morning, some of the shelter guests would get their prescribed medications to take with them when they left in the mornings. People would gather outside of the building, most of them from the eastside of town looking to score on the prescription drugs for their own consumptions. Some of them would do the opposite. They would come down there to purchase the drugs to sell them to people in the more affluent neighborhoods while others would come there to sell street drugs such as heroin, marijuana, and cocaine. During the daytime, people would be on the side of the building that was off the side of the street to smoke weed, cigarettes, and drink beer there, or at the back of the building. In the evenings, when the majority of the residents were inside the shelter, there were some who would go to the back of the building with the local crack heads and heroin addicts to smoke rocks and shoot up. This area at the times that I've mentioned was affectionately known as the "Drug Stores."

After being there for several months, if a shelter guest wasn't able to acquire or secure a job, the staff of the crisis assistance network and the shelter would attempt to provide the guest an opportunity to work into a re-entry program. This allowed the guest an opportunity to work at the facility as a stocker, runner, laborer, or anything that was needed in the form of getting the help for the shelter and the crisis assistance department. There was plenty of work to do there, because of the wing of the crisis assistance network at the Rowan Helping Ministries. People from the local community from local churches, nonprofits, and community-based organizations were there to assist in the food pantry for the people who received food stamps when they didn't have enough food at their houses to last them. Other people of the community would request assistance from the crisis assistance to help residents of the community with their financial needs. If they were eligible, people could receive financial assistance with the heating utilities, rental/mortgage, and electric bills when they were about to lose those services in their households. Shelter residents who worked in the food pantry were the stockers. Stockers were responsible for stocking the shelves in the pantry, and the clothing department. When they weren't stocking these two departments for the shelter, stockers helped the people who received this assistance by getting the groceries to their cars. The runners would go to the warehouse to get the canned and dry goods and replenishing the pantry. Runners would also go to the clothing warehouse and would get the clothes so that the stockers could also restock the clothes for the people who needed to receive the donated articles.

That process would happen several times a day, because many of the people throughout Rowan County would come there throughout the month to receive assistance. There was also work for the people from the shelter to work in the soup kitchen. The shelter would not only feed the residents who resided there, but also the community that surrounded it. Every day between the hours of twelve noon and 1:00 p. m., they would open up the soup kitchen to serve the unemployed and homeless population. Rarely would the administration have a resident from the shelter work in the capacity as a professional. I can only recall one time when the head of the volunteer, Emily, would actually allow a shelter guest to work as an intake assistant. Prior to living at the shelter, I would come there to receive food assistance when my food stamps didn't last me to the end of the month. When I went there was when I first met Elizabeth. She was an intake assistant who would help with the acquisition of clothes, food, or money to help with your bills. Most people would call her Liz. She moved from my home state of New Jersey a couple of years before I did after the death of her husband. She worked there as a volunteer before falling on hard times herself. She was forced to move into the shelter, and after a brief stay, she would go back to work again in the crisis assistance network. Liz resumed her duties as an intake assistant and was very good at doing that.

It goes to show me that you had to believe in that old saying that "it's not what you know, but who you know" to get ahead. The administration was happy to get any volunteer help that they would receive. It was always better for them to get the help from the outside with the different organizations, agencies, churches, and businesses of the community. By doing this, it gave the impression that more good is taking place at the shelter than it really is. I'm learning that perception is more important than the facts. Prior to moving into the shelter when I was looking for a job, I would patronize the services that the crisis assistant network would offer in the food department. I was eligible to come there once a month to ask for food to supplement where I was staying. I did that when my rations at home were running low, and since I was a social worker by trade with an honors degree in child and family development, I thought that it would be a pretty good idea trying to see about doing some volunteer work there. The one time that I'd inquired about doing some volunteer work there was when Liz was doing my intake, and she told me that I should ask at the front desk. I did that and I was given the contact name of Emily with the phone number. I called there to make an appointment and was told to come in to fill out an application to volunteer. I came in, filled out an application to volunteer, and was never interviewed to do any kind of volunteer work.

All the work that they wanted from the volunteers were people who've been what they consider be the pillars of the community, or someone who needed to do their community service from the county department of probation. It was always easy for the shelter and the crisis assistance center to get the *Salisbury Post* to post a photo op when they could get some students from the cosmetology school at RCCC to come and do some haircuts for the guest who couldn't afford to get them. It even looked better when they had a local chiropractor to come in and to make adjustments on the backs of the guest who need them because of sleeping on the cots provided by the administration. A better thing was to get either some local high school or college sports team or auxiliary club to either clean up the grounds or serve a meal for the shelter guests. Appearances are always better than the reality that no one wants to hear the truth.

When I first admitted myself as a guest into the shelter, I was given a reality check by my case manager. Just a little over a month and a half, I had applied for a position at the local HBCU in town, Livingstone College. They had posted a position on their job board online and were looking to fill a position for a resident hall director. I, looking to secure employment, figured that this would be a good way to utilize my degree and to continue to work in the educational setting. I received an e-mail telling me to call for an interview with the college. I called and set up the appointment for the afternoon for the following Tuesday. I asked my caseworker, David, if he knew of anyone that was employed at the college to see if he would be able to put in a word that I was a shelter guest who has the credentials and qualifications to fill the position. He told me, "I don't know anyone who works at Livingstone College, but I have to be honest with you. I'm not used to working with someone who has a degree. I'm used to helping place people who need to get their GED or people who work in the manual trades," Now if that's not a reality check, then life as you know it shouldn't exist. How was it that a case manager who held a degree didn't have any connections with any of the human resource managers at any of the four local colleges—Livingstone, Catawba College, Rowan Cabarrus Community College, and Pfeiffer University? No connections with the human resource managers at city or county government levels, and most importantly, none at the corporate levels with the biggest corporations being Food Lion, the largest grocery store chain in the Carolinas with stores also in Georgia and Tennessee Freightliner, the freight trucking division of Daimler-Chrysler; and the Carolina Beverage Corporation, the makers of Cheerwine and Sun Drop sodas?

What happened here was that the light bulb in my head finally went off for me. They're paying this man good money for sitting on his ass not to do a damn thing. One of the first things that I can recall is David asking me during the process of my intake into the shelter if I was depressed. I told him that, yes, I was depressed. I told him that I came here with the hopes and inspiration of working and that I was disappointed that I wasn't after living in Salisbury for the past nine months. He then suggested that I may want to check myself into a clinic for depression and substance abuse. I declined, because I knew that if I were to start working and earning an honest living would help solve part of my problem with depression.

When I think about David wanting to me to go to the local hospital for depression and counseling, I noticed that there was a young guy by the name of Brian. He was a very jovial young guy who was going to Life Works, the program at the local hospital for substance abuse and depression. He was a very outgoing guy who liked to leave the shelter in the morning, get a hustle on so that he could have a beer or two during the day. Sometimes Brian would be a customer at the drugstore in the back of the shelter and would buy a little weed to smoke, but that was the extent of his partying. He was a character who would love to play the dozens with you, but all in all, he was a young guy with a great personality. Well, David and Rodney had put stipulations on terms of him staying at the shelter. Brian had blown into the breathalyzer positive one time too many and was instructed to go and admit himself into Life Works and follow up without patient services at Daymark.

Once Brian was released from there, he was never the same. He came back and would do the recommended follow-up appointments, but he wasn't looking for work the way he once did. His demeanor and attitude changed as he was sleeping heavily on the benches in front of the shelter, or in the waiting area of the crisis network. The clever funny man with bad hearing and the outgoing personality wasn't the same. I asked Brian how he was feeling. He would say that he was always tired and that he couldn't get enough sleep. I told him that, since going to the hospital, he wasn't doing his normal things. I told him next time he went back to his doctor's appointment at Daymark to let them know that the medication that they've prescribed for him was keeping him drowsy and to have the doctors lower the dosage they were giving him.

He would go to his appointments and inform his doctor and pharmacist the medication that's been prescribed had been too strong. When he came back after having the medical professionals change up the prescriptions, overtime it appeared that Brian's condition had worsened. If he went to the library, he slept there. If you went past the bus depot, you could find him sleeping there along with the normal places in front of the crisis center or outside on the concrete slab. I made a point of going to visit my caseworker about the condition of Brian. I don't know why I went to him, but maybe it's the training as a social worker I received when I was a college student, or my genuine concern about this young man's welfare. He seemed to do nothing about it at first, stating that his body had to adjust to the medication. That was until one day everyone was going into the shelter for the evening. Brian was waiting in line. He was one of the first to wait at the door to enter into the facility. It was customary for the guys to let the women and families enter into the shelter first. Well, after that happened, Willie, the shelter aide, was at the door having the guest blowing into the breathalyzer. When it was time to have Brian blow into the device, he was asleep. That wasn't the unusual part, but what was unusual was the fact that he was sleeping and standing up at the same time. He wasn't leaning on the wall to support himself, but standing unassisted. This was just too dangerous.

After we woke him up so that he could gain entry into the shelter, I went ballistic on Willie. Maybe it was unjustified to go off on him, but I wanted to make a point to get the attention of someone who worked there that this man needed some help. Brian would have a few dollars in his pocket still even though he wasn't hustling like he did prior to his Life Works and Daymark mandate by the shelter. I feared for him that someone would try to take advantage of him and would hurt him to get what little money that he had. David was still there by the time that Brian was about to come into the shelter. This was unusual, because when the five o'clock hour comes around, David got like a ghost and disappeared. Willie brought David out to see about Brian's condition. I was livid and let them know my frustration with him and his handling of the situation. I was in danger of getting kicked out for several days.

I realized one thing that the sign on the building wasn't at all what they had advertised it to be. The sign reads that it is the Rowan Helping Ministries. I questioned them and myself, what kind of ministry would allow a person to suffer after seeing the result of this kind of behavior? Once this incident happened, I didn't think much of this place or the people who were running this show. How could you look yourself in the mirror knowing that you're having mentally sick individuals come there without giving them any kind of guidance or assistance to get them the help that they needed? Maybe living underneath a bridge would've been better than for me to stay here. This wasn't a good idea to move myself into the shelter, let alone Salisbury, North Carolina. Maybe I should've been more selective and careful before I made my decision to move here. Maybe I shouldn't have checked my bag in at the door. There I go looking back in hindsight again when I needed to be looking ahead.

CHAPTER 3

What Are These Accommodations?

Staying at the shelter you would see people from all walks of life. One of the people who would come to mind was an old woman named Ms. Dora. When you first laid your eyes upon her, you probably would think that she was an old man. Dora was an eccentric elderly white woman who was rumored to have a large nest egg stashed somewhere. I wouldn't doubt it, because she fit the profile of someone who could be that. She often wore soiled clothing, had silver-gray hair, a lot of wrinkles in her face, and would be chain-smoking cigarettes like an old mill factory. Every morning, she would bring out a comforter and would set up her camp either on the ramp leading into the entrance of the soup kitchen and shelter, or on the hill where the parking lot was. Dora would pretty much keep to herself and have a pocket radio with her for entertainment.

She would sit out there all day everyday regardless of the weather conditions. The only times that she would go inside of the crisis assistance network was if the weather conditions would get extreme. If it got to be extremely hot or extremely cold would be the only time that Dora would go inside to get some comfort. She wouldn't want to be bothered with anyone otherwise. Rumor had it that she had a nest egg hidden somewhere, because she would always leave at the first of the month and would be gone for several days at a time. This wasn't unusual for shelter residents to do this, but what was unique about her was that she always had cigarettes throughout the remainder of the month. The majority of the guest at the shelter would use up their disability or welfare money well before the fifth of the month would roll around. Cigarettes at the shelter are the same as they are in jail. They're a valuable commodity and are almost as good as cash.

Everyone in the neighborhood knew Ms. Dora and wouldn't bother her for anything. One would learn not to mess with Ms. Dora quickly. For example, if you didn't have any cigarettes, you dare not ask her for one, because she would curse you out by telling you that she didn't have any to support your habits You were persona non grata (not welcomed) with her. Now if the shoe was on the other foot, Dora wouldn't hesitate to ask you for a cigarette, and if you gave her one at the first of the month, she would be kind enough to buy you a pack. She wasn't as crazy as many people perceived her to be. In fact, she was another one of the brightest lights at the shelter. She knew how to pull the strings of the people who lived and worked there and was playing those strings like a concert violinist plays a Stradivarius.

Dora was another person who suffered with mental illness. She would normally be one of the first people to leave the shelter in the morning to set up her camp for the day, and one of the last women to return there in the evenings. During the daytime, always with her cigarettes and Pepsi, she would be sitting at her camp doing cross-word puzzles, word search, or crocheting. It wasn't unusual to see her go around to the side of the building for her to use it as an open restroom. Seldom would she use the restroom facility at the crisis center. The times when she would use it was cases when the weather was extremely cold or inclement. If she wasn't able to make it into the building to use the bathroom, there were many days that she would urinate or defecate on herself. When night time came, it is the policy of the shelter that all guest had to shower before they sat at the table for dinner. When she entered into the shelter, she didn't like to shower before dinner. The smell was so pungent stinking of urine and shit that the residents often complained with good reason. The staff had to make her take one before dinner, but Dora's biggest battles came when the staff had to make her give them her clothes so that they could be washed.

She was the only person who had carte blanche to leave and return to the shelter at will. Dora was the exception to the rule of once you left the building you couldn't return until it was time for dinner. The administration of the shelter knew about her situation and condoned whatever she did. So what's wrong with this picture? In my mind, I thought that this was supposed to be a support network to assist people who suffer with these kinds of situations. Here you have an older woman who was receiving disability that couldn't obviously take care of herself. This person needed to be in a nursing home or an assisted living facility. I found out one reason why the administration would want to help the people is because the government and private foundations will give money through grants to shelters, transitional housing, and other places for the guest who reside there. For the shelter to assist someone and direct them to a facility that is better suited would mean that they're literally throwing money out of the window. See, it pays to keep someone with mental health, drug addiction, and physical disability issues. To move them to another facility would be like biting off the hand that feeds the staff at the shelter and crisis assistance network.

Another example would be the cases for disabled veterans. Salisbury is also the home to one of the North Carolina full service veteran's administration hospital, and quite a few of the residents at the shelter are either disabled vets or applying for their military disability benefits. This was a sweeter deal for the shelter, because the VA would pay the shelter to house the vets. The shelter would receive more money from the VA then it would get from the government and private foundations to house civilians. It only makes sense to accommodate the ones that pay the bulk of your bills happy, while you keep the people who aren't paying a dime to leave them ignorant, oppressed and hopeless about the future prospects for a better quality of life. Once you've been in there for a minute you've got to have a plan of action. You've better have a strong will and determination so that you can get out of there to become a self-sufficient person.

If you're living at the shelter, and didn't have a plan of action to get out then the administration would make one for you. They had an operation for those who were just hanging around the grounds of the facility without prospecting for work, or anything to do. The shelter had a working arrangement with a church around the corner from it, and the program that they called it was given the name New Tomorrow. This is a place that the shelter guest who didn't have any kind of skills to go to learn one. They would assist you with the basics in job searching skills. Something like I was doing when I was working at the Urban League of Essex County in Newark, New Jersey. Participants in that program would learn how to properly fill out a job application, learn how to produce a resume' and how to go through a mock job interview. New Tomorrows would've been good if they had done more to bring employers there to screen potential applicants for jobs. They would bring people from several local business to have forums about meeting the expectations of employers. New Tomorrows would have its participants creating acrylic paintings for a silent auction. This isn't bad, because the participants were told that they would receive the proceeds from the compositions. I can't confirm it, but I'm sure that administration was get a small percentage of the auction bid for their own operating cost.

The administration would do an excellent job of promoting itself with public relations. They had a great pipeline to the Salisbury Post newspaper, and the CBS television station that had a news bureau in town. It was easy for them to bring the attention of the work that was going on there. Using New Tomorrows was the easiest way of doing its own self-promotions. If the grounds of the shelter were looking bad and needed to be cleaned, it was easy to call one of the editors of the newspaper to send a reporter and photographer around there to take some pictures of the director of New Tomorrow supervising the shelter guest as they were cleaning the grounds of the shelter. Throw in a couple of quotes from the guest and it's was a quick fix to get donations from the community members. The sad part about that is the director of New Tomorrows and the shelter director would find someone who wasn't very educated to give the newspaper or the television station their quotes.

Don't get me wrong. I know that the participants are very appreciative of everything that they received. Now their hearts were in the right place, and doing the cleaning duties, along with working in the warehouse, displayed a sense of pride. It gives people a sense of being part of something that's good and important. I don't see anything wrong with having guests doing the work that needs to be done, but when the administration directs the media on who to interview to exploit them. This was for the benefit of the shelter and crisis network. It's like winning the home run derby for the administration. That's something that makes the administration look like they're doing more than what they truly are.

New Tomorrow would've been a great idea, but it doesn't work in the favor for the people who are enrolled in the program. Having the participants cleaning the grounds of the shelter, and working at the warehouse to retrieve supplies for the shelter and crisis center isn't a bad thing. It's better when you can get people to do it because they want to volunteer, not because it's a directive. Having employers come to New Tomorrows to show participants how to fill out applications is fine, but it doesn't fulfill the prospect of work for the participants. This was something that I've questioned about the program at New Tomorrow. If your company, agency, organization, or firm have open positions, why wouldn't you have your human resources personnel screen these participants for potential applicants? Having the participants taught how to produce resumes, applications, and drilled on interviews techniques is a moot point if you're not doing anything to help them build on those skills. Getting the program participants to make paintings, bird houses, potholders and other crafts are good as a stress reliever but it doesn't give people a sense of security. These are the skills that people acquire when they're are living at a senior citizen adult day care service and more importantly, it doesn't get them out of the shelter and into a place for them to call their own.

One of the things that the administration has is a near zero tolerance level for is the abuse of prescription and illegal street drugs. The administration would conduct a monthly meeting with the people residing there, and randomly the administration would select guest from the shelter to test them for the use of drugs. Breaching this agreement once you sign that you will abide by the rules would result in facing the consequences of the administrative staff. The consequences for the first time offender you were given three days out of the shelter, and have to go to Daymark for substance abuse classes. The second offense could result in being out anywhere from ten to thirty days out and required to attend substance abuse classes and a third offense could result into an indefinite suspension of residing at the shelter. Now if you are placed on an indefinite suspension you can always appeal it, and they will amend the time of the suspension so that you can return into the shelter. Intervention was recommended, but wouldn't be followed up or monitored properly by the case managers. The time management, monitoring and follow up on the people whom the case manager would service was extremely poor.

On this day, the administration was holding their monthly meeting, and not much to my surprise was testing several of the shelter guest for drugs. Rodney and David were calling in several of the guest to go into the back offices so that they could test them for drug abuse. They would test the people by swabbing them in the mouth. The monthly meeting would have Rodney the shelter director, the caseworkers David and Linda, the shelter aid workers Will and Willie attend the meeting. Making a rare appearance this time would also included Ms. Foster, the executive director, and Nate, the director of the food pantry and soup kitchen.

That first night they caught ten people and had asked them to leave the facility. They were asked to leave, but they still could come into the soup kitchen for lunch. Most of the time, I noticed that the random testing would occur when they had an overflow of people staying at the shelter. The shelter would normally house approximately about fifty to sixty people a day. There would be times when the shelter would have as many as seventy people staying there, and when you need to make room to accommodate the new guests, then it was easy to test the most suspicious people. There's a pretty good chance that you may get one or two of them who have the dirt on them that they're doing become exposed. That day they caught ten people, two women and eight men including Janice, Joe the artist and CW. Janice got caught for abusing prescription drugs while Joe the artist had had weed and alcohol in his system, and CW was for having crack cocaine in his. All of them had three days, and every one of them having to attend Daymark for outpatient substance abuse classes.

CW would stay at the crack house that he frequently visited, and for him that was good. He could continue to work at the construction site that he was at and still enjoy the luxury of beaming up to Scottie. He could indulge all the way up to three days before he has to stop smoking the rock. You see, it only takes crack cocaine three days to get out of your system as opposed to weed that takes up to thirty. Joe the artist had faced the same consequences of doing three days out of the shelter, but he was charged for having weed in his system. After he was asked to leave, Joe would spend a lot of time at the Eastern Gateway park sitting around drinking a beer first thing in the morning trying to hustle some business from the people at the bus depot adjacent to the park by displaying his artwork. For Joe the artist he was able to survive because of the money he would bring in on a pretty frequent basis. Joe was a good artist, and he was in demand by individuals and businesses for the work that he could produce. He was enrolled at RCCC, so if he wasn't at the park, then he was able to hustle the staff and students at the college. Any way something was about to go down with the penalties being handed out by the shelter. Joe the artist was going to survive this and find a way to prosper behind it.

Janice was only one of two women to get caught using drugs. Janice was using prescription drugs and cocaine at the time she got busted. This wasn't the first time that she was caught and was asked to leave the shelter. A year earlier Janice and her husband entered the shelter. He's an African-American and a vet who was working on trying to receive his disability. They were a couple when they first came in together, and before the year was over, they were separated. There has been several times when they left in the mornings that they would be seen by the park stopping, or at the gas station to get a forty-ounce bottle of beer to return to the park sitting there and drinking. At one time or another, they would get into an argument like a married old couple would do. I recall that he was mad at Janice, and was screaming at the top of his lungs. He called her a stupid black bitch. Now let me remind you that she's a white woman. She replied to her husband, "So what do you think you are, white?" One weekend the two of them went out on a drinking and drugging spree. They both blew into the breathalyzer and it showed that they were positive for alcohol in their system. The next day when they wanted to re-entered into the shelter, Janice was able to enter but her husband wasn't. I don't know the reason for him not entering, but I do know that I didn't want know the reason for it. He remained out of the shelter for several days, before going into the VA for a substance abuse program. He was admitted into their program and hasn't been seen since. The one thing that you can count on at the shelter is that people will talk and start rumors. Rumors aren't uncommon when it comes down to living in a communal environment. I've seen and experienced being part of the rumor mill first hand. I try to ignore it, because I had only one goal in mind to get the hell out of living in the shelter.

The meeting started at nine o'clock sharp, making it mandatory that all of the shelter guest having to be there. None of the people who were asked to leave were at the monthly meeting. They had to leave before the meeting had commenced. Rodney lead the meeting off telling everyone that he had asked ten people to leave the shelter because of violating the substance abuse policy. He reiterated the position of the shelter that abusing drugs will not be tolerated. Next he told the guest about smoking on the grounds of the shelter, and that there is only one area of the shelter that you are allowed to smoke. That was on the concrete slab patio area where the staff had placed outdoor ashtrays for people to extinguish their cigarettes. He was giving the residents a warning that if they were to see cigarette butts on the grounds, or seeing them smoking anywhere other than the designated area that the administration would make the facility smoke-free.

When he announced that was a possibility the residents who smoked cigarettes were all up in arms. This was within good reason, because the residents weren't the only ones who were smoking in the unauthorized areas. Anyone could come there on any given day into the crisis assistance network for help and wait for a volunteer assistant to see them, but it was the process of waiting to see the volunteer. If the person who was waiting was a smoker they would go outside to take a smoke, and they would just drop off the finished cigarette on the ground. I've personally seen some staff members hold a conversation with one of the people who would just be hanging around the shelter while they were smoking without asking them to go into the smoking area. That same staff member told me that I need to move into the smoking area, and I told her respectfully not to bother because I was just passing through as I was walking to the bus depot.

Rodney then addressed the residents about smoking and drinking on the side of the building reminding them that there are cameras set up all around the building that they can see all that's happening. Cameras are set up everywhere on the grounds and inside the shelter and crisis network areas. The only places that they're not set up is inside the restroom areas, and I wouldn't be surprised if they had the phone lines wiretapped. Now I can confirm that there is a camera on the side of the building and that if they wanted to they could see through the monitor that there is quite a bit of unethical activity going on around there that has never been addressed until now. How come they hadn't address the fact that people, and not just shelter guest were drinking alcohol and smoking weed and crack I don't have the foggiest idea why! He also warned them if anyone was caught there doing anything *un*-authorize that they would be in jeopardy of losing their privileges of staying at the shelter and would be subjected to getting days out for the infractions. Ms. Foster would step in and try to explain why letting the residents know that there are certain things that their insurance policy wouldn't cover, and these were the reasons why the staff was going to have to start enforcing these rules more strictly.

Nate would come in to try to reinforce what Rodney and Ms. Foster stated. Nate would try to do that by attempting to add some comic relief, but in the process he's condescending to those who didn't realize how he's talking down to them. He would continue by telling the guest that there's a program that if some of the residents would be interested in joining the program. This will assist those people who didn't have any success finding jobs. The program would include working with the shelter and the crisis assistance network on whatever work that they needed to have done at the facility. A resident would have to do sixty days of service and would be eligible to get assisted housing at the eagle's nest, and earn a maximum of seventy-five dollars a month. Rodney would inform the residents that they will need to do their chores when their names would show up on the list failure to this would also result in consequences of being asked to leave the shelter for several days.

Nate would add his two cents in here also. He would take the chore list and, in his own sarcastic way, call the name of the person who had a chore. He would tell them their duty and explained what that chore would be. On this night my name was on the list, and my duty was to police perimeter of the building for loose trash. So when he called my name I raised my hand, and he told me "Leroy, you've got to police the outside of the building. You know what that is and can you do that job?" I told him of course I do, and that I could do your job because I have a bachelor's degree in child and family development. Until then none of the other residents knew that I held a degree. They kind of knew that there was something different about me, because I never wanted to be homeless let alone look like one. I would dress the way I did as if I was going into an office working a regular nine to five job. When I told Nate that bit of information you should've seen the look of astonishment on his face it was priceless. He was standing there with his mouth wide open, because someone used his own sarcasm back on him. Some of the guest were laughing when I told him that. Others were probably thinking, wow he's got a set of balls on him to talk to Nate like that. Both of my parents are dead, and it would've only been them or my grandparents that I would've let talk down to me like that. With my snide reply that was given I was sending a message to him, the administration and the rest of the staff to know that you're not dealing with a passive person. That you will speak to me with respect, and you will know that you're talking to an educated man.

After I said that I notice that the executive director Ms. Foster was making a beeline to the door, David still didn't show any emotion holding steadfast with his normal poker face and Rodney opened the floor for questions, but none of the residents had any outside of the question about the designated smoking area. Much to my surprise I thought that there would've been more questions about the program that was mentioned earlier, and other matters that would've concerned about their own welfare. Rodney would then close out the meeting letting the resident know that unless they have a medical reason, guest were required to tell their caseworkers if they had any prescribed drugs and failure to do that would result in penalties for them. There weren't any other questions to that fact, and shortly the meeting was over.

At the end of the meeting Nate had come over to me and asked me where I got my degree from. I told him that I received my education from Benedict College a historically black college in Columbia, South Carolina I guess that impressed him. Soon Rodney would join the conversation, and the both of them asked me if I would be interested in joining in the program. Apprehensive at first, I told them that I would give it a try but I wouldn't commit to doing long hours and days. I'm still on top of my goal of trying to get out, and try to secure work in the social services areas. I told them that I would be open to working two days a week in the morning until twelve noon. By doing this it would allow me to use the rest of my afternoons to look for a job. I also realize that the best time to look for a job is in the morning time. Looking for a job in the afternoon is harder because you only have a limited time on the computers at the places that have the internet access since I didn't have a laptop at the time. I was willing to do something that I know would benefit the shelter, crisis network and just as important for myself. After hearing what Rodney, Nate and now David too joined into the conversation giving me their sales spiel I was asked to come into the crisis assistance network when the doors opened up at eight. I was told to see the Emily who was in charge of scheduling the volunteers.

The next morning after I woke up and had breakfast, I stuck around the shelter so that I could meet with Emily. Normally I would've gotten out of there not long after having breakfast unless it was cold outside. If it were cold, I would've stayed inside until the last possible minute then go into the lobby of the crisis assistance network and leave about ten minutes before nine to go to the library, unemployment or the career center. Me working around there wasn't what I wanted to do unless it was to work at the crisis assistance network. I didn't mind working with the food pantry, or the clothing department, but it wasn't what I was interested in doing assisting the patrons with the crisis assistance network. I did the work regardless of my own personal feelings. Whatever they wanted me to do there I was going to do it, and be the best damn person at the task that they asked me to do.

I met Emily and she told me that I would begin working with Nate on the dock where they would do the intake of the food for the pantry and the soup kitchen. I was told that they only needed me to help them out just two days during the week. I was thinking that this would be good, because I didn't want to take away too much time from me continuing to stay on my goal. One of the things that I would do was to spend as much time away from the shelter as I could possibly do. I had an agenda: in the mornings, I would leave to stop at the career center, unemployment office, or the library to do my online job searches. Staying around the shelter too long will make you complacent, and you'll lose your focus on whatever it is that you're trying to do. I couldn't afford to lose that focus. I had to continue to work on the goal that I've set for myself. Now I didn't alienate myself and didn't socialize very much with the others who lived there with me. Doing that was damn near impossible, because of the fact that you lived there. Some of the residents wouldn't let you be to yourself unless you almost had to threaten to use violence against them.

When I started volunteering there, I was told by Emily that I would start working with Nate in the food pantry. Going with him to pick up supplies from the warehouses, and working on the loading dock when businesses and people would drop off the food donations. Working on the loading dock, the food pantry volunteers would have to weigh the food, log in the name of the person or business who made the donation, and give them a receipt for tax purposes. Going to the warehouses, you would assist others by getting the canned and dry good items as well as getting the toiletry supplies. Nate would also go to the stores or food banks to pick up the USDA food for the participants who qualified to receive it. I was told that I would work part time in the crisis network because of my educational and work background. This was the part that I really had an interest in working with. Prior to moving to Salisbury, I had several years of working with nonprofit social service agencies. I worked four years with the Urban League of Essex County in Newark, New Jersey, as an admissions and recruitment director. Working in Newark, I was responsible for recruiting new trainees for free job training in computer operations and Word processing classes, but I would also assist in recruiting businesses to assist the trainees in the placement of the students. I also worked another year with an Urban League affiliate when I move from New Jersey to South Carolina. I was employed at the Columbia Urban League as a program coordinator for an after-school and summer enrichment program for at-risk children ranging from elementary school to high school. I thought if they knew about those skills, it may show them that I can be a valuable person to the causes that they do.

The first week, I was working with Nate and the other volunteers in the food pantry and the warehouses. We would do everything that was required by checking in donations, gathering supplies from the warehouses, and giving assistance to those who needed it. I would eat lunch just before the soup kitchen would open about twenty minutes before, and when the clock struck twelve, I was out. Doing the work there wasn't necessarily my favorite thing to do, regardless of me being compensated for it or not. Some of the people were wondering why I would leave out so early, but that wouldn't bother me. I was hoping that I would be working in the food pantry for a short term, but to my knowledge, that wasn't going to happen.

I continued to work in the pantry with Nate for another two weeks. At the end of each day, Emily would make a point to see me to inquire about my availability for the next day. During my first two weeks of working, I actually worked four out of the five days in the pantry. I thought that doing this, it would afford me the opportunity to start working in the crisis network, but that wasn't going to happen. What I was doing was for the betterment of how the staff there could use me. There were days during that period when there wasn't enough people to help in the crisis assistance network, but looking at me, they must've figured that I looked like someone who didn't know what they were doing. I felt that they were judging me on my appearance and not by the experience that I bring to the table. I wear my hair in locs, and many people take to the assumption that I may practice the religious faith of Rastafari. If they bothered to do the research, they may have thought that I didn't eat pork because Rastafarians, like the Jews and Muslims, practice not eating pork as a part of their religious doctrine. A ritual that some Rastafarian practice is smoking marijuana, but this wasn't something that I did or considered. I had no urge to do it because I stopped over the past five years, and the only time I strayed was when my mother passed away.

I continued to work in the pantry for the next three weeks. I stuck to my goal of working toward becoming a self-sufficient person. I was only going to work the two days during the week, because the more days that I gave them, the less time I would have to look for a job. On my last day that I worked in the pantry, I had finished weighing the food from one of the local grocery store chains that made a food donation when Nate summoned me to come with him and Barry so that we could pick up supplies from the warehouses. As we were leaving, Nate and Barry were sitting in the front of the truck while I was sitting in the rear reading a newspaper that was left in the backseat. Nate looked over at the concrete patio where people were sitting and smoking cigarettes. He was talking to Barry before he posed the question, "Don't these people have somewhere to go?"

That struck a nerve with me, and it truly made me furious when I heard this. I was thinking to myself, "Is this fool for real?" I was wondering what in the world this jackass was thinking. First of all, this was a homeless shelter and a crisis center where people live and come to this facility to receive assistance. These people, as he put it, were homeless, unemployed, and disenfranchised. How he dare he come out of his mouth by labeling them "these people" was well beyond me. Later, he and Barry were talking politics, and Nate affirmed that he was a republican in support for Mitt Romney and his social agenda. At that point, I was about to become Harry Belafonte and call him a house nigger, not short of calling his ass an Uncle Tom.

Every so often in my lifetime, I would run across an African American man or woman who has worked his way up to become a socially acceptable African American in the eyes of white people. I like to call this the OJ Simpson syndrome, because once they became successful, they will do things for charitable organizations. Doing good deeds for these organizations normally meant that the person was getting their names out there for the affluent people to recognize them and, in return, forgetting about the place where they came from. All of a sudden, they became too good to recognize the same people who they themselves grew up with, went to school with, and more than likely, the same people who they went to church with. This is what I call being a good nigger! I was given the impression that now since he has arrived that Nate was the kind of person who grew up on the other side of the track but now has a big house on the other side of town and now probably worships at the church that can raise the most money for a fundraising event. I was so ready to read him on his comment about "these people." This was definitely one time that I had to pray hard to ask God not to let me lose it.

When you went to the warehouse, Nate would have his pickup and a mini-trailer with the name of the Rowan Helping Ministries on the sides and the back of it. We would make two trips to the separate warehouses. The first trip was to the warehouse that housed the canned and dry good supplies, and the second trip was to the place that housed the toiletries. Nate would make sure that the trailer and the bed of the truck would be stocked to capacity. Doing that was good because it minimized the number times that they should've made trips to restock whatever was needed. Barry was normally the guy who would go along with Nate, and another person would go with him. Most of the time, it was another volunteer, but when there wasn't a volunteer to go with him, then I was drafted like a Vietnam inductee to assist them.

Once the truck and trailer were stocked to capacity, we would return to the shelter to unload everything to restock the pantry and the supply closet. Barry and I would be the ones who would have to do that and, in between, unloading and replenishing the pantry and supply closet. We also had the responsibility of accepting food donations and logging in the information of the records for the shelter and the donors. If there wasn't anyone donating food, then the unloading and restocking wasn't hard, and it could be done in a timely manner. That was if Barry wasn't eating, drinking, or chain-smoking at that time. Now Barry would work and did a great job of what he was supposed to be doing when he did the actual work. Barry knew what it was like to work his way out of the shelter and into the Eagle's Nest. He worked there for a period of ninety days before he was asked to come to work as a staff member. I wasn't mad at him for not pulling his weight, because he had worked many months before they would symbolically accept him as an equal employee of the shelter. I knew that in my heart after seeing how they treated the people who had to move into the shelter and wouldn't view them as an equal but more or less as someone who wasn't capable of doing better for themselves.

The more I thought about it, I knew that this would be my last day volunteering in the program. They would never give me the opportunity to work in the area of the crisis assistance network. This was something that I had an expertise in, which I received my degree in. Emily and the people in human resources never took an opportunity to check my background or to call anyone to verify if I even graduated from the college. They didn't do that because they had no intentions of doing that.

Now I don't know why I felt so sensitive when I heard Nate say what he did, but I was truly outraged when I heard it. I don't know if it came to me from my days as a child. I was one of the first kids on my block whose parents were able to afford a pair of canvas Chuck Taylor Converse sneakers. Like all kids, when you got something new, the first thing that you'd do is to go around the neighborhood to show off what you had to the other kids. I got those sneakers and went bragging about how cool it was that I wore a pair of Cons and not the PF Flyers or Pro-Keds. As I was bragging to my friends that I had these sneakers, little to my own knowledge, my father was coming home from work and heard me as he was walking behind me without me knowing that he was even in the area. Once I noticed that he was there, he asked me to walk with him to the house. He explained to me that I shouldn't ever try to make anyone feel bad because of material things that I had and they didn't. He told me that our family wasn't rich and that me being able to wear nice clothes was a blessing that I shouldn't ever take for granted. That was a lesson that he told me that has stayed with me to this very day. Maybe this is why I have a passion for wanting to work in social services, because of that lesson that he taught me so many years ago.

One of the biggest unknown variables about living at the shelter is that the people there are a very tight-knit blended family unit. The bonds that are built there are closer than some biological families that you may grow up with. It almost resembles that of a high school community. When I was in high school, everyone was in a clique of some kind or another if you weren't a loner. People in the shelter are compassionate about the welfare of one another. When one of the guests would get kicked out for whatever reason, the guest who stayed there would help those who were out by supplying them with cigarettes, a bag lunch, and some spare change that they could afford to let go. People who lived in the shelter can pick and tease each other, but have an outsider come around there and pick a fight with one of the residents there, and they've made a near life-threatening mistake. Almost like a visiting high school football team coming to your school's stadium wanting to start a fight, and they find out that they bit off a little more than they can chew. Several of the shelter residents would come to the aid of another who was there and wouldn't allow some outsider trying to infiltrate and hurt one of their own.

I just couldn't understand why I was feeling as offended as I did when I heard Nate say what he did, but then it hit me. I was a member of this blended family. Whether I wanted to become a member or not, I was part of something that was bigger than me. This was the second reality check that I realized as a resident of the shelter. I had built bonds with CW, Joe the artist, Forbes, and the others. I didn't look down on them, because I wasn't in a better situation than any of them. For me to look down or to try to put myself on a pedestal would've made me a hypocrite. Whether I wanted to admit it to myself or not, I was now part of this kinship. This wasn't a bad thing, because not everyone at the shelter is a derelict, addict, or criminal as some people may want to perceive them to be. Shelter residents are displaced mill workers, retired veterans, teachers, truck drivers, high school dropouts, college students, writers, musicians, actors, bankers, and social workers. They come from every ethnic, economic, religious, and social group from every part of the state. They are single mothers who may have been in an abusive relationship and don't have the resources to move into a home that will provide the security from their abuser. They are people who are working to get a hand up and not a handout. I was now one of them, and they were now a part of me. This had been the toughest thing that I'd ever experienced in my lifetime. I wouldn't want anyone to experience being in this situation, including my worst enemy. Meanwhile, I missed the times I spent with my granddaughter, taking her shopping and going to the nail salon. It's been close to a year now since I had the opportunity to see her, and I know that she misses me as much as I missed spending time with her. This was something to make me keep my focus on getting out of this environment.

CHAPTER 4

Time To Make Some Rounds

I had a little history in this town before I moved to here to Salisbury. I was a student at Allen University before I transferred to their 'cross-the-street rivals at Benedict College. I played basketball for the Allen University Yellow Jackets at the age of thirty-five. At that time, I was probably one of the first, if not the only, person to play on a college basketball team in three different decades in the country. I was a walk on basketball player for the JV team at Northwestern Oklahoma State Univerisity in Alva, Oklahoma. I played during the first half of the season in 1979 before the Christmas break. After the Christmas break, I was in jeopardy of not playing the rest of the season when I returned in January of 1980, because I didn't take my psychology final before the break. When I returned, I had to take it and I passed it. I played only one game when I came back from the break before I found out that my fraternal grandmother passed away and then returned home. I didn't return back to school until sixteen years later, and when I did, that's when I met the coach at Allen University. I inquired to him and asked if I could learn the game from him working as a student assistant coach. He took one look at me, asked me my name, and told me to come to tryouts. I told him that I wasn't interested in playing, that I was too old, and that I didn't believe that I had any eligibility left. He told me not to worry about that and to be at the gym for tryouts at seven thirty. I did that in 1996 and played my first college exhibition game on Halloween night against the legendary Laurinburg Academy at the gymnasium on the campus of Denmark Technical College in Denmark, South Carolina, for a tournament classic.

Later that year, our school came to Salisbury to play in a holiday tournament that was held at Catawba College. They had four schools represented at the tournament, the two local schools, Livingstone College and Catawba College and Belmont Abbey University along with Allen. The very first game of the tournament I was sent into, the game and the coach had a play ran for me. As I was making a cut toward the basket, I sprained my knee and missed the next four games. Although I finished out the season, I knew in my heart that it was the end of my playing days competitively.

One morning, as I was taking the bus to go to the career center, I was looking out of the window, and as I was passing by the Meroney Theatre, I looked at the marquee. I saw that the Piedmont Players were holding auditions for a play that I've performed before, and they were auditioning for *Dreamgirls*. In the morning, if I wasn't at the library, there was a pretty good chance that I'd be over at the career center mainly because I had more computer access without the limitations of the hours on using them. When I saw that the Piedmont Players Theatre Company was holding auditions for what I knew, it was something that I wanted to do. This was one of the things that I wanted to do once I got here and saw that they had a community theatre in town.

They actually had two performing arts theatres in the middle of downtown Salisbury. One was on South Main Street where the Meroney Theatre is and around the corner on North Fisher Street is where they have the Norvell Theatre—that's the children's theatre. This was one of the few attractions that made me want to move to Salisbury, that a small town this size has a theatre district for the performing arts that produces Broadway-quality stage plays. There is another smaller, more intimate theatre venue on Lee Street just outside of the main business district called the Black Box Theatre. Looking at what this small town has to offer, I knew that I could benefit from it and build on my performing resume while still working on securing a job here. With three theatres and the two colleges had me thinking that this wasn't such a bad suggestion that my cousin encouraged me to do.

Livingstone College has two theatres on its campus. Livingstone is the AME Zion historically black college in town and was named after the philanthropist and explorer Dr. Livingstone who was lost in the jungles of Africa before being found by Dr. Stanley. They have the Varick Auditorium, a larger, more modern facility with adequate lighting and moderate sound equipment. They also have smaller older theatre on campus that doesn't have the more modern sound or lighting equipment but has some of the best acoustics without a sound system that I've ever heard. It had a very nice-sized elongated stage and is called the Tubman Little Theatre.

Before the Piedmont Players bought the Meroney Theatre, they did many of their performances at Catawba College. When I went back to get my bachelor's degree, I was a non-traditional student and basketball player who would normally drive my own car when we left our campus to play away games. I couldn't play the game against Catawba with a sprained knee when I first visited their campus, so I let the coach know that I was going to the gym early and that I would meet him and my teammates over there. When I arrived at the gymnasium, I toured the athletic facility and viewed their athletic hall of fame. I had some extra time on my hand, because it was still about three hours before tip-off. So I went across the campus and saw that they had a planetarium and ran across the theatre. What I saw was that they have a wonderful state-of-the-art theatre with studio lighting and a high-tech sound system.

I wasn't trying to make a career out of acting, because there's too many people who had more experience and training than I. Too many things to consider when looking to pursue that avenue as a career. You have to be ready to leave at a moment's notice when it comes down to doing auditions. You have to have good training and constantly working on the craft. You have to be willing to go work on seminars and workshops for acting. It was something that I wanted to do as a child, but later, as I got older, I fell in love with sports, and the acting bug was gone. I fell back in love with the stage in my senior year at Benedict. My professor Charles D. Brooks III, from my theatre appreciation class, informed the class that the fine arts department was holding auditions to be performed for one of the first national conferences on reparations. The play was performed in the banquet hall of the school, and if I'm not mistaken was called *Life and Death on the Plantation*. Because of the lack of the presence of white students at the school who were willing to participate in the program, I was asked to do the role of the slave master. Little did I know how big this production was going to be. During rehearsal, there was talk about having a Caribbean band to underscore the music in the background while the performance was taking place. This wasn't a speaking role, but a role in a play that was narrated with very few speaking parts.

While rehearsing for the performance, I was told that I need to use a whip as a prop. I learned to follow the instructions of my teacher who was the director of this production, but I was catching hell trying to get this whip to crack but did it successfully only a few times. After three rehearsals, countless times trying to master that role of the slave master, it was figuratively time to crack the whip. It was showtime and time for me to put what I've learned into action. The show was going off without a hitch—the narrator was doing their thing, the musical performers doing theirs, and my co-star were acting before it was my cue to come in. When that cue happened, I remembered what stage fright was once I saw the audience. There was a flashback from the last time that I was on stage in the sixth grade. For me to get over it, I always remembered that your best friend in a situation when you didn't want to fail went by the first name of Frankie and the last name was Fear. I remembered that from an old "*Rocky*" movie with Sylvester Stallone. I had Frankie Fear on my shoulders as I entered into the banquet hall. Thank goodness that I didn't have any lines, because I probably would have forgotten them. I entered the staged area of the banquet hall in coveralls, a straw hat, and in white face along with my whip in hand. I was allowed to improvise and say, "Get back to the field, workers," but I made it a point to say that after I was to successfully make that whip crack. I was so proud of myself, because it sounded so good and crisp like the way you heard a whip crack just like in the introduction to the TV show *Rawhide*. At the end of the performance, my director thanked all of the actors, but it was something that he said to me that had stuck. He told me and said, "That was acting." I've been bitten by the performing bug ever since.

I was going to the career center more and more instead of the library, because of the accessibility of the computer usage. The library only allowed for library cardholders to use the computers for only two hours but they did have access to the Wi-Fi for an unlimited time period if you had a smartphone, tablet, or laptop computer. I was spending more time at the career center than ever before. Now my morning schedule included going there, looking online for a job until three in the afternoon, and making my way toward the library afterward. I did that every day until it came down to going to the Meroney Theatre for the auditions. I was hyped about doing the auditions, because I did the show before several years after I graduated from college. I performed in the role of Marty when I did the play before, but this time I was looking to try to land the lead male character of Curtis.

Certain things about performing that I like most are the rehearsals. That is without a doubt my favorite part about doing a show. The things that only the cast and crew members see and experience are priceless. The mistakes that the actors make when it comes to remembering their lines, where they need to be on stage concerning the blocking are things that make it fun for me when it comes performing a play in the rehearsal itself. It's like how the TV networks would do showing the outtakes that happens when they're videotape a program. It happens just like that when you're rehearsing a show, but for me it's a joy because I'm there to experience it firsthand. I'm part of all the action. I was going to be blessed to have this opportunity to do that all over again. I couldn't explain it, but I've had many moments of euphoria that couldn't compare to acting. It's a high that I couldn't experience when I was smoking weed or drinking. Acting comes a close second only to that when my granddaughter in kindergarten, and she made a Mother's Day card with her picture on it. She gave it to me, but I told her to give it to mother. She insisted that I have it and gave it to me instead. Acting comes a close second to that one experience.

It was time to go to the audition, and I wasn't as nervous as I would've normally been. Maybe it was because I knew the play like the back of my hand. I remembered all the song numbers, but believe it or not, I didn't remember any of the dialog from it. I was confident that I had a part in the play. I was trying hard not to land the part of Marty that I chose not to read for. There was singing and choreography involved in it, and I felt confident in my dancing more than the singing. I've been dancing ever since my days of going to the high school dances and Saturday evenings after a football or basketball game in the school gym.

I hate open auditions, because I always had to revisit my stage fright. There were several people from town and the surrounding communities coming for their chance to become locally famous if not nationally. During the auditions, the director would ask everyone to fill out the standard applications. This would include the name, address, contact information, clothes sizes, and past performance history. Performers would also have to sing a few bars and read some lines from the script. This was one of the few times that I've gone into an audition where they didn't ask if you had a prepared monologue to perform. The producers gave all the performers a number after their applications were completed, and once that was done, they would call the performers to come to the middle of the rehearsal hall and sing a song. Most of the performers who came without any sheet music would sing "Twinkle Twinkle Little Star" or "Happy Birthday to You."

It was my time when they called me, and I was ready to sing. I chose to sing "My Girl" by the Temptations. I knew all the songs from the show, but my honest feeling about singing a song from the show that you're auditioning for is too much like copying the original performer from the soundtrack. My singing was pretty good, but in my own biased opinion, it's not the strongest part of my performing component. It's probably the weakest part of that aspect for me performing on stage. If I had to do it over again, I would've done it differently and sang a song from that show. It would've been the one titled "My Dream," the same song that the lead actor had to perform in the show.

After all the people had sang their songs, the producers gathered together to see how all the actors read for the speaking parts. While waiting there, I had made a few good connections with some of the guys who auditioned for the show. I connected with this brother from New York named Malcolm who moved down to Salisbury to go to college at Livingstone. His mother was a resident there, and she'd moved back home bringing Malcolm with her. He's a cool brother who was looking to do this production, but he had a dry monotone sense of humor. Joe the actor was another brother who I met at the audition, but this actor brought something to the table. After talking to him for a minute, I saw that he had some credits doing some shows at Livingstone College in their theatre department. The last person who I was talking to was my main man, Tony. Tony was from South Carolina who moved here when he was a student at Livingstone. He was a seasoned performer with the Piedmont Players and I knew that he would be my biggest competition for the part of Marty if I wasn't cast in the part of Curtis. Most of the other people in the cast were younger than I, and there were a few of the cast members who were my peers.

Auditions lasted for two days, and at the end of the second day, the director and producers of the show made the final list for the shows cast. I was really hoping that I was selected for the role of Curtis. I was very excited, because of my familiarity the show and the characters from it. The director thanked and dismissed everyone for coming out to the auditions. He informed everybody that the list was on the table by the entrance to the rehearsal hall. With the same kind of anticipation like a child looking for that gift on Christmas or their birthday, I was expecting to get that role. I waited until the bulk of the people who auditioned left the table after seeing their results. When I arrived at the table I saw that my name was on the list, but it wasn't for the part that I anticipated. I was given a dual role. I was a supporting actor in the opening scene for the Trutones, and in act two, I was in the role of Jerry Norman. The other times that I wasn't onstage I was singing in the background off it, and when I was onstage, I was in the choreographed numbers.

I kind of felt cheated, because of the fact when I did the application process that I listed that I did perform this production in Columbia, but that didn't seem to matter to the producers of the show. They knew what kind of performers and who they wanted to have do the roles for the show production. They whiffed at the opportunity to get a couple of people who were really talented.

One person that comes to mind was a woman named Tionne. She's a sister who's a seasoned performer out of Winston-Salem. She performed spoken word and had done some good stage credits to her resume, including *Ain't Misbehavin'*, *Don't Bother Me I Can't Cope*, and *The River Niger* just to mention a few. The sister had a good set of pipes to boot and caught on to choreography very quickly. Another person the producers whiffed on was a sister named Cassey. She didn't have the stage credits like Tionne, but was a strong soprano who would've been perfect in the role of Lorelle. The last of the females who could've been cast as one of the premiere roles would Tameka. She too had done some stage work before and had an excellent singing voice. All of these women were placed in the secondary roles, and as members of the chorus for the choreographed numbers, and when it called for the big ensemble scenes. They were cast in parts for the Stepp Sisters and Le Styles who are the girl groups of the production.

I was thinking to myself that the producers of the show were strictly going on what they had seen in the movie. If they were going for the talent, then they missed the target on the talent all together. They were typecasting, and they were doing it according to what I believe would be a selling point to the audience. One example was the woman who they cast for the role of Michelle. She looked the part, but it was obvious to all the cast members that she was uncomfortable on stage. She didn't have a good singing voice, but this was the choice of the producers. Now there was a good choice for the role of Effie. The only thing about her that didn't make it an excellent choice was that she didn't train her voice to sing the songs in the key that the songs were written in. She was an amazing talent. She could sing, act, and dance in the choreographed numbers. She could've bought the house down if she had trained her voice to sing "And I Am Telling You," the show's premiere song the way that audiences are accustomed to hearing the song.

Miscasting wasn't only on the side of the female characters, but the male ones as well. The one that comes to mind most was the role of Marty. That role was given to Malcolm. He's a nice guy, but I found out as the rehearsal went on that he didn't like to commit his lines to memory. He worked in Charlotte and it was hard for him to make rehearsal, because of his work schedule didn't allow him to make a good portion of the practices. With that obstacle, and the fact that the director was lenient of the cast members' schedules, he used that fact to his advantage. The closer we got to opening night was when he started to make an effort to commit his lines to memory. It got so bad that when opening night came, he used a leather-covered binder as a prop to hide his script as he went on stage. When he returned off stage, he would read his lines in between the scenes he was to enter and still flubbed some of them when he returned. He committed a show business taboo by going on stage with his script in hand. I know directors who would've dismissed an actor for doing something like that, and he would've been replaced in the second act. He was blessed to work with this director. I realized that since Salisbury is such a small community that whatever they felt was appropriate was going to be the standard.

The person was the one who was cast in the role of C.C. was a good choice. He had some previous experience on doing stage productions. He had a good stage presence and a nice singing voice. The most talented out of all the characters was the one who played Jimmy Early. As rehearsal went on, I found out that he was a student at the University of North Carolina-Charlotte and had known my niece who was a couple of years older than he. Tyler has been performing in the theatre since he was in high school and has done stage work all around the Charlotte metropolitan area. Most of the principal male characters didn't have to do a lot of choreographed numbers throughout the production, but it wasn't the same for the women. Most of them had choreographed numbers that they had to perform when it came to the singing in the show. The role of Curtis was well cast when they chose the guy to play that role. He was a good singer and danced well also. Marvin lived in Charlotte and performed with several other performing companies. He didn't commit any taboos, and he picked up his lines very quickly.

I was still disappointed about not getting the part for Curtis, but I was willing to do the part that was assigned to me. The one thing that I notice that there were a lot of the guys who were in the production are either gay or bisexual. Once the public performance started, people who saw the production told my colleague Tony, that they knew how many of these guys were gay. Tony flipped the statement back on them and asked them to tell him how many of the men there that weren't gay. It's no secret that there are quite a few talented and gifted people in the circle of Broadway and Hollywood who are gay, lesbian, or bisexual. In this production, there was more fruit on the stage than there was in a box of raisin bran cereal.

Although the production had a lot of talented and gifted people, there wasn't any crew for the show. This was another show business taboo that shouldn't have been. Performers who weren't on stage were asked to double up as a crew members. The first time that I was asked to do that I had honestly considered to leaving the play. I thought that I had nothing to lose. I had done this play before, and not to do it wouldn't hurt me, but not doing it would bring down my credibility as an actor. I never turned down a part that I auditioned for, and I have always given it my best. My parents have never let me quit anything that I had started, and I wasn't going to start doing it now.

I noticed when I was in the rehearsal hall that they had posters of the past productions that they've done at the Piedmont Players theatre. I was particularly interest in the productions of African American plays, and the one thing that I noticed was that the only plays that they've done were for African Americans were musicals. I don't know why, but this unnerved me. Everything that I saw was a well-acclaimed musical production, but there was more substance to African American theatre than singing and dancing. The producers of the shows would open up their season with one of these plays that featured an African American musical. These shows would bring in a good crowd and a lot of money to the Piedmont Players, but the main part that made me conscious was the fact that they only saw the need to put the African American performers in musical stage productions. Personally, I felt insulted by the theatre company doing this. As a performer, I was pleased that they did do theatre that address the need for African American productions, but as a person of color, I know from my experiences that there were other productions that could be performed.

Theatre is more than just musicals. There is also comedies, dramas, and other genres of performance than what they are doing at the Piedmont Players. The ones that come to mind are by writers like August Wilson and Lynn Nottage who earn Pulitzer Prizes for their compositions. African American theatre for drama are plays that have substance. Just think about plays like *Fences, Intimate Apparel, The Piano Lesson,* and *Ruined.* These plays tell the story of African American life through the expression of acting with the absence of singing and dancing numbers not included in the performance. In my mind it is almost the same as telling African Americans to continue doing the minstrel theatre with the song and dance routines of the late nineteenth through the early twentieth centuries.

I had made an acquaintance with a famous Hollywood director Jama Fanaka from my college professor at Benedict College Professor Charles D. Brooks III. Brooks had done some screen work in Hollywood when he was working on his graduate degree at UCLA. He worked on two films with Jamaa Fanaka, who was best known for his trilogy of the *Penitentiary* movies that featured Leon Isaac Kennedy and Mister T. I had made his acquaintance through Charles and found his page on Facebook. I've been in touch with him two years prior to moving to Salisbury. I've spoken and chatted with him several times. I had mentioned to Jamaa about the progress of how the current production that I was working on is going.

I was talking to him about how many things that I was told were taboos that were being done with the current production that I was a part of. Much to his amazement, he was shocked as much as I was. I was telling him about wanting to present to the Piedmont Players the play written by Charlie Russell, *Five on the Black Hand Side.* He concurred that it was a good idea to do that, and that I should find out when their board or committee meets to suggest doing that play.

Days after the run of *Dreamgirls* was over, I thought that I better have a plan B in place just in case the committee of the Piedmont Players rejected my suggestion for the play. I decided to think of forming my own African American production company. After seeing how the city of Salisbury seemed to be stuck in the mode of keeping things on the historic level. I thought that forming my own production company would be a good idea. Another interesting fact about this town is that they have a large statue that stands on the center aisle on West Innes Street just off the corner from the Rowan County Administration and the *Salisbury Post* newspaper. There stands a figurine on a pedestal of an angel holding up a wounded confederate soldier commemorating the men who served in battle of the Civil War. This isn't an unusual thing for southern cities to attempt to hold on to the good old days of Dixie.

In South Carolina, a group had commemorated the treasonous act of secession from the United States with the 150 year anniversary by throwing a formal ball for the occasion. Another thing that comes to mind that also happened in South Carolina is the confederate flag that once was on top of the state capital continues to fly on the grounds. Many other southern states have found ways to incorporate it into their own state flags. One other state that comes to mind is Georgia. There was controversy when the 1996 Olympics were held there, because members of the International Olympic Committee were starting to second guess their choice of Atlanta being chosen as the host city for the centennial games when officials of the games noticed the way that the Confederate battle flag was incorporated into the state flag. Having this display was a blatant act of disrespect for social progress, but the fact that descendants of southern sympathizers tried to classify it as southern sovereignty doesn't surprised me. Even when my younger brother Lance who graduated from Columbia High School in the state capital of South Carolina in 1982, one hundred and seventeen years after the end of the civil war, his graduating class had to sing "I Wished I Was In Dixie."

I started taken the first step to start forming my own production and theatre performing company on this on my younger brother Lloyd's birthday coincidentally. I already had the logo that I knew that I was going to use. It had evolved from an art assignment while I was a student in college. My art class professor was giving the class a lesson in symmetry. We were given an assignment by using food coloring to develop a Rorschach test. My professor instructed her students to attempt to draw a figure out of what the result of the prints that we made. We did several prints and I produced some images of insects mostly, because the patterns of the ink made me think of butterflies and dragonflies. All of them made me think of insect but one, so I was thinking what I could do with this print. When I first saw it, I envisioned that I saw the continent of Africa, but the shape of Africa isn't a symmetrical figure. I knew I wanted to give it an ethnocentric theme so I decided to make it look like a tribal mask of some kind. I gave life to the figure into by giving it some eyes, and in an attempt to make the middle of the face with a nose like that of a Mandrill except I drew the line in the nose the wrong direction. The colors of the design were blue and yellow, and I loved the idea of it so much, that once I completed it two years later, when I was on vacation in North Dakota, I got a tattoo of it and placed it on my upper right arm.

Now that I had the beginnings of what I wanted to do as a production head, I had to research what kind of plays that I wanted to present to the public and where would I be able to perform them. I called the production company that I formed Updaway Productions, a name after a colloquial term used to describe the south side of my hometown in East Orange, New Jersey. I asked several of the cast members from the *Dreamgirls* production that I worked with from the Piedmont Players if they would be interested in doing more plays that addressed the issues of African Americans. Several of them told me that they would be and if there was a project, they wanted to be a part of that it would be a good thing to do it.

Little did I know what I had to deal with. I had to find a place to rehearse, a venue to perform it in, work on marketing, finding sponsors, and learning how to budget things so that the cast and crew could get paid. Getting the interest of people in the town was the easy part. It seemed that everyone who I ran into was interested once I told them that I started writing, producing, and performing plays for an all-African American cast. The public appeared to be ready to accept the productions of an African American performing company in Salisbury. Trying to get people to contribute as a sponsor was another objective, that I had to overcome. Trying to get the local businesses and community-based organizations that were African American owned was almost like being a dentist trying to pull at a wisdom tooth. It reminded me of when I went to a jazz concert to see Miles Davis perform when I was living in New Jersey. He was an African American performer, but when I went to his concert, the majority of the faces that I saw in the audience were white. I was almost ashamed that our people would rather look for another way to get over. We would rather find a black market DVD of the latest Tyler Perry movie than to spend the money to view it at the theatre or find a way to covet an illegally downloaded song by Prince instead of going to his website to do it legally.

Trying to start my company was something that I knew would be a high hurdle to jump. Some people who have the opportunity to make a difference are willing to leap that hurdle while others will talk about doing something while continuing to sit on their hands. While trying to make this change happen, I felt that there was somewhat of a reluctance to continue with it from the people who I've encountered. They appeared reluctant to change here in Salisbury, as much as things change they very much remain the same. People always say that change is good. While living in Salisbury, change doesn't try to keep up with the times. It comes slowly, if any change comes at all. When President Barack Obama won his first term in office, the *Salisbury Post* printed a small story of his historic victory. This was truly a monumental occasion having the first African American male being elected to the nation's highest office in the land. While the news that had taken place making headlines in the television and other news media outlets, the *Salisbury Post* decided that this event wasn't big enough to warrant a full page coverage so it made the news in the county and state as the bigger headlines on their five star edition. Again, this was something that shouldn't have surprised me, but it was disappointing for me to hear this. The one thing you can count on in life is change. Change is something that is constantly evolving. Sometimes change comes for the better, or it comes for with the worse. In Salisbury, I'm still wondering when change is going to come.

CHAPTER 5

The Elevator Ride of Instability

Nothing had changed as far as my employment situation as I embarked on this new business venture that I decided to pursue. The reason that I was looking at trying to start my own business in entertainment industry was, when I would go to the career center or the library, people would stop and ask if I was in *Dreamgirls*. I would reply that I was, and then the questions would follow as to when I would be doing another show. It started to become a constant thing. I could walk to the Family Dollar store, Walmart, the supermarket, or a fast-food restaurant and would always be recognized. All the time I was still going to the career center and library trying to secure some means of employment to help me get out of living in the shelter, and using the income to help get the business off and running to establish some credibility?

When I was going to the career center I would look at several website for large corporations, non-profit organizations and small businesses to try and get any kind of employment. I was there so often that people who would visit there thought that I was one of the employees who worked at the center. One reason they probably thought that was because I never wanted to look like a homeless person. That being said, I would dress going there as if I was going to work in an office. Most of the clothes that I've invested in over the years are suit jackets, dress slack, suits, shirts that had cufflinks, and expensive shoes of snake, alligator, and ostrich skins. I knew all of the employee at the Goodwill Career Connections and a few of the people like myself who would come to work on their job search and employment prospecting.

Nancy was the director of the center when I first starting going there. She was from Elizabeth, New Jersey, and had graduated from Ohio State University. She was a short white woman with hair as white as snow and was a lover of dogs. She was nice and would sit in the front where the computers that the people would use to do their job searches are instead of taking a private office in the building. Nancy would help those who needed it, but there were times when she couldn't because of the other obligations of her job. They had blocks on the computers set up so that you couldn't go on any unauthorized site. You could stay in there all day as long as you didn't go on those unauthorized websites.

Eric was the other employee who worked there under Nancy. His job title was career specialist. He was good at helping people with their resumes. He was from a small town just outside of Charlotte, North Carolina. He has an associate degree in computer graphic design, but he was assisting others in career counseling. Dealing with Eric was pleasant, because he reminded me of some of the people who I had met when I was still living in Jersey. Right off the bat I was able to talk to him about sports and get into a pretty good discussion about what's happening at the time with our favorite sports teams.

The Goodwill Career Connection was a good place to go to. I used it for all it was worth. They would have job postings that they would list on their whiteboard on a weekly basis. I liked going there because it gave me an outlet to get away from the daily drama that took place at the shelter. It gave me a place where I could have some peace of mind while living in the most stressful time of my life. There I could look for a job without being disturbed, and if I didn't want to talk to anyone while I was pursuing my employment endeavors, it was respected. I didn't have to answer any questions to anyone about what I was doing or why I was so quiet. When I get that way, it's because I need the solitude to concentrate on getting whatever I needed done.

One thing that I notice whenever I was applied for a position, I had the qualifications for the job. I knew that I was qualified for many of the positions that I had applied for, but one thing that was holding me back was the fact that I had a misdemeanor assault record that happened in 1994. This was a charge that I had served my time in the Lexington County Department of Corrections in South Carolina, and I paid restitution to the victim. This is something that is going to be held over me like a noose to hang myself. I had asked the victim for their forgiveness and received it. More importantly, I asked God to forgive me and I can live with the fact that I was wrong for doing such an impulsive act. I know deep in my heart that God has forgiven me. I was taught that God forgives people for their past acts of indiscretion, but man doesn't do that. Thinking about this made me think of a song that I heard years ago by a group called the Last Poets. The name of the song is "The White Man Has a God Complex."

Now that I know that I have this obstacle to overcome I don't get discouraged about trying to fulfill my ambitions to work. I can't let it, because if I do, then I know that I will become a beaten man. I refuse to succumb to the notion that I have to settle for anything. I can't, because I have too many obligations that I have to do. I have an eighty thousand-dollar student loan payment that hangs over my head, and I've only been able to visit with my granddaughter only a handful of times since I've moved here. If there has anything to help keep me grounded while living here, it's been the love of my grand-daughter that keeps me going. Shaylee has been with me ever since she was four days out of the hospital. She's been a great child and has been the one constant thought about wanting to succeed since I moved out from Columbia. When I had made the decision to move from Columbia, I told her that, once I started working, I would come back to get her so that we could spend some time together on the weekends. I miss the time that I would take her to the mall so that she could do her own shopping. I'd give her a small allotment of money and told her that it was hers to do what she wanted with it.

On the last Christmas before my mother passed away, she gave all the grandchildren money so that they could get their own gift. I took her to the mall so that she could treat herself. We stopped at the store where every little girl loves to shop at—Claire's. She bought some cheap jewelry and was about to purchase some sunglasses. She asked me, "Granddad, do you like these glasses?" I told her to put them on and told her that they were cute on her. She took them off and looked at the label and said, "I'm not going to pay ten dollars for some sunglasses." I told her that I would get them for her since she's just missed making the honor roll. She said no and put them back. When I told her that the money that I or my mom gave her was her money, she had a harder time spending it. Now if it was something she wanted and she had to ask me for it, there was no problem spending my money.

Another example of her not having a problem spending my money was when she was in the second grade, and she was a member of the school's steel drum band. The band was going on a school trip to the Carowinds amusement park in Charlotte, North Carolina, at the end of the year. They had several fundraising events throughout the year, but the band members were still short when it came for paying for the trip. She told me that she wanted to go and asked me for the cash. I asked her how much was it, and she told me it was forty dollars. I told her that I didn't have it, and I asked her if she asked her mother who was between jobs. She answered that she did, but she didn't have it. Then I asked her if my ex-wife had it, and I knew what that answer would be. Shaylee told me that she asked her, and she didn't have it either. Then I told her that I didn't have it either. This child told me that it's only forty dollarsgranddad. I asked her one last question. Earlier in that school year, she told me that she wanted to be a doctor, so I asked her did she still want to be a doctor when she grew up.

She said, "Yes, sir."

I said, "Good. I tell you what I'll give you the money, and in return when you become that doctor you'll have to buy me a forty thousand dollar used jaguar car."

Being away from her for the long stretches at a time hurts me, because during the times that we talked, it bothered me to hear the hurt in her voice. I miss taking her to get her favorite ice cream from Baskin Robbins, going to McDonald's so that she can have her chicken nuggets and fries and spoiling her while the two of us would get a mani/pedi together. I asked her one time while we were out why did she think I was doing these things for her. She replied that I did those things because I loved her, and she wasn't far from the actual reason. I told her the reason that I do those things is because when she gets older, she's going to like boys sooner or later, and she should expect that person to treat her like a queen. I also informed her that if the young man who she'll go out with will do that for her, that she should reciprocate the same treatment to him as well.

One of the people who I met while I was at the Goodwill Career Connections center was a woman by the name of Dee. She was one of the few people who was raised in Salisbury that didn't conform to the ass backward system of being part of the good ol' boy network of doing business as usual. Dee suffered the same fate that many of the people who were unemployed from the bank crisis of 2008 did. She had worked several years in the corporate world and also at some nonprofit agencies around Rowan County. There are several qualities about her, but the one thing that I admired most is that she was one of the few black people living in Salisbury that didn't have a problem questioning people or situations with a simple word—why? She has a quick wit about herself and was definitely one of the sharpest pencil in the box. We would sit at the computers talking about the different formats of resumes and proofreading each other's cover letters all the time. When I told her about my plans to start my own business, she was one of the first people to give me advice about the things that I needed to do in order to get myself started. She told me the difference between a non-profit and limited liability corporation. She's been willing to give me any advice or assistance in order to get my first production.

I felt that I had the base of a good foundation to start my business, and I wanted to do a show. I was thinking that I should do one that I'm familiar with, one that I've performed in the past or that I've seen, and it had to be one that addressed the issues of bringing a play to the stage that displayed the love and complexity of the African-American people. The one play that I knew I couldn't do was the one that I just got finished performing *Dreamgirls*. I wanted to stick to the format of doing a play and not having it as a musical. I wanted to perform something that displayed the versatility of the actors who were going to be in it. I decided to do the Charlie Russell classic "*Five on the Black Hand Side*." This was a large production, and this being my maiden production as a producer/director, I didn't realize just how large of an undertaking this show was going to be.

I had taken the advice of Dee and decided to get the word out that there was a new stage production company that was in Salisbury. I decided to do a business page on Facebook. I called the production company page Updaway Productions. I was able to acquire pictures of some of the previous stage work that I performed and posted them on the page. I was letting all my friends know that I was bringing something new to the table, and that I would be holding auditions soon. Shortly after posting the information that Updaway Productions was up and running, people around town were very inquisitive about what I was about to do.

Word got to my former director Charles D Brooks III, and he corresponded with me about my new endeavor. Mr. Brooks was still teaching in the theatre arts department at Benedict College, and during his time off, he hosted a talk show program on blog talk radio. He asked me if I wanted to do his show to help promote my theatre company. He was giving me an opportunity to not only let my friends on Facebook know about this new company, but a larger listening audience all around the Internet. This was one of the few times that I felt that I was making a difference and getting the recognition for the years of work in acting. By trying to promote the broadcast I had to try to hype up the interview by posting it on my Facebook page, and any of the other social media networks that I am affiliated with including LinkedIn, Black Planet, and Multiply. I wasn't on Twitter then because they only allowed you to use a small amount of characters to hype up your post. I regretted that I didn't have a Twitter account until afterward.

I asked to call in about five minutes. Before the show went on the air, I called in to Charles and it was a good show. He asked why I was starting a theatre company. I told him what the purpose was, and soon after that, several calls started coming in with listeners asking questions about what were my intentions with my production company and what play was I doing. This was a great thing because it accomplished what I needed it to do. It helped establish me as a new player in the arts community of Salisbury, and it made me known in other parts of the country that have a relatively strong theatrical reputation. Doing the show with Charles was good from that viewpoint, but it was great to share some of the things we've done together. We spoke about some of our stories and most of all the memories that we shared again with each other and to the public.

After the show aired, I was on a mission to start working on the production. The first thing that I thought that I needed to do was to audition people for a cast. My cousin had let me use her establishment where she would host the venue for live music and spoken word recitals for the auditions. I made several flyers and posted the information in the *Salisbury Post* newspaper and my other social media networks for the dates and times. I passed out flyers and received approval from Livingstone College. Things were looking like this was going to happen with the cooperation that I was getting from many who I encountered around town. Some of the people who I had performed with from the Piedmont Players had auditioned for parts, as well as the people who patronize my cousin's establishment. The most surprising of all the people who auditioned was my own sister who drove up from Charlotte to read for a part.

The next thing that I needed to do was probably the first thing that I needed to do. I needed to secure a venue to put on the performance for *Five on the Black Hand Side*. After performing with the Piedmont Players, I found out that they had already booked their theatre through until August of 2012, and that included both the Meroney and the Norvell theatres. I thought about doing it at the Black Box Theatre downtown, but when I inquired about the price, it was out of my range without any startup capital. I looked at the schools that were located here in the town, and my first thought on using a school venue was to see about securing one of the auditoriums at the local colleges to choose from.

I had learned by talking to Malcolm and researching my facts that before the Piedmont Players had purchased and renovated the Meroney Theatre, they held many of their performances on the campus of Catawba College. I went online, viewed their theatre schedule, and they were booked for the next couple of years. I know that I would've loved to perform there, but Catawba was definitely out of the question. I inquired about doing something at Rowan Cabarrus Community College, but I was told that their auditorium was for the use of the school's drama staff and students only. Livingstone was the other school that I inquired to use their facilities. I loved the fact that they had two theatre venues located on the campus to choose from. The Varick Auditorium was the most modern of the two and had better stage equipment of the two. For me personally, there is truly something special and appealing about the Tubman Little Theatre. There is a certain ambiance about that place that draws me to it the same way that a magnet is attracted to steel. The more that I thought about it, the more idealistic I thought that doing this play on the campus would've benefited all the parties involved.

Livingstone is a historically black college or university that has its own drama department with instructors. Located on West Monroe and Thomas Streets, in between South Craige and Partee Streets, is the area where of town where the college is. The campus itself is like most HBCUs, in that most of the buildings on the grounds have been added gradually over time and have a story of historical significance behind them. Most of those building are within that square block area including the football stadium. The main entrance is on West Monroe, and just across the street is the historic house of the former college president J.C. Price. The house is listed as a national landmark and still is inhabited by his descendants at the estate. The more that I thought about it, the more I fell in love with the idea of holding the show there on this campus. It's located in the historical African American part in the city of Salisbury, and performing this production there could bring in money that would benefit the community. My plan was to cast not only people who were interested from outside of the college, but use the students who wanted to audition as cast members as well. Others who weren't able to make it as cast members, I was going to use them as crew members, wardrobe managers, makeup artist, and hairstylist. I was trying to accomplish by using the students in this capacity so it would have allowed them to earn some service learning and work-study hours if they needed to receive them.

The next thing that I had to do was to make up a proposal and submit it to someone who was in charge at the college that could get this show on the road. I met Professor Connor when I first moved into Salisbury when I applied for an admissions recruiters position at Livingstone. I ventured away from the human resources department after I applied for the position. That was when I found out about the Tubman Little Theatre on the campus. I saw when I arrived at the theatre that the department was holding auditions. It was scheduled for about a week later, and I went to the audition. This was my first encounter with Professor Connor and another fellow thespian that I would have the pleasure of working on future productions with B.J.—Lewis, a comedian, actor, and student at the college.

I contacted Professor Michael Connor to inquire about what was the procedure needed to secure the auditorium to do a show. Once I told him about my venture and the mission what I was trying to accomplish in Salisbury, he was very supportive. He told me that I would need to go to the theatre department chair to get their permission to use the venue for the show. I was informed that I would need to contact Ms. Linda Hunt who was the department chairperson, and that I would have to go through her. I thanked Professor Connor and then proceeded to go toward her office. When I arrived, I met her secretary to ask if Ms. Hunt was available, but she wasn't. I asked the secretary if I could make an appointment to meet with her. She asked me why I wanted to meet with her. I told her that I wanted to submit a proposal for doing the play at the school. She was kind enough to look at her schedule and penciled me in for a date for the week before the students were to do their fall semester finals. I was finally feeling like I was starting to shake up some things around this town. Word started spreading in this small town like a sexually transmitted disease at a nudist colony. There's a good idea that people would want to jump on the bandwagon and this seemed to it. I was responsible for this idea that everyone wanted to jump on, and now I was the straw that was stirring the drink.

During this time I was asked to do a Christmas performance at my church after the conclusion of the *Dreamgirls* run. It was a good production that was written, produced, directed, and acted by the pastor's wife, Mrs. Theresa Phelps. It was a well-thought-of play that was a gospel-based musical comedy. This wouldn't have been my first choice to perform, but as a performer, you have to do work that you may not feel the full conviction in doing. The reasons I was working on this production were truly selfish ones. I did this to help build up a following for Updaway Productions and the upcoming work on *Five on the Black Hand Side*. My character in the church play was the lead male who had cheated on his wife, but came back to be with his family after he found the Lord or his conscience, whichever was first.

It was the first time that I actually played a character that had the same name as did. The thing that I didn't like about doing this particular character was that he was a scumbag who cheated on his wife and acted as if he didn't care too much about the welfare of his family. I knew that I could do the role, because I was always looking for ways to diversify my craft as an actor. Most of the performers weren't professional, so I kind of knew what to expect. The woman who played my wife happened to be the writer's daughter and sang some of the lead numbers on the praise and worship choir as well as the gospel chorus. She didn't appear to have much experience when it came to doing lines in front of an audience, but she was convincing enough to hold her part. What I liked about doing this play is that some of the people who viewed me in *Dreamgirls* felt comfortable enough with me to allow me to give them some advice. I advised them on how to project their voices, assist with the blocking on stage so that their backs weren't facing the audience, and the importance of accentuating the physical features by using makeup.

Just like many things in this town that I found out to be too good to be true, this production was one of them. After being with the cast members, orchestra, and director for the brief period of working on this production, I found myself liking it more as I mastered my script and worked out a rapport with the woman on her role as my wife, but just as much as I liked many of the intangibles about the script, I felt a bit of uneasiness as we got closer to the production. The main thing that I didn't like was that the script made me feel as comfortable about doing this role the closer that it got to the show's opening. I kept hearing whispers from others of just how perfect I was for this role of the sleazy husband. Now it's normally a compliment when an actor can do the role so well that it can make an audience gravitate to them, or they can make that same audience resent you. An example of that is the actor James Woods. I loved him in movie *The Boost*, but despised him in *The Ghost of Mississippi*. Maybe being an outsider originally from New Jersey with most of my natural-born accent still intact made me feel more self-conscious about this one particular role.

The other thing that turned me off and really embarrassed me more than anything was the day of the production. Now being that this was a gospel musical comedy, the last scene of the play had taken place in the church where all the characters were going to attend a church service. When it came down to the part of the service when they were praying for an offering and the prayer was over, the mistress of the play immediately stated that they were soliciting an actual offering. Now I personally wouldn't have had an issue with that, because I felt that the director should've informed the cast members if they were going to do an actually offering for that ministry's auxiliary, then everyone involved in the production should've been informed. I've invited several people and informed them that the admission was free. I felt bad that when the show was over, I apologized for having them give out any money. When they solicited an offering at the last minute, I felt that it was classless act. I felt embarrassed for the cast members because they were scrambling to donate an offering more than the people in the audience.

There were a few mistakes in the production where the actors may have forgotten their lines and ad libbed, but the majority of the play was a success. It was a one-night-only show, so for me, it was a bittersweet engagement. One-night engagements are not my favorite shows to do. I don't like them because they don't give you enough time to get your chemistry with the other cast members together so you get the timing of how to respond when you're performing in front of an audience. Just like any other show that I have ever done, my favorite part of performing a show regardless of how long the run is whether it's a single show or ten and that's the rehearsals. When a show is done then all the fun that the audience doesn't see is over, and then it's work to give the audience a perfect performance. When the run of the show is done, it's over and that's it!

When the show was over, all of the audience would greet us and congratulate us on how well the show was. Many of them inquired if there would be another show, but I would inform them that this was a one-night-only performance, and if you didn't see it you've missed it. The church didn't have anyone to videotape the performance so if they didn't get there to see the show, I felt so bad for them. If it were videotape, that would've suited me fine, because I like to keep a video record of my performances. I may want to do a video collage of my performances and post it to an e-mail just in case a producer or director would want to see it as an audition tape of my previous work that I've done.

With the success of the church production and more people knowing that I was starting up my own stage production company thing, we're starting to look good. People who attended the presentation showed their appreciation. For some of the cast members, this was the first time that any of them were actually asked to sign their autographs. The play that the cast just got finished performing was well received, and the audience wanted more. The director, like the audience who viewed the performance, was pleased. At the end of the show, we spoke at length about doing another show together. We both agreed that it should be ready for a presentation around the Easter holiday season, so she asked me to come up with an idea for a show. I told her that I had never written a show, but I was willing to give it a try. I worked on this project immediately the next day when the show was over.

I wasn't as excited as I thought I would've been when it came to writing a stage drama. Having total autonomy in writing, it may have been one of the reasons that I wasn't as enthused as I thought I should be. I wanted it to keep it simple, but do something that came to the resemblance of a person who was practically being resurrected from their deathbed. I thought about that to mirror the season of the Easter holiday, the same theory but not exactly how Christ had been resurrected from the grave. It had to have a modern appearance to the story setting, having it take place in the late twentieth, or the turn of the twenty-first century. Personally, I knew that I wasn't able to omit or add any musical numbers for the production. Making it a musical wasn't my choice. I wanted it to have more of dramatic suspense than the musical theme, because I wanted to keep it true about African-Americans having the ability to act.

A couple of weeks passed since I've made my appointment to meet with Ms. Hunt at Livingstone College, and all the time I was continuing to work on the script for the Easter play during the daytime hours. I would make way to the Goodwill career center or to the library, going online to do about three to four hours a day of filling out job applications, and then dedicate the rest of the time to work on writing my first stage composition. If an idea came into my head, I would write it down no matter where I was. If it came to me in the middle of the night, when I went to the bathroom at the shelter, after I finished using bathroom, I would pull my notepad from under my cot and put that idea down on paper. I found myself being more committed on trying to make the current script that I'm writing better than the last production that I just performed.

Meanwhile I was obsessed with getting the presentation of my proposal for *Five on the Black Hand Side* when I meet with Ms. Hunt. Fine-tuning the selling point of my proposal to the college, I was making sure that I had crossed every "T" and dotted every "I." I made sure that I included the synopsis of the play as well as the background of the writer. Also included was the mission statement of Updaway Productions and the board members that I classified as my creative team. The most important member of the creative team was Dee, because of her familiarity with the social and political climate of the city. She was my insider to helping me get my foot in the door. She attended high school locally and was a graduate from Catawba

College. Some of my important business connections wouldn't have been able to occur if I didn't have her in my corner. I also solicited my cousin who was a senior marketing director for a major oil company for fifteen years prior opening her boutique in town and her husband, a retired military vet who owned a construction business prior to moving to Salisbury. He came in handy for his expertise in constructing the set while his spouse knew how to produce creative ways for marketing the show.

In the proposal itself, I had taken the time to define and redefine all the fine points. I wanted it to be reader friendly enough that there wouldn't be any misunderstandings about what it was that Updaway Productions was attempting to do. I've made a concerted effort that I didn't want to leave any stones unturned. The proposal opened with the company contact information, title of the play, author, and publisher. The proposal began with the production overview. I was giving the college the goals of what Updaway Productions was attempting to present to an audience, and other ways of promoting this event so that all the parties involved would be able to acquire some money behind it. This was important to make it look attractive enough so that Livingstone College would want to invest their resources. This way they would be able to reap some financial benefits from it.

The next part of the proposal was to lay out the goals and objectives of the project. I wanted to acknowledge that this was a play that was written by an African American back in the 1970s that addresses some of the same types of social issues that are very much present today. The issues of these goals that were presented to the college were to develop student opportunities, acknowledge the social issue in the African American community, to facilitate and interchange of cultural ideas, and experience and to promote community outreach of the local community. Each of these focal points were important, because they were mentioned to promote the college itself along with the students, faculty, and staff. The goals would also promote the African American historic district on the west side of town.

The community outreach portion was probably the most important aspect of the proposal. For many years, the community around Livingstone College has fallen to decaying with many of these houses that are just across the street from the campus on West Monroe. Some of those houses hold historical significance as it relates to the college. If you've ever been there, you would be able to view that this neighborhood was probably the Hyde Park equivalent for the very affluent of the African American Community in Salisbury. When traveling in that community, one could picture that some of the houses on West Monroe Street once had beautiful manicured lawns, with the grounds and street immaculately pampered. It was an upscale community where the well-to-do African Americans resided at one time. Over time, many of those residents who possessed the pride in their community have either moved away from the area or passed without leaving their homes to a relative to care for their residence. Some of the newer tenants who moved into the community didn't care for the property as well as the previous owners.

The Duncan Elementary School is located in the same neighborhood. It is a property that symbolized how this area was once a very progressive and socially thriving neighborhood. Duncan Elementary School is just right across the street from Livingstone College and takes up a whole city block. It was operated by the Rowan Salisbury School System until the late 1980s before its doors closed for good. The building and the property remain dormant until the school and the property was purchased by Livingstone College. About a mile and a half down the road on West Bank Street was the J.C. Price High School. It was named for the one-time principal of the school and former president of Livingston College—J. C. Price. This was the African American high school in Salisbury during the era of Jim Crow. Just under twenty years after the landmark Supreme Court decision of *Brown v. the Board of Education,* Price High closed theirs by the early 1970s. The thing that had my mind wondering is here you have a community that has the educational and cultural benefits that were taken away by the city council or the county. My next question, was why did this have to happen to this community? Was is better to bus the people who lived in this community out to another school? Another question was, why couldn't compromise happen to the point that the people from the suburbs would be bussed into the schools that were closer to the city limits? The last thing that came into my mind, but certainly not the least important was, what did the community do to stop it? When everything was done to this area of town, this community had never recovered. When this process happened, it took away the cultural, social, and economic infrastructure of the African American community. It took away more than the aforementioned; it also was to take away the communal pride of the African American community and raped it of its most important resources its people. When a community like this is stripped from its resources, it's a prime candidate for eminent domain or genderfication.

I believed by submitting this proposal that all parties involved would've been able to make a little money. I hoped that Livingstone would've taken a little bit of the money to help offset some of the cost to start with the renovations of the Duncan School, or the worst-case scenario was to use it to help purchase equipment and materials for either one of the auditoriums on the campus. By using the money earned toward the purchase of new stage equipment would've been right in line with the city of Salisbury being a growing arts community and demonstrated the school's willingness to look at the possibility of attracting other independent entertainment producers to use their facilities as a venue to host events on the campus. Personally, I was also hoping to make enough money so that I was able to pay off my actors so that they could have a little spending change and use whatever what was left to build upon what I've started with Updaway Productions.

I gave them the background information of the production company and what our intentions were. The goals that I set for Updaway Productions were to give the audiences the finest quality performance and to tell the story of the African American life and cultural experiences through the expression of the theatrical arts and to combat prejudice, stereotypes, and ignorance about African Americans and other minorities. I understand that anyone who has performed onstage wants to give their best performance, but my main goal was to do plays of substance that have received a high-critical acclaim or an award-winning production for excellence. These productions were going to be a Tony Award or a Pulitzer Prize-nominated or winning plays. If they weren't, then it was going to be a project that was written with a good enough story line that I believed could keep the interest of the audience.

The proposal was then concluded with the synopsis of the play and the members of the creative team for Updaway Productions. The creative team members included the marketing of the play, and I was putting that responsibility into the hands of my cousin. At that time, she was still a business owner of a women's boutique in downtown Salisbury called A Little Sumthin' Sumthin', and prior to her having her business there, she was a senior marketing director for a major petroleum oil company for over fifteen years. I included her husband who had his own construction business prior to moving to Salisbury as an independent construction contractor in Alexandria, Virginia. I would leave the responsibility of having him as set designer and props manager. The stage manager and costume director was my friend Dee who I met while going to the Goodwill career center. She was enthused about getting this production up and running as much as I was. She was my insider to trying to get the people in this town excited about the production, and she knew who to talk to when it came to opening up doors. She was a graduate from Catawba College with her bachelor's degree in business administration, but her concentration was in communications arts. I found out that she would become more valuable to me, because of the fact that she has her own non-profit company, Ainavad, where she was the CEO and president. Since I created Updaway Productions, I appointed myself as the creative director and founder of the company. I included the fact that prior to this undertaking, I had done eight previous productions as a performer and two as an assistant director. This was going to be my maiden production as a director of a play, and I was looking forward to doing so.

I was set and ready to meet Linda Hunt and anyone else to give them the best presentation that I could possibly do. As far as I was concerned, this was going to be my version of the Royal Command Performance. Even though I was living in a homeless shelter, I always attempted to dress to impress, because you never know when an opportunity comes so you better carry yourself professionally. Since

I've moved into the shelter, I always tried to believe that there's an opportunity for something good in terms of becoming gainfully employed. I had to believe this, because if I stopped, then I was a defeated individual, and the life that I was once accustomed to will never return to me.

A couple of days before my appointment to meet with Ms. Hunt, I practiced just as I would do. I when I was rehearsing lines to be delivered for a play. I would look into the mirror and rehearse my spiel as if I was talking to the person who may be interested in allowing me to perform the show. The one thing I found difficult to try to rehearse for is the responses to the possible questions that she was going to ask me. This wasn't like any other interview that I have done previously. It wasn't like they were going to ask me about the best practice modules I was going to use when it came to counseling adolescent youths. It was something altogether different from anything that I experienced before, but I knew that I was going to have go into a salesman mode. I was going to have to try to sell ice cubes to an Eskimo and sell them a lot of them too, but I was ready.

After a couple of days of rehearsing my spiel and building confidence in the process, the time has finally came for my moment of truth. This was the day that I waited for since the time that I spoke with Ms. Hunt's secretary's in her office to make this appointment. I arrived at her office according to the Lombardi rule. I made a conscious effort to get there to the building at least fifteen minutes before the scheduled time. When I arrived, I informed the secretary that I had a 2:00 p.m. appointment with Ms. Hunt. I told her that I was early, and that Ms. Hunt could take her time if she needed to. After sitting around for about ten minutes, the secretary informed me that Ms. Hunt was ready to begin the meeting. I tried to remain calm as I stood up from my chair outside of Ms. Hunt's office and took a deep breath. As I entered the door to meet the person who I was going to negotiate this deal, I find myself looking into the face of the woman who worked in the shelter as the part-time evening caseworker for the shelter guest.

Once I saw who I was going to have to talk with in order to get my agenda underway for Updaway Productions, my emotions were running through all kinds of extremes. The first one that came to mind was frustration. I was furious because I had applied for a position of a dorm resident director on the campus. I asked my own case manager, David, if he know anybody who he could talk to about maybe helping to place a qualified person to fill that position. David replied, "I don't know anyone over at the Livingstone College who would be able to help, and I'm not used to dealing with a person of your credentials. I'm used to helping people who need to be placed in a labor job, or people who need to acquire their GED." When I realized who I was meeting with, the initial feeling that I had was outraged, but I had to remember to stay cool regardless because this could be the first step to becoming self-reliant. I had to remember to keep my game face on even if it was bullshit that my case manager fed me.

I met with her for about forty-five minutes and tried to make sure that I didn't leave anything undone. Much to my surprise, she was impressed enough that she wanted me to leave her a copy of the Charlie Russell script. At first I was reluctant to do so, but as a measure of good faith, I did. I told her that I didn't make it a practice of leaving material, because of the fact that the college has the resources if they wanted to do the play they could. I didn't want to be stuck with nothing to show for my research and hard work. It was the week before the college was about to have their students do their finals for the fall semester. She mentioned that she would have to go through the proper chain of command to submit my proposal. It would have to be screened by the dean and possibly the school's president also. I told her that I understood and that I was happy that she had given me this opportunity to meet with her. I mentioned to her that this proposal wasn't written in stone, and that the terms of the agreement were negotiable. I left there feeling that our meeting went better than I expected, and I was hoping that she was willing to try to push forward this effort.

After leaving the campus that afternoon, I met with my cousin and her husband to discuss how we should try to proceed with the rehearsal schedule for the show. We all agreed that until we were able to secure the venue, practices should be held upstairs at the lounge above the boutique. I called Dee after I met with my cousin and her husband that same day to inform her how we should go about the matter of blocking the actors for the production and looking at the resources for costumes and props. I didn't tell any of the people who were cast in the production yet, but I did tell them that we were going to start holding rehearsals upstairs above the A Little Sumthin' Sumthin' boutique on West Innes Street. I felt pretty optimistic about our chances of doing a show at the college, and I thought that this would've been just the kind of infusion of new ideas that this city needed from the African American community.

Just a couple weeks after meeting with Linda, I received an e-mail from her telling me that she would get back to me about the show when she and the rest of the administrative staff return from the winter break early the following year. Just to recap the year, I did a production with the Piedmont Players Theatre that was a big success, I was requested to do an interview for blog talk radio online by Charles D. Brooks III who asked me to talk about the production company, another production with my church's ministry of theatre, and getting my own production was about to start doing rehearsals for our premiere production. It looked like the year that's started off poorly was finishing strong. My optimism was high, and I was looking forward to the next year. I thought that things were finally starting to take a turn for the better.

CHAPTER 6

I'm In the Wrong Place

With the new year came changes and I started the year with the conception that I was going to make positive changes in my own life. Even though I was still living at the Rowan Helping Ministries, I was feeling pretty good about the turn of the events that ended from the previous year. I was part of two successful plays and got myself some good exposure from doing a couple of Internet radio interviews. Whenever I walked around town, ate at one of the better restaurants, or went to the local stores, people who frequented the theatre recognize me and inquired if I was going to work at the Meroney Theatre again. This let me know that the people who witnessed my performances appreciated what they saw and acknowledged me as a professional theatre performer.

Meanwhile, things were changing at the shelter. Rodney and David would still hold their monthly shelter meetings on the first Thursday of the month. The administration was making different rules as a way to accommodate the people who needed to stay there. Starting at the beginning of the year, there were more people who admitted themselves into the shelter for a temporary residence. The facility was only built to house up to fifty people at any given time, but during the winter months, the staff would accommodate anyone who needed to come in off the streets for a place to stay.

One of the things that they started to do was to enforce their policy of smoking in the designated areas. They would reinstate that it was the policy of the shelter for their guest to smoke at the patio area located at the corner of East Liberty and North Long Streets by the entrance of the shelter. If their guest were caught smoking outside of those designated areas, the administration would make the shelter a smoke-free campus. Another rule that would be enforce was that there was to be no public display of affection. What this meant was that all couples, whether married or dating, were no longer able to hug, hold hands, caress, or kiss on the grounds of the shelter and the crisis network. Anyone intentionally caught breaking the rules would be subjected to getting the night out for the first offense, and subsequent offenses would result in more time out of the facility, ranging anywhere from three to ten days or even indefinitely out in the cold. Both Rodney and David confirmed that these recommendations came at the request of the board of directors from the shelter.

Residents at the shelter suggested that the board members change the name on the building from Rowan Helping Ministries to Rowan Hating Ministries. Everyone was questioning where the help was for the residents of the shelter. There were caseworkers who have self-admittedly mentioned that they didn't know or have any employment or business connections when it came to getting their own assigned caseload of shelter residents with any type of stable work. Their answer to helping the shelter clients was to make them go to a grant-funded adult day-care program where the residents get tutored by people from the human resources departments of some of the bigger companies from Rowan County. The people who come from these companies work predominantly in the human resources department, and they tutor the shelter guest in the area on how to properly fill out an application and produce a resume. That wouldn't be such a bad thing, but the administration of the shelter did not ask the people from these human resources departments if they could screen the shelter guest to see if they qualify for a position at their company. When the shelter guest weren't doing the job readiness skills or arts and crafts, then they're working at the warehouses sorting out supplies for the other people in the county who are requesting the assistance from the crisis network. The most of the participants wouldn't mind doing it if compensation was accompanying their efforts, but they're doing the work as an unpaid shelter staffer.

Meanwhile as these new rules have been given to the residents, there was an air of rebellion by the residence. One thing that wasn't allowed was smoking inside of the establishment. Some of the residents who would come in late in the evening would take a late shower and, while they were in the process of that, would smuggle in their cigarettes and lighters so that they could go into the shower and hold the lit cigarette by the vent. The only problem with that was that the ventilation system was inoperable. This was a restroom that accommodated three men in a shower at a given time, and the ventilation system was broken. One day I inspected this for myself and was appalled at what I found when I took a closer look at the place where I had to use for my personal hygiene. The vents in the showers were not only in operable, but clogged with dust also. The walls in the restroom had black mold on them, as well as mold and hard water soap scum buildup on the tile in the shower area. In the shower area was a wooden bench attached to the back wall away from the showers, and underneath there was where the heaviest of mold build up was.

Joe the artist would do his best to make sure the bathroom, if nothing else, was thoroughly cleaned before he left the shelter in the morning. He was a fanatic about the cleanliness of the restroom area. Other residents who were conscious about the pride it took to maintain the place inquired to Rodney about getting some cleaning materials and equipment to maintain the facilities properly. We were informed that the shelter guests couldn't use any kind of mechanized equipment because it was considered a big liability for the shelter's insurance company to cover. If the residents wanted to use a gas-powered leaf blower to keep the parking lot and the smoking area maintained, that was out of the question because to the insurance liability. If the residents wanted to use a pressure washer to help clean the walls of the bathroom, that was out as well. The only cleaning supplies that were furnished to the residents for cleaning was cleanser and a purple disinfectant that didn't have any scent to it. Shelter residents asked about using a cleaning agent that had bleach. We were told that when it mixes with urine, it makes a gas that can be lethal, or that some people are allergic to it so it's recommended that bleach wasn't used for health reason. This was some more bullshit that the administration didn't think that people know about. They attempted to keep ones who they can ignorant, but a small minority of the residents chose not to remain that way.

Besides Joe the artist, there were several others who would take pride to care about living at the shelter. One person who would come to mind is a woman by the name of Diane. She would mainly stay to herself majority of the time and wouldn't say much to anyone except when it came down to waiting in line to enter into the shelter for the evening. She was an African American woman in her mid- to late-fifties who took pretty decent care of herself, but from my own educational evaluation, she may have suffered from some sort of mental illness. There were times when Diane's temperament would go through extremes. She would be very receptive one minute and then shut you completely out as if you never existed or that she was holding a conversation with her the next minute. Her claim to fame was that she would pick up the loose cigarette butts by hand throughout the parking lot and would do this several times during the week.

Most of the others who did try to make the best out of the worst possible situation were the vets who applied for their disability. Maybe it was their military training, but the majority of the vets had no problem cleaning the men's bathroom. Darryl was one who came to mind. He was a brother who was original from my neck of the woods out of New Jersey. He came there to the VA hospital to apply for his benefits and was placed there by the VA to stay at the shelter until there was an opening for the thirty-day program that he needed. Whenever he had a chore, he would switch with someone on the list to do the bathroom even if it wasn't his turn to do it. One day I was assigned to do the bathroom when he happened to be on the chore list the same day. I asked him why he always wanted to do the bathroom when it wasn't his assigned duty to do. He told me that the reason that he didn't mind doing it was that when he cleaned the toilets, sinks, mirrors, showers, swept and mopped it, it was going to be cleaned thoroughly." That made a lot of sense to me, and it reminded me when I first moved to South Carolina and stayed with my sister. One weekend, I noticed that she was up exercising at 5:00 a.m. before she cooked breakfast for her son at 6:00 a.m. I asked her a similar question. Why do you get up so early on the weekend? Her reply was that "I work hard during the week, and I'm going to play just as hard as I worked." From that point on, as long as I was staying at the shelter, I didn't need to get upset about cleaning the bathroom after some of these trifling ass people who stayed here, but I needed to take stock in the fact that the bathroom was going to be the cleanest one that I'd be proud to put my own ass on the toilet that I just got finished cleaning.

Living in such close quarters, you'll find that there will be times that some of the personalities can cause some tension. Entering into the building to be admitted for the evening, the possibility of tempers flaring and clashing were higher than at any other time during the day. Trying to get into the showers was good example of conflicts happening. The shelter was powered by solar energy panels for heating in the winter and cooling the facility in the summer. People would complain about the water in the showers turning cold to Rodney and David. Guest were informed by the administration that, when there were cloudy days, the system that worked with the water heater wouldn't make the shower stay as hot as they normally would as oppose to when it is sunny outside. This was a fact that I found hard to believe. I felt that what the administrators would need to do was to turn the temperature on the water heater up so that it would stay warmer longer. I believe that the administration wouldn't do that so that they could save money on the power bill.

As the winter months got colder, there was a rush for the residents to get to the entrance into the facility early so that they can get into a hot shower for the evening. When it happened that the water got cold early, some of the residents wouldn't take or delay taking a shower until after they ate their meal. It's the policy of the administration that the residents take their showers before eating. There were some times that people wouldn't let the water hit their bodies for a week or better. Most of the people who wouldn't take showers were the ones who suffered with mental illness. When their hygiene became offensive, it would almost come down to the point that the men of the shelter would get verbally hostile to the person who wasn't showering. It nearly came to the point that blows were nearly exchanged, because of the lack of self-respect that the person who neglected to shower had for themselves.

Another thing difficult about living in close quarters at this shelter was the fact that when an epidemic or illness occurred, be it a cold or flu, the symptoms would spread so quickly. At times three quarters of the population there would contract whatever illness was being spread. Couple that with the fact that the ventilation ducts appeared like they haven't been cleaned since the day that they were installed at the facility. If you were to look at them you, can see where there are dust balls and possibly even mold that was beginning to build up on the vents. When you went to bed in the evening, the sleeping area where the majority of the guest resided was appropriately heated. It wasn't too hot, and it was comfortable to sleep in, but approximately about an hour and a half before it was time for the staff to wake you up, the air blowing out of the vent would be cold. Not necessarily my favorite way of getting up in the morning. I have to keep reminding myself that I didn't reserve a room at the Pierre Hotel in Manhattan, but this is the Hotel California in Salisbury, North Carolina. People would be in their beds coughing, sneezing, and farting so much that if you had recorded of all the sounds when everyone fell asleep, you could've cut, mixed, and made the sounds you've heard into a symphony. A lot of the people who were sick with illnesses such as the cold or flu wouldn't cover their mouths or put their forearm over their mouth to reduce the spread of the germs that their bodies were discharging. This made for a lot of sick people who didn't have any medical insurance or any of the resources to get the medical attention that they so badly needed. The majority of the people who stay in the shelter were grateful for having a place to lay their heads and receive a meal for the morning and evening, even if they didn't stop by in the afternoon for the soup kitchen for lunch.

When I wasn't at the shelter, I was spending the majority of my time at the Goodwill career connections, utilizing the computers for prospecting jobs and grants to help produce the show that I've submitted the proposal to Livingstone College. There were many times that I've met Dee there to go over strategies about how we were going to market this show and where we should be looking for grants to fund the show. She was great at finding the grants for funding the performing arts and had several ones lined up for the team to examine. Eric who worked for Goodwill wanted to see what he could do to be a part of the production as well. He informed me that he was really working out of his field and had received his degree in graphic arts and design. I informed him that I would allow him a chance to produce the flyer and playbill cover the closer that we go to the show. I believe in giving people an opportunity or another so they claim that they have the skills to do the work. Eric was employed by Goodwill as a specialist who assisted the people on how to use the resources of the career center for assisting them with their job search skills. He was particularly good in helping them produce their resumes.

I would continue to go the career center during the daytime, and in the afternoon, I would use the library. I did this pattern for the next couple of months and started to use my evenings to go for rehearsals with the cast of the play. I was beginning to learn a valuable lesson when it came down to getting everyone to rehearsal. I learned that you've got to be flexible for rehearsal time. Not everyone is going to be able to make it because their work schedules vary. Some performers may have to be concerned about child care responsibilities, so you have to keep that into consideration. I informed the cast that I was flexible with their schedules, but the closer that we're going to get them to the opening of the show was when I was going to need them to be totally committed. I also told them that if they couldn't do it or perceived that they were going to have a problem to let me know. This would allow me the time to see about getting an understudy for them.

For the first month of the year, I had assembled the people who I've cast to hold the readings and rehearsal upstairs at A Little Sumthin' Sumthin' in the evenings after the boutique downstairs had closed. Rehearsals were held on Monday and Wednesday evenings from seven to eight thirty, and the majority of the cast would make an effort to get there to go over lines and allow me to give them motivation for the direction of the play. The rehearsal were going good, and after the third week of rehearsal, many of the cast members were starting to feel comfortable that we were able to start blocking the first scene with the actors. For the actors who made the rehearsals, there was a feeling of confidence that the play was going to come off well. Enthusiasm was up on all who were there, and the main objective was trying to get the commitment from Livingstone College to allow Updaway Productions to do the play there.

One of the other objectives that was difficult to overcome was trying to fill out all the parts that needed to be cast for the production. Most of the principal characters were in place, but there was still room for many of the younger characters who could be young adults in their early to mid-twenties that needed to be filled. The month of January was a difficult month trying to work with the college due to the fact that the administration of the school was busy enrolling students for the spring semester. My original objective was to produce the play at the college to have the production for black history month, but if we had to do it, we could push it back to the month of March. March would've been just as good because it's women's history month, and the synopsis of *Five on the Black Hand Side* is centered around a woman as the main character. The only downside about doing the play in the month of March at Livingstone College is that the institution, a member school of the Central Intercollegiate Athletic Association better known as the CIAA, holds its conference basketball tournament in the city of Charlotte, so you wanted to be careful about scheduling the show around the same time as the tournament.

I knew that early enrollment for the spring semester would be a problem, so I consciously didn't make an effort on trying to pin down a date for the performance until after the Martin Luther King holiday. I informed my cast that I wouldn't be making contact with them until then and explained to them the reason why. By doing this, I also knew that I was taking a calculated chance of losing some members of the cast. To my very own surprise, the company stayed in place with much of the same enthusiasm that they had when we had from the beginning of this project. I kept good to my promise of trying to contact Linda Hunt at Livingstone College. Efforts were made over those couple of weeks to attempt to get a meeting with Ms. Hunt, the dean of the school, or the president of the college. I've sent phone calls, written mailed correspondence and emails to her without a reply.

The circumstances weren't getting better for my cousin with her establishment. The year-end sales that she done in December didn't help put her in the black, and she was losing money. Couple that with the health of her own father that wasn't getting any better made it difficult for her keeping the doors of the boutique open. My uncle was on COPD and wasn't feeling his best when my cousin would make her way to visit her parents in Virginia for the holidays. I would open and close the shop for her and assist any customer who needed to purchase any products. Normally, on the weekends, she and her husband would have the upstairs lounge open. Because the money was tight, they decided not to open it until after the New Year. I didn't hold rehearsals during that holiday week either.

Upon their return from Virginia, my cousin, her husband, and I sat down to discuss our new plan of action for 2012. We discussed how we going to work together to get each other out of the hole that we've found ourselves in. Our plan was to continue to open the lounge upstairs with live music and spoken word on weekends, host a Super Bowl party, and host a talent show with people paying an entry fee. We hoped that this would've helped because the sales from the store was struggling. Tony, who I worked with from the show *Dreamgirls*, would work security when they had the upstairs open, and I also cast him for the lead male character as Mr. Brooks for "*Five on the Black Hand Side*." I would be there working the crowd as the Bartender. Salisbury has a unique alcohol sales law that would allow a business owner to have their patrons the opportunity to bring their own beer or wine for consumption on the property when they were hosting a party. If they wanted to consume hard liquor, then they would have to apply for a temporary license to serve. The owner would need to file an application with the North Carolina state Alcoholic Beverage Commission and they would have to go through the local municipality to confirm that their business was registered with the city before getting final approval for a temporary license to sell hard liquor.

There was a couple times that she hosted some parties upstairs after going through the proper protocol for serving liquor. Several groups would pay to host their functions there, because she made valid attempts to keep her clientele more on the upscale and mature crowd where the people who patronized her business were professionals as well as blue collar workers. Being that this club was placed in the downtown business district, she felt it was important to have the patrons represent the establishment with a certain amount of sophistication. To acknowledge that this was an establishment of class and sophistication, she included a dress code. This was an act to display that African Americans don't go out for a night on the town without the women having their skirts above their hips, and the men not having their pants sagging below their waist showing their underwear.

In the beginning of this endeavor, it was pretty successful. The boutique was beginning to develop a strong following, and once word got out that the upstairs was open to the public and that the lounge featured music by a live band and spoken word was being held, then a following of loyal patrons grew. Shortly after several successful functions, my cousin had applied for a license to serve alcohol. Once the local newspaper the Salisbury Post found out about this the newspaper began a smear campaign against her. The newspaper falsely accused her claiming that her establishment was selling alcoholic beverages without the proper permits. Initially, after she applied for the license, she was originally approved by the city council, but the very next day after she was approved, the *Salisbury Post* printed an article that she was selling beverages illegally, and the city council delayed granting her the permit. She had to appeal the decision and wait another month before she would have to go in front of the city council to defend herself. In the process of doing that, many of the patrons who used to purchase products and goods from the boutique cease almost immediately. Townspeople would only come into the store to look at the place that the paper wrote about. Very few, if any, would open their wallets or purses to acquire any of the goods from the boutique. The people who frequented the lounge wouldn't come as often as they once did. This was a calculated move by the people who were in control of the businesses that they wanted to see in the downtown area of the city.

The people who didn't want to see the success of A Little Sumthin' Sumthin' found that the best way to scare people off from patronizing their business was by using the power of the press. It was easy to persuade the residents of Salisbury once the newspaper printed the story incorrectly. In Salisbury you're still dealing with some people of whom haven't moved their mindset out of the era of Jim Crow, so it was not just for some the white people who didn't want to see change or the competition against the other clubs in the downtown district, but it was easy to manipulate many the blacks who were accustomed to the status quo and knew nothing else. The action taken by the newspaper was the easiest way to devastate the business.

After a month and a second meeting with the city council, they were approved for the license. By then, the damage was done. Like anything that is worth having, there's always something worth working for by finding other resources of keeping your dream alive. The current plan of action was a good idea, and the execution of this plan was in motion. For us to turn back and stop what we put into motion was too late now. The boutique continued to stay open, and on the weekends, the lounge was open. The Super Bowl party didn't bring in the crowd that was anticipated, but everyone used any and all opportunities to inform the public about the talent showcase that was going to take place in February. It was an all-out campaign that included print and social media. Participants were to have an entry fee to be part of the showcase of talent. People inquired from all over, and this was the biggest response that I witnessed since the day that the doors opened. All was in place when the night of the showcase happened.

This was a night that I would never forget. It was February 11, 2012. Just before we opened the doors, my cousin received the call from her sister that my uncle had been admitted into the hospital. We decided to keep with the program as scheduled, because the response from the public was so good to the point that it was almost overwhelming. The musicians were warmed up and ready to give the show of a lifetime they stated. The DJ was warming up as the crowd was coming in steadily for the first time since the opening of the lounge. People who wanted to perform in the showcase were coming and paying their fees. At one point, before we began hearing from many of the people who entered that my classmate's sister and pop superstar Whitney Houston died in her hotel room earlier that afternoon in Los Angeles. The food was in place, the bar was well stocked with everything that was needed, and everyone was ready and raring to perform. Things were starting to look great as my cousin, her husband, and I put on the finishing touches for what appeared to be the biggest social event for the New Year. It appeared that this event was about to live up to the hype that surrounded it. About a half hour after we opened the doors and moments before the MC was about to introduce the opening act, everyone in the place received the news that my uncle had passed away.

After the announcement came everyone who paid the cover charge at the door and their entry fee had the money refunded. The once-festive mood that encased the place was shortly replaced by sentiments of condolences. Everyone who was involved in this had to do a complete three hundred and sixty–degree turn in the opposite direction. Instead of a celebration of a triumph of overcoming an objective, we all found ourselves preparing for the funeral of my uncle. As quickly as everything was happening, it eventually wound up being the funeral of what business was being left at the place that the people who were loyal have grown to know and love as A Little Sumthin' Sumthin'. As the crowd was dispersing from the lounge, everyone there made an effort to see my cousin to extend their condolences on the loss of her father. Once the place was emptied, I told her to leave me the keys so that I could lock up everything, set the alarm, and make arrangements to care for her shop and her pet at their house.

The next day she and her husband left for Virginia to handle the business of preparing for a funeral. I didn't have to go to open the shop until that following Tuesday. Since the showcase hadn't gone off as expected, there was an urgency to sell the majority of the items in the boutique at closeout prices. Without the performances that the showcase would've provided exposure of the store, traffic coming into the boutique was minimal to say the least. Even though the city council had approved the license for alcohol sales, a lot of the people who did come in were interested in seeing what the fuss was all about from the article printed in the *Salisbury Post*. While she was going through the early stages of bereavement, it was agreed upon that I would open the boutique from Tuesday through Saturday, and that the upstairs lounge would remain closed until they returned from Virginia. I would also go to her house to retrieve the mail for them and feed their dog, Jackpot.

I found myself in a very unfamiliar situation. One where I was going to have to make some critical decisions. I knew that I had to make a strong effort to contact the administration at Livingstone College so that I could get a commitment from them so that Updaway Productions could do the performance of *Five on the Black Hand Side*. Performing this show was still my priority. It was the main thing that I wanted and needed to accomplish in establishing myself as a major player for the performing arts community. One day, while I was running the boutique for my cousin, one of the patrons who heard that she lost her father came by the store. She was one of the few people who was in her corner when the newspaper did their smear campaign. This was a meeting that came at a very opportune time for me personally.

Ollie Mae Carroll was the commander of the J.C. Price American Legion Post in Salisbury and was one of the first people to come to the aid of my cousin. She came to see if there was anything that she could do to help. I told her that my cousin was out of town taking care of the family business and that she would be back in a little over a week. I told her that I was only there to help her out while she was out of town and that I had been acting at the Meroney Theatre. As we continued to talk, she told me that she has a son is an actor living out in Hollywood. Mae then inquired if I was going to do any other acting projects around town. I told her of my plans to do *Five on the Black Hand Side* at Livingstone College for either the month of February or March. After giving her the synopsis of the play and an overview of what my goal was for Updaway Productions, she invited me to come to a meeting of a group called West End Pride. This is a nonprofit civic organization that researched grants to build businesses and to revitalize the economic infrastructure of the historically African American community of the west side of town. I informed my cast members that we would have to put rehearsals on hold until after my cousin returned from Virginia. I was also hoping that going to the meeting for West End Pride would be a stepping stone for securing the one of the venues at Livingstone College.

After my cousin returned from the Virginia, the meeting with the West End Pride group commenced the following week. Their main concern was to find financial resources to revitalize the community. I was very impressed with the members who convened, because the majority of them were people who had their own businesses on that side of town. These people were barbers, funeral home directors, members of the American Legion lounge, nurses, law enforcement officials, and representatives from Livingstone College. This group wanted to bring in a national retail businesses discount store like a Dollar Tree, Dollar General, or Family Dollar as well as men and women's clothing stores and restaurants to name a few other businesses to help stimulate the economic structure to the area. They also wanted to do something unique to the Duncan School. There were plans to convert the former elementary school into a cultural museum arts and community center, as well as using the cafeteria facility into a school for the culinary arts. The final component of the deal proposed was to refurbish the historic houses that ran along Monroe Street just outside the gates of Livingstone College, also to bring affordable housing to the civic low-income housing development that was conducted through the Salisbury Housing Authority. Their goal was to secure this grant money from the federal government, so that it would be reinvested in the historically African American community and stayed in the community to reinvigorate it.

The meeting started off talking about the importance of conducting a voter registration campaign, because 2012 was the election year. It was important to get the vote out in order to attempt to have the elected officials get our proposals pushed through, so that the grant would be approved for the revitalization of the West End community. All members of the committee agreed that this was a vital campaign to their cause. That was one of the only things that everyone would be in agreement with. The rest of the meeting would be based on what would need to be done to secure the grant and what role would Livingstone College take. Most of the time members would talk about how the money should be used to refurbish the houses in the neighborhood, and the other part of the time, the members would talk about the business that they would like to be placed there.

The hot topic was how Livingstone College could help, and would they help in this joint venture? State Alexander who was the assistant to the college president was the main representative from the college. When the meeting began, it was about putting together a united front and solidarity, but as it progressed it turned into a Livingstone College bashing. State Alexander explained that Livingstone College was willing to help, but it would be conducive if they were to work together. By bashing the college, it wouldn't be tolerated if this was going to be a campaign of beating up on Livingstone College. I took an opportunity to speak to address the group. I let it be known that bashing the college wasn't helpful for anyone, and that if we were going to acquire the funds that we would need to put any differences and the past behind us. The majority of the members agreed, and State then proposed that we should hold the next meeting at the president's dining room of the college.

At the end of the meeting, I took another opportunity to speak to State Alexander. I introduced myself to him and told him about the proposal that I had sent to Linda Hunt. He appeared to be genuinely interested in the play and wanted me to send him a copy of the proposal via e-mail. We exchanged contact information, and I was looking forward to the meeting in the next couple of weeks with the rest of the committee members. By now I had a few decisions made for me. I had to inform my cast what has transpired and that we weren't going to be able to put the show on before the month of

April. I had to let them know that if they had other priorities that they should keep them. I wasn't able to afford to keep them.

By this point in time, I was still putting all my hopes and aspirations on the belief that doing this show was the break that I need. I had to keep saying to myself that if there was going to be an opportunity to make something happen, that I had to be the one to do it. I haven't been successful in trying to receive the cooperation from many of the people at this new town that I call home, but the one thing that I do know, keeping my faith was the only thing I have to hold on to. It hasn't been easy, and there were nights I found myself going to sleep and waking up with tears in my eyes. During those times, I find myself waning in my faith, wondering if I would ever be delivered from this ordeal, and doing something that I know I shouldn't do by questioning God on the ultimate three letter word that ends as a question as to why?

The one thing that I started doing shortly after moving into the shelter was to visit the churches that would have the two volunteers who served the residents. I would continue to go to my own church that I became a member of Gethsemane Missionary Baptist Church, but I didn't attend the worship services there as much as I did since moving into the shelter. I wanted to take the time attend services at these other churches as an act of appreciation for the volunteers who would come to serve. In the process, I would also get my fulfillment of getting the word of God in and fellowshipping with others. Just like when I would leave the shelter to go to the career center or the library, I found contentment and peace being in the sanctuary of the church. Hearing the testimonies and sermons of others helped me realized that some of my problems weren't as big as some of the others. There were people who lost their jobs, went through custody battles, and had their houses and cars repossessed. My problems next to theirs seemed to be minor, but still in all, it was a problem that I needed to get help with. Still I feel that I have a lot of things that are incomplete. I have always been told by my parents not to start a project that I didn't intend on finishing. I was still living at the shelter with my prospect for jobs that have been far and few in between interviews.

I had a play that had no rehearsal hall, no venue, and no characters to perform them. I got to the point that I got desperate to do anything to bring some income into my life. I wanted to do it on honest work, because I was too old to have to constantly look over my shoulder wondering if the law or somebody would want to take me out for doing the wrong things. I guess that we have to learn how to live in the moment, because tomorrow isn't promised to anyone. I know that sooner or later something has got to change for the better. I didn't know what the future holds, but I had to believe that there is a future. It's like a quote that I saw on one of my friend's Facebook pages, and it stated by saying "Yesterday is the in the past, tomorrow is the unknown, but today is a gift and that's why it's the present." I just wished that this gift came with some frills, but that's not the case in reality.

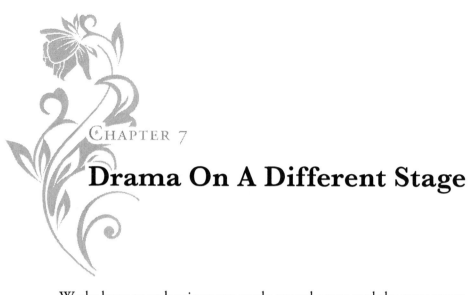

CHAPTER 7

Drama On A Different Stage

Weeks have gone by since my uncle passed away, and the new group that I joined, the West End Pride, have met with the administrators at Livingstone College. I have still been going to the career center, prospecting job leads while in the process of trying to manipulate things so that I can put on *Five on the Black Hand*. Things haven't exactly gone according to plan when it came to getting this production underway. It's now the month of March, a year later since I've admitted myself into the shelter. This was the latest time that I originally wanted to put this production out for the public to experience. The original intentions were to perform the production of this play in the month of February for black history month or to do it in the month of March for women's history month. This story is centered around the main character, Gladys, who is an African American housewife who's been sheltered and submissive at the beginning of the play, but blossoms into a determined, strong, independent woman by the end of it. This story has so many different topics that were addressed in the 1970s that are still very much prevalent today. Doing a performance of this play is something that everyone can relate to, regardless of race content. It is still my focal point of getting this production done.

Being at the career center was great for me, because it gave me the solitude that I couldn't get when I was at the shelter. There were times when I was at the shelter trying to put down notes in a notebook and someone would take away my attention from the thing that I needed to focus on the most. When that would happen, I would lose my train of thought and forget what it was I need do. I struggle with that, and having to keep my concentration strong was the thing that I needed to have the most. One day at the career center, the management at Goodwill had posted jobs on their bulletin board of jobs from the area. Most of the jobs would cover that Salisbury/Rowan County area, and some of the other jobs would cover the Charlotte or Winston-Salem areas. Goodwill posted an opening in the local office in Salisbury for a career connections specialist position. This was a part-time job that only covered twenty to twenty-five hours a week. I didn't care how many hours a week it was, but I wanted this job as if this was the best job that I would ever have for the rest of my life. The attraction that I found appealing to me was it was related to what I acquired my degree in.

I applied for the part-time position of career connection specialist and was asked to come back for an interview a couple of weeks later. I was praying that my experiences working at the two different Urban Leagues in Newark, New Jersey, and Columbia, South Carolina, would've made a difference. I was interviewed by Nancy who ran the center. I made sure like I always do that I had attended to the interview dressed professionally and didn't do anything that was over the top like wearing a strong-scented cologne. Shoes polished, clean clothes, and fingernails clipped and filed. I felt good going into the interview, and I had copies of my resume revised. I always try to make a practice of the Lombardi rule to be there at least fifteen minutes before the interview, or you're considered being late. I kept the interview professional when I addressed Nancy by addressing her by a title of Ms. Rominger. The question she'd given me were the simple ones to answer, and at the end of the interview, she had asked me if I had a question. I always believed that you should always ask your interviewer at least one question, and it really shouldn't deal about the compensation. I inquired about the reason that this positioned opened. She replied that the company was expanding the office and that they would need someone to assist with the duties of performing the task equivalent to that of an administrative assistant.

I was blessed to be called back after a couple of days to have a second interview. Nancy told me that I would be interviewed by the people out of the Winston-Salem headquarters the following week. I would be screened by Sheila Padrick from that office. It reminded me of a line that I remembered from the original *Superman* movie with Christopher Reeve, when Jackie Cooper the former Our Gang child star portrayed the role of Perry White said, "This would be the most important interview in history since God had spoken to Moses!" I was treating this interview as such, because I viewed this as a sign of a positive change coming. Working the part-time morning hours would've been allowed me to do some work for four hours a day, and I could still pursue working on my passion, which was to produce a theatrical production. Going into the interview, I felt confident about acquiring the position without being cocky. This was a position that I went to school to work with, and I thought that my experiences from working at the two different Urban League offices would be to my advantage.

I made sure that I followed the Lombardi rule of being at least fifteen minutes before the interview, but this time I was there a half hour before. I wanted to have time to look over my resume so I could make any adjustments that I might need to do. I wanted to be there so that I could also screen the other candidates for the job. I wanted to see what kind of advantage that they might have or vice versa. If there was any kind of advantage that I could find I would try to use something to my advantage. I felt the need to find something to give me the edge over the others who were competing for the same position that I was.

Much to my disappointment, there didn't appear to be anyone that was slack coming in for their interviews. Everyone who was chosen by Nancy to come in for the follow-up interviews were some of the sharpest knives in the kitchen drawer. The interviews began early that morning as they started screening candidates at eight thirty. There were eight people who were vying for just one position. My interview was scheduled for nine thirty, so I had the opportunity to see Reni Geiger and Sheila Padrick, two of the managers for Goodwill out of the Winston-Salem office. The Winston-Salem office is the headquarters for the northwestern North Carolina region. The first couple of people who were in the room with the interviewers appeared to have been interviewed pretty quick. Whenever I had experienced a fairly quick interview that didn't seem to be a very good possibility of me securing the job from an employer. Now it was my turn to prove to these interviewers that I was ready to assume my position and accept the responsibilities with Goodwill as one of their employees. My main goal was to try to remain cool and not look too excited.

When it came my turn to meet with the hiring authorities, it felt to me just like an audition, and just like any other audition that I ever had done as a performer, I had those butterflies working in my stomach, not knowing if this was a good or bad thing. I had the visit from my friend Frankie Fear. It's amazing how, in a time of stress, fear can work in your favor if you have a grasp of not wanting to have a failure go against you. My interviewers were very thorough asking me the questions, and our session lasted about forty minutes before Sheila asked me if I had any questions for them.

Again it's always a good thing to ask the interviewers questions, but when I did, I wasn't going to inquire about the salary unless the interviewer doesn't tell me how much the salary is. I try to avoid asking about the compensation, because most of the time, I feel that they will pay me fairly even if that doesn't always happen. I asked them several questions, and the first one was, how did the position become available? The reason I inquired about that is because I needed to know if this job has a high-turnover rate, and I wanted to be careful before I take the position if there's a high-turnover rate. My next question for her was, is there the possibility for getting overtime? Being that this was a part-time position, the work week was less than forty hours, and I wanted to get as many hours a day that I could. Another question that I asked them was, how soon would they need to fill this position? I needed the work ever since I moved to Salisbury. When I moved to Salisbury after my old job reneged on allowing me to work from home, I wasn't able to collect any unemployment. I liquidated my savings and my 401k in order to survive. Anything that I had of value I needed to sell or pawn in order to survive. I pawned my electronic equipment, silver, gold, and even sold the bedframe to the junkyard for scrap in order to put a little change into my pockets. My last question for them was, how did I personally measure up to the other candidates who they've interviewed to this point? Maybe that may have seemed a little too presumptuous, but I remembered my parents telling me that the only dumb question is the one that was never asked. Reni expressed that she was impressed by my background and that my chances are equal to all of the candidates. Sheila told me that she was equally impressed with my previous work history from working at the Urban League of Essex County and that I would probably be a better candidate for another position with the organization maybe as a mentor retention specialist. At that point, Reni agreed that if they had a position available, I would've been a better candidate for that one. When the interview was over, I shook their hands and thanked them for the opportunity for the interview, still not knowing if I was going to be considered seriously for the position that had opened. I immediately went to the computer in the career center to use the computer to write each of my interviewers a thank-you letter.

No decision was conveyed to me about the position being filled until two weeks later. One day about the same time that Goodwill was to announce who was going to get the position, I entered into the career center and noticed that Nancy and Eric were training a new person. I knew at that time that was my confirmation for not getting the position. I was so high on the hopes that I would've secured that position that I was ready to make plans to move out of the shelter. Once I got my hopes up and not being able to get the position was the biggest let down. I felt as if I was so high that looking down, I could see the country from outer space. For me not getting the job was one of the hardest things to try to rebound from. The one thing that I never stopped doing while waiting to hear about the position from Goodwill was to still put in for other positions for other employers. Now that I didn't get what I needed, I had to keep my focus on getting a source of income.

When the job opportunity with Goodwill fell through, I made a stronger effort to revisit the opportunity of presenting the play at Livingstone College. The negotiations had now gone past the deadline for the month of March, and now I needed this production to be performed before the students graduated in May. Several times since the initial meeting with State Alexander, I was told that I would be meeting with him and Dr. Kelli Randle the dean of the fine arts department. The reason for the delay was due to the fact that Dr. Randle was in a car accident. That incident had delayed the production from six to eight weeks. I made it a point of letting the people who were cast know, and also Mae Carroll from West End Pride that the negotiations have been stalled because of the accident of Dr. Randle.

It was April before I received the e-mail from State that Dr. Randle was well, and I needed to make arrangements to present my proposal to them. I finally had hopes of a breakthrough for the play. I had called his secretary to schedule a time, and I was told that he would get back and confirm with me to when all parties involved would meet. With my birthday coming up, if all would go according to plan, then this was going to be a birthday present that I could enjoy. Still waiting on the meeting, I didn't want to inform the cast or committee members over with West End Pride and the officials at Livingstone College. I didn't want them to experience the rollercoaster ride of the emotions that I was going through with this process of securing the venue. Before a single act, musical selection, or wardrobe change would be made, I needed everything to be in place. I needed everyone who was part of Updaway Productions to concentrate on the product of giving the finest performance that the public was expecting to see. Already there was a buzz going around the town that there would be a performance, and the public was just itching for something that they never experienced before.

I received the call from Mr. Alexander's secretary the following week and got confirmation that the meeting would take place the next week on a Wednesday. Understanding what had transpired at Livingstone College with the CIAA tournament and the accident to Dr. Randle, I accepted the date for the meeting and felt pretty much prepared for it. Shortly after getting the notification from the secretary, I made a call to Jamaa Fanaka, the director of the *Penitentiary* movie trilogy. I told him of my current undertaking and explained what my goal was in presenting *Five on the Black Hand Side* to the people in this area of North Carolina. Jamaa understood that it was important to do this performance, because of my previous explanation of how things went with the casting that I experience at the Piedmont Players Theatre Company. I told him about the meeting that was going to take place with the college and asked if he wouldn't mind if I had to call him from there to be a reference for me. He told me that he was available at that time and that he was happy to help me in any way that he could.

Now I'm just days away from my meeting with the officials from Livingstone College, and I made contact with an established Hollywood director. Next thing I did was to contact my creative team and asked Dee if she would be available to come to the meeting. She, being a graduate with a degree in business and her concentration in communications, we began work on a PowerPoint presentation and developed a web page. We had completed both endeavors within a two-day period. If we were going to be turned down, it wasn't going to happen because Updaway Productions wasn't prepared. It looked that we've finally had all of the puzzle pieces together with every "T" being crossed and every "I" being dotted. I was so hyped up about the meeting that I had to remember to try to stay calm. The people who were scheduled to attend from Livingstone were State Alexander, Dr. Kelli Randle, and Linda Hunt. I had my own team lined up with Dee Addison, Jamaa Fanaka on speed dial to comment in on the meeting, and myself. I felt pretty confident about the pending meeting, and that I had a pretty strong line-up that would've been able to persuade any respectable theatre company.

All things were in place just a day before the meeting. I was at the career center with Dee going over the final strategy for our meeting with the officials at Livingstone. As I was sitting at the computer going through my e-mail, I got one from the college. I was notified that, at the present, they would not be able to do the production, because the staff was getting ready to do finals for the spring semester. Needless to say, by the time I received this information, I was livid. It felt to me like a baseball analogy, coming up to the plate against a pitcher who toys with you by throwing fastballs and your timing is just slightly off. You swing and foul off one fastball after another because it's just outside of the strike zone. Then when you finally guess the right location of the next fastball, the pitcher serves up a curveball and you miss the whole thing. It's strike three and you're out! I didn't know what to do next. I wanted to cry openly, because this was six months of hard work that was just pulled away from me. If someone had a raw egg and put it over my forehead, it would've cooked instantly.

I wanted to beat myself up knowing that I put myself in an area that was resistant to change. If I was going to enter into the inner sanctum of the performing professionals in this town, then I needed to accept the way things were in order to fit in. When I got the information from State Alexander that the play wasn't going to happen, I made sure that when I saw Linda Hunt that evening at the shelter, I request the return of the master script. I wasn't going to give her, or the theatre department, the satisfaction of keeping it for any future productions that they may have had in mind. The one of the hardest things for me to accept was the fact that it wasn't time for me to produce the show at this time. It wasn't the right play for this town. The more time that I thought about it, the bitter I became. For the next couple of weeks, I really didn't do much of anything. I stopped looking for a job, because I wasn't getting any responses from the applications that I put in, and I stopped trying to work at growing the business that I started. I was experiencing a state of depression that saw my whole attitude change about the way I felt about where my presence is.

It's been over a year since I've been living in the shelter, and since I've last worked. I was staying at a place that called itself a ministry. This is a ministry that forbids the residents there to show any kind of public display of affection. PDA is what the residents of the shelter called it. If you're a married couple who had to move into their facility, you weren't allowed to hug, kiss, or even hold hands on their property. Doing these public act of affection can get you kicked out of there for several days at a time. When you check in for the evening, you have to turn in your cell phone, money, and any kind of sharp instruments that can be considered to be used as a weapon, including nail file, pocket knife, and box cutter. Even if you were wearing earphones, your portable video game, mp3 player, radio, computer tablet, or laptop computer had to be turned off when they call lights out at ten o'clock at night. The case managers do very little to help you find the residents employment. The first thing that they want to know when they did the intake procedures of the new people entering into the shelter is if you are depressed. When they asked me that question, I reciprocated by asking them the same. The majority of the people who I know that are depressed if they're not working and want to. So for me to dignify that question with an answer was a moot point. The caseworkers want to admit you into Life Works, which is the psychiatric institution at the Rowan Regional Medical Center, or Daymark, the outpatient center for depression, substance abuse that's also located in the same town. Since my time as a resident being a guest of the shelter, I haven't been given a job referral for a lead or referral by my caseworker, David. Since being there, I've been told nothing but lies by him, and he hasn't made an effort to put me on a case plan of any kind.

Now there have been several changes that have happened at the shelter. The director Rodney Harris has resigned, and his position has opened. The news came out weeks later that he and several officers within the Salisbury Police Department were being indicted for abuse of authority and for illegal searches. I was thinking that this would be a good opportunity that works twofold. This would allow me to work in the field of my degree and with my familiarity with the people, policies, and procedures of the shelter. Personally, I thought that it would be the perfect situation for me. I was hoping that I was the perfect candidate for the position. Against my better judgment, I saw my case manager David and inquired to him about the position. I received the application, filled it out, and returned it to the receptionist at the front desk of the crisis center. I still didn't have the enthusiasm that I did when I was pursuing the opportunity to present the play at Livingstone.

I still tried to keep the hope that there will be an opportunity to work at the shelter. There was always the possibility that they may hire a candidate from within the shelter. I didn't lose sight of the fact that there would be another opening or two possibly. If they were to give the position that Rodney held to one of the employees who work at the shelter, I knew that there was going to be another opening there, and I was hoping to land one of them. I knew that this was going to be a lengthy process when it came to the authorities to screen for the next director of the shelter. It could take a week or it could take several months before they decided to fill the position. While he was the director of the shelter, Rodney ran a pretty tight ship. He had zero tolerance level when it came to having guest fighting on the premises, and he was constantly drug testing the shelter guests for marijuana, cocaine, and other narcotics. These were the most commonly used drugs at the facility, and to test for them was easy. The most ridiculous thing that I could think of is the guest who were on probation or parole from the law enforcement officials were jeopardizing their own freedom by taking these drugs like it was candy. The majority of the people who were on probation or parole wouldn't use while they were on those restrictions, but there would be others who didn't care about the consequences and would use them anyways.

In the process of trying to secure a job with anyone, I notice that my tolerance level had dropped to an all-time low. I found myself wanting to be isolated from the rest of the shelter population. I didn't speak to many, and when someone would ask me a question, I would give them a close-ended answer. I was irritated and really didn't want to be bothered with any of the people who lived in there. I just wanted to find a way to get out of the shelter, and I didn't see anyone who was living there that was really trying to make an effort of getting out. Once in a while you would run into someone who was at a transitional point, and they needed to use the shelter as a temporary means of staying before they move into their new dwelling. I needed a job, and I was dissatisfied with the progress that I was making in order to accomplish my goal. I was missing the things that I was accustomed to doing and having since I've moved in. The simple things as far as talking to a friend on the phone in the evenings, watching a basketball game on television at night, cooking the kind of foods that I wanted to eat that kept me healthy. Living there at the shelter, you were at the mercy of whatever they had to serve for a meal, and this being the south, the main staple of meat is pork. Pork is king of the region, and don't let anyone else tell you otherwise. The breakfast that I was used to eating would consist of corned beef hash, beef or turkey sausage, and beef bacon. While at the shelter, they would serve nothing but the pork products that I've mentioned. The one thing that I missed most of all was the freedoms and liberties that I took for granted when I was living outside of the shelter. Being around and in contact with my granddaughter was the liberty that I missed the most.

My granddaughter was just about ready to graduate from elementary school, and she called me to let me know. She was about to take the next step from elementary to middle school. When she first started school, this child struggled, and it was so bad that after her first year in the second grade, she wasn't ready to move forward with the rest of her classmates. Her mother decided that it wasn't in her best interest for Shay'lee to advance to the next grade level. She had made me proud, because she did the hard work of excelling pretty much on her own. The only time that she wanted my help was at the beginning of the school year. I received the call from Shay'lee, telling me that she had homework on the first day of school when she was in her fifth grade, and that she wanted me to help her with the answers. What I figured out was that she was trying to con me into giving her the answer on a social studies assignment. I told her that she was going to have to read the material over several times, but the answers were there in the materials she was assigned. She made the A/B honor roll earlier during that school year and made honors in mathematics and physical education. I was disappointed when she asked me for money that she wanted to learn how to play the string instrument for the year and then changed her mind to sing in the choir instead. That disappointed me, because I was struggling on a monthly basis just to support myself in cigarettes, but I had sacrificed them just so that she could learn to play the viola. If that was the worst that happened, then I could live with it.

I still haven't told her to this point that I was living in the shelter. I was embarrassed to let her know that I wasn't able to move forward after fourteen months of not working. I almost felt helpless to the fact that I wasn't able to give her a graduation card with a few dollars so that she could get herself something nice as a reward for accomplishing a great thing. I was able to save the money from the sale of my food stamps to go and celebrate her graduation from elementary school. It was just the fourth time that I was able to go into Columbia to visit her since I moved into Salisbury. The best way for me to travel was to take the Greyhound from Charlotte to Columbia, so I had to travel to Charlotte first. I had to leave the night before because there were only two buses to go into Columbia in the morning and another one that leaves late in the afternoon.

When I arrived in Columbia, I caught a cab from the station to the school. I just made it into their cafetorium where the ceremony was being held shortly after the graduates started their processional. After the graduates finished, the rest of the guests were allowed to come into the facility to enjoy the ceremony. All the young ladies were dressed in white dresses, and the young men had white shirts and black dress slacks. I saw where my granddaughter's mother and the rest of the family was sitting, and I found a seat close by and sat there. I felt so proud when they were doing the awards for the department awards to see my granddaughter walk toward the podium three times. The next time that she would go there was to be her last act as a student to receive her graduation certificate from elementary school.

Seeing her receive her awards brought tears to my eyes. It brought back the memories of her going through the struggles as a kindergartener. Me having to go over her house in the evenings to tutor her on how to do her spelling word by writing out each of the words five times. There were times when she was trying to learn how to read and she would tell me that she couldn't. I would tell her that she will learn how to read. The biggest part of advancing that made me feel the proudest is that she was able to achieve this on her own with the help of the after-school programs that she participated in. I felt very responsible for her not advancing when her mother made the decision not to let her continue on with the rest of her classmates. It was me who didn't realize what I was doing when I had her audition for a stage play that my alma mater, Benedict College, was presenting. The fine arts department was doing their annual fall presentation, and Mr. Brooks told me that it was going to be *The WIZ*. I was informed about the play back in August of 2007.

I agreed to audition for the role and was told that he was looking for children performers to play the roles as munchkins, mice, and citizens of the emerald city. She came to the audition with me along with her stepsister Tamia. Everyone who auditioned was given a line of dialog to read, and since it was a musical play, we were also asked to sing a song. If you had a sheet of music, then it needed to be provided for the music director. When she saw that the children were singing, she said that she didn't have a song to sing. I told her to sing "Lost without You" by Robin Thicke. I remembered her singing that as a child. Shay'lee was the kind of child who was trying to sing before she was talking. Once before she got out of the babbling stage as an infant, she tried to sing "Fallin'" by Alicia Keyes. She was still undecided about what song she needed to sing, but when Mr. Brooks called her name to come to the stage, she did her thing. Brooks had asked all the children their names, ages, grade, and the school they attended. He gave them a dialog that he asked them to repeat after him and then he asked them if they had a song that they could sing. As soon as he asked Shay'lee if she had a song, that surprised the hell out of me more than most of the audience who were at the audition there too. She sang a song by Mary Mary, "I Got Myself Together." I never knew that the child could sing that well. The other actors and actresses stood up and clapped their hands as if they were holding service in a chapel. The cast members who I acted with started turning around to me and gave me a look as if I was coaching her. I was so overwhelmed with joy that I couldn't help but cry, and when my former and current co-stars were giving me the thumbs-up, I would wave my hand at them as if I was telling them that it's all her talent. I had nothing to do with it, and she's the one who truly has the talent in the family.

That was her way of letting me know that she was ready to perform and she wanted to do this show with me. Due to the rehearsal schedule and her age, it was hard to ask a seven-year-old to do homework, have dinner, and go to rehearsal from seven to nine in the evening. Shortly after she was a cast member, she found it difficult to stay awake in her classroom. She was struggling in her daily classes and was falling behind in her grades. Her mother told me about this, and we both mutually agreed, at this time, it would benefit her to concentrate on her studies instead of worrying about performing in the show. This became evident for her struggles in school, and her mother and my decision for her to repeat the second grade that she was in at that time.

I feel responsible for her having to do that, and I don't know if I will ever get over that. I believed that I wanted her to perform in this production more than she did. Looking at it in hindsight, I may have wanted her to perform in this production, because I wanted to influence her into looking at making a career as a performing artist. Maybe I was wanting to live vicariously through her by trying to guide her into a career in show business at a young age. I don't regret the fact that I introduced her into the world of theatre. It helped develop a love affair that she has for the discipline of the theatre arts. I do regret that I didn't think it out by pushing her to do the production, because she had to repeat the second grade over again.

It was now that I needed to find a way to get things back on track in my personal life so that I can do whatever it was to help my granddaughter. I encouraged her to do this, and I didn't foresee the consequences that could occur from her working like a child performer. When I think of it, I wasn't any better than any other child performer parents who had put them on a stage because they were talented enough to entertain with the potential of making a living out of it. Still to this day, when I called her to let her know that I'm doing a show when one comes my way, she still asks me if she can perform with me. That would be a dream that I would love to see come into fruition.

Before any of that can happen, I have to get myself in a stable situation. Still holding on to the one thing that I know won't fail me is the belief that this was a test of my faith. I had my moments when I doubted if I would ever be able to weather out this storm of a bad decision I made by moving to Salisbury. There were times that I have my moments and doubt did set in. Some days were better than others, but I know I will have to make better choices. I prayed to God that it would get better. I know that things didn't go the way I hoped for, but God was working hard for me and I had to let him do his thing, not mine. It will happen. I just had to trust God.

CHAPTER 8

Sign of The Times

Now, I've been at the shelter for sixteen months, and the prospect didn't look very bright. Nothing was happening with me securing the job at Goodwill, or anyplace else for that matter, but I was still putting in applications for jobs in North Carolina and all around the country. Some of the people who I have come across with told me that maybe I was aiming too high for a position. One person who worked there at Goodwill told me that the McDonald's restaurant was hiring, and I should try to get with them. So to prove a point to them, I applied. I went there on a Wednesday because they take the applications and do interviews on the spot. I filled out the application but had omitted the fact that I acquired my bachelor degree. I completed it, I turned it in, and I waited for the interviewer to tell me it was my turn to talk to her. By the time that she finally got to me, all was going great until they asked me if I went to college. I told her yes and that I hold a degree. She said, "I thought so. You know that you're overqualified for the position you're applying for."

I figured that something like this would happen. Maybe it was the way that I answered the question while she was interviewing me, or the fact that when I go to the interview, I dress professionally. I was taught that from my days working at the Urban League of Essex County that when you go to the interview, you should dress to impress almost to the point that you want to be the owner of the company that you're interviewing for. I let her know that I was willing to do anything to work for the company. I was willing to work part time if that was the only hours that were available. I needed a job and would do anything that I could in order to get it, because this has been the longest that I've been out of work. By the end of the interview, she told me that if I was to work for them, they would notify me. I told her that the best way to contact me would be in the afternoon by telephone, and if they could please call me before six in the evening.

I knew when I left there that the interview went fine, but they weren't going to be interested in hiring me. They knew if an opportunity had arisen where I could use my degree, I wouldn't be an employee that would stay there long term. I understood that and respected their decision. Days went by and I didn't get a call from them, but this was something that I expected. I ran into my friend Dee at the career center and told her about that experience. She asked me did I have another play that I could do that didn't have such a big cast. She liked the idea of me wanting to do theatre here and told me that I shouldn't give up so easily. I thought about it, and I remembered the play that I wrote for the church that was turned down. The church wanted to make it a musical with some of the performers singing, but I had a different vision for it. I wanted to do a dramatic comedy. Too many times since I've been involved in theatre, the audience in the Piedmont region feel that African Americans only have to sing and dance in order to perform for an audience. My intention was to dispel this notion, that it's the only way that African Americans to perform on the stage.

I revisited the play that I titled as "Sign of the Times" and fine-tuned it during the edits. Just like the last time when I cast people for *Five on the Black Hand Side*, I didn't think that I wouldn't have a problem casting the production, but trying to secure a venue. I had Dee look at the script, and she fell in love with it. The next thing I did was to revisit what venues that could hold this production. I thought about it, and it came to me that I needed to see Mae Carroll at the American Legion Post. I made an appointment to meet with Mae so that I could pitch my proposal to her so that she could ask for and get her board members' approval. Originally I wanted to put on this production for October, but shortly after doing the proposal, the Piedmont Players Theatre Company was advertising that they were going to do the musical production of *The Color Purple*. Their shows were going to run late in the month of October and early November. So I felt that it would better to for me to do it after the run of *The Color Purple*. I thought it would've been foolish of me to try to run my production during the same time that the more successful and established Piedmont Players Theatre were going to do theirs.

When I met Mae, we had lunch with two other members of the post at Ryan's buffet. I was prepared and had copies of the proposal for everyone to view. We discuss all the specific of the production—marketing, casting, crew, and the other amenities that go along with producing a stage play. For the first time since I've started Updaway Productions, I had the positive hope that this will finally go off. Mae and her people were happy that I wanted to do a show there, and I was equally happy that Updaway was going to have this opportunity to perform a show. By the time that the meeting was over, the optimism was good by all parties involved. I let Dee know what was happening, and together, we began the process of using social media to start promoting the show and casting individuals to fill the parts.

Meanwhile things at the shelter have changed a lot. Rodney was no longer the director of the shelter. Rodney resigned shortly before the *Salisbury Post* had written a story about a lawsuit filed against the Salisbury Police Department. The story stated that four people have filed a lawsuit against Salisbury and members of its police department, claiming officers conducted illegal searches and abused their authority. The plaintiffs were suing at that time a current officer on the force, a former officer, the predecessor of Rodney before he was the acting police chief, Rodney, and the successor after Rodney's resignation from the force. I don't know if Rodney was pressured by the administration or the board of directors to resign, but he resigned his positions as the shelter director only days before the story hit the streets. Prior to taking the position as the director of the shelter, Rodney began active police duty with the Salisbury Police Department in 1990 as a patrol officer. He served twelve years as an investigator, followed by four years as a police sergeant.

He was promoted to lieutenant in 2008. Lt. Rodney Harris served as acting chief following the retirement of Chief Mark Wilhelm in December of 2009. He was investigated by the North Carolina State Bureau of Investigations and place on administrative leave with pay prior to the current charge. I applied for his position as the Shelter Director, because my background is in the human and social services. Unfortunately, the administration and the board of directors didn't think it was a good idea for me to have that position, and one reason that I was given was that I needed to be away from the shelter at least six month before I could apply for a position.

The board of directors approved David, my former case manager, as the new director of the shelter. I used to joke about how strict to the letter Rodney was about the regulations of the shelter by calling it "Master Rodney's slave quarters." Little did I know at the time when David acquired the position as the director how dramatically things would change, and not necessarily for the better. Compare to the way that David was going to run this place, Rodney ran the facility like a preschool campus compared to David. David had every intention of using it as a true slave quarters. David was now the puppet master, and he was going to pull any string that he wanted to get the residents to do whatever bidding he needed them to do. It's true whoever said the proverb that you never miss the water until the well runs dry was right.

Almost immediately, David started laying his own law down, and he was going to have a zero-tolerance level on everything that was installed before he took over, and he was going to make up new rules as he deemed necessary. One of the first thing that David did was to institutionalize the residents of the shelter. When a guest was first admitted into the facility, they were issued a set of pajamas to sleep in that were donated by the volunteer groups from the church or other community-based organizations. Immediately he used money from the budget of his department to invest in hospital scrubs for the residents to sleep in. This was nothing more than a blatant effort to intentionally ostracize the residents from making them feel as if they were a normal part of the community. This was an effort to demoralize the residents that they were slightly better than the inmates at the county department of corrections. The only difference in having the shelter guest dressing in uniform hospital scrub from the inmates in the jail was the fact the guest didn't have the letters DOC for department of corrections pasted on the back of their pajamas. It was insulting and very degrading for the residents to wear those scrubs, but it was a successful effort on behalf of David and the administration to break down the drive to succeed of many of the residents. For many of the residents who came to stay in the shelter, they were returning to life on the streets after spending time in the county or state penal system. So for many of them, it was a return psychologically to being incarcerated.

The biggest threat that he was going to do to the guest was to make the whole outside of the shelter and crisis assistance network into a smoke-free environment. There was a designated area on the grounds where people were supposed to smoke. There was an elevated brick patio in the front of the building that the residents and the guest were asked to smoke at. The majority of the residents would followed the rules to smoke in the designated areas. Many of the people who didn't follow them were those who would come into the crisis network and food pantry to receive assistance. David told us that if we were caught smoking around the shelter that was not in the designated area, he would cease the smoking policy immediately.

He also instituted that all guests of the shelter would need to have only one set of clothes washed on a daily basis. This wasn't so bad because it was still the summertime. The thing that I was wondering was what would happen when it started to get cold. People were going to have to dress in layers, and granted that it's not the same kind of climate that I've experienced in New Jersey. Still there was going to be the need for people to stay warm. I was wondering if the roles had been reversed, he would've appreciate the fact that he would possibly have to walk around town with funky clothes. I questioned him about that, but he didn't want to move on his position. Another rule that he instituted there was that all guests were required to have their shelter pass with them at all times. Anyone who didn't have their shelter pass after the crisis network closed was to be considered trespassing. Guests would be required to show their pass before entering the facility. He stated that he informed that the Salisbury police department had been notified of this and that the police had the right to remove the people from the grounds of the shelter. David reiterated and was extremely adamant about their position on the personal display of affection, and if we were caught, he would immediately give whoever was doing this, the both parties involved, give a three-day suspension from the shelter.

Whenever a person would get written up for a suspended stay, you could always appeal it. Most of the time, the director would reduce the time of the suspension, but there would be instances where he would prolong it. There have been a couple of documented instances where I don't believe it should've been deemed necessary to do so. The first time that I saw this happened to someone first hand was when a young kid who was nineteen years old at the time got caught drinking on the property. JP was a young man who has been going in and out of the North Carolina foster care system, and by the time he was nineteen years old, he was too old to remain in the system. At that point he became a member of the homeless population. Still not mature and somewhat impressionable, he went around the corner of the shelter that many called the drugstore and was drinking in that area with others who didn't stay at the shelter. There was a surveillance system that was located around the exterior and the interior of the building and the transitional housing area called the Eagle's Nest. David viewed this action from his office, and when JP wanted to gain entrance into the shelter that evening, he was told that he had to go around to the front of the main entrance to see David before he could gain admittance. When he went around to see him, David gave him a notice that his privileges staying there were suspended. He was given thirty days because he had been written up previously.

I'm not condoning the actions of JP, but here's a kid without any family in the town, no resources, and not working anywhere. Now let me remind you that before David became the director of the shelter, he was a case manager for the residents of the shelter. David didn't do any form of intervention with JP until after he was admitted back into the shelter. The intervention occurred when JP returned to the shelter. He was instructed to go into the outpatient treatment center for alcohol and drug abuse at Daymark. While he was on the streets, JP had to rely on his friends, the kindness of strangers, and his own street savvy to survive. He wasn't allowed to be on the property and he couldn't go to the soup kitchen for lunch. There appeared to be very little done in the form of assessing this individual, and shortly after JP had appealed David's decision, he was still denied entrance into the shelter. This was a display of David exercising his authority over the people who had no other choice or resources but to live in the shelter. If this was just the beginning of him going into a power trip, then a lot of people who like to play with fire were going to get burned.

Before selecting David as the director of the shelter, the board of directors must have been looking at someone who was familiar in working at the shelter. By putting him in that position, they knew he understood the policies and nuances of how to operate their facility. David didn't have a degree in social sciences, but his was in business. When it came down to working on budgets, he's the one you want to do that kind of work. He came off as a person who was selfish, and outside of being concerned about his paycheck, the only other important thing to him was him. These were going to be harder and more difficult times ahead. If anyone didn't recognize that things weren't going to get any better for them before things get worse, this was going to be their wake-up call. David was going to do whatever it took to get anyone who wasn't abiding by the rules out of the shelter or punish them so that they had to feel dependent on the services that the shelter provided.

When David became the director of the shelter, I was given a new case manager. Keona was the former program manager of New Tomorrow's program that was held at a local church a couple of blocks away from the shelter. The only problem that I had with New Tomorrow was that it's a program that was grant funded to assist displaced individuals. Where I saw this program falling short was there was little effort to assist the participants in securing employment. Those who attended the program did learn some valuable skills for job searching techniques. Participants learned the basics of producing resumes, cover letters, and interviewing skills. They also participated in the religious portion of the program where they would have to give testimonials and talk with the religious leaders who would visit the participant to inspire hope. That was a mandatory component that had to be implemented because this was a faith-based program. There wasn't any drawback to this program for Rowan Helping Ministries, because whatever participants that they had in the program, the administration would receive money from the grant to do the training of the participants. So instead of helping the participants with the need to secure employment and housing, it would just as good as putting money in the pocket for the people who were running New Tomorrows. For the participants who were expecting to receive housing and employment assistance, New Tomorrow meant no future.

Keona was promoted to be the case worker and I was assigned to her. I was hoping that maybe she had a clue of what case management was about. I first recall seeing pictures of her when I went on an audition at her alma mater, Livingston College. In the hallway of the fine arts department, there were some still shots of a production that she was in as an undergrad student. It was directed ironically by the woman who would become her colleague at the shelter, Linda Hunt. Another time when I visited New Tomorrow I briefly met her there. They had a company there that was testing people for HIV/AIDS, and had a condom distribution program.

So when I met her, I asked her if she had my resume on file. Together we looked over my file and attempted to work out a case plan to see about what we could do to try to secure employment for me. I wanted to make sure when I met her that there wouldn't be any questions about what I was doing, and I wanted her to know what I needed from her. I didn't want to get it twisted on either hand and made sure that we were both on the same accord. I told her that I was constantly going to the library or the Goodwill career center looking for a job, and that I was in the process of producing a show that I wrote. She told me that she had done some acting and we found something mutual that we had in common. We both had a love for the theatre. I informed her that the production was going to have a rehearsal schedule that would run into later hours of the evening, and

I asked if I could get permission to rehearse. I got her approval, and I felt pretty good about our meeting. I was hoping that she had a clue and could assist me on getting my life back on track.

Before I left, I had inquired about her old position at New Tomorrows. She told me that in order for me to be considered for that position, I would need to be out of the shelter for a minimum of six months before I can be considered for a position. This was disheartening to hear, but I was grateful for this information. My old case manager David didn't have the balls to give me this information. In my mind, I didn't see any reason why they should deny me to work at the job, let alone to apply for it. From viewing what the administration said about their vision statement from their Facebook page, it states, "The mission of Rowan Helping Ministries is to serve, through cooperative community action, our neighbors in Rowan County who are in crisis, by providing essential life needs and educating and empowering them to break the cycle of crisis." Who would be a better candidate for this position but someone who knows first-hand from the experience of being a guest there? I knew what was expected of the guest and the regulations that they had to follow.

A couple of weeks later I found out that they had filled the program manager's position at New Tomorrows by a woman whose daughter performed with me when I was in the production of *Dreamgirls* at the Piedmont Players Theatre. Theresa came in as the new program manager of the New Tomorrows. She remembered me from the days when her daughter and I performed on stage together. I guess it was easy to remember me, because I was the tallest cast member in the show, and I had a distinctive snake skinned coat that I wore during the performance. I recalled meeting her before when we had a cast and production party for opening night. We've spoke briefly shortly there and I was telling her about my production for *Sign of the Times*, and that I would be interested in having her daughter do a part for the Updaway productions of that play. She told me that her daughter had an engagement during the time we were holding rehearsal, because she was doing a series of spoken word recitals.

By now it was August, the membership at the JC Price American Legion Post had approve of us using their facility for Updaway Productions to rehearse and put on the show. I had assembled the cast for the *Sign of the Times*. Just like any other community theatre show that I've been a part of, there are always some parts that take longer to fill than others, but it was all good. For once I was out of the shelter to do something that was productive. It was a way of getting people who were interested in the theatre involved, and it was a way of me getting my name out into the inner circle of the local community production companies. Also at this time, it was harder for me to get some actors due to the fact that the Piedmont Players Theatre was getting ready to start their 2012 season. Their opening play was going to be the stage adaptation of the Alice Walker's novel *The Color Purple*. Many of the more seasoned local actors were looking to perform in the Piedmont Players production more than mine. Finding bodies to fill certain parts was harder than it would've been if I wasn't doing the show for Updaway Productions after the Piedmont Players play.

One of the other dilemmas that I had to put into consideration was should I audition for *The Color Purple*. I asked Tony who I performed with in *Dreamgirls* if he would be able to do my play, but he was committed on doing the production for the Piedmont Players. He in return asked me if I was going to audition for *The Color Purple*. Originally I told him no.

I wanted to concentrate on doing the *Sign of the Times*, and I didn't have any intentions on acting in *The Color Purple* or the *Sign of the Times*. My concerns with the play for Updaway Productions was to concentrate on every aspect of the play itself. The marketing of the production was already underway, because Dee was working on it with me on a daily basis. I needed to get in touch with Cliff Roseborough as my music director from my church to head up the orchestra so that the music could be scored. I didn't have the money for any sound equipment, but the blessing in doing the play at the post was that the acoustics were great because it was an intimate setting. Also the most important aspect of this production for me was to direct. I needed to show the actors what they needed to know about motivation and blocking. Still I was debating whether if I was going to do the production with the Piedmont Players. Just days before their auditions occurred I decided to give it a go.

Like every time I go to an audition, I wanted to take the lead male role, but this play of *The Color Purple* wasn't like anything that I expected. It was a musical, and I didn't know what exactly to expect. I have seen the movie version of this classic, and I was thinking that there would be more acting than singing in it. Once I got to the audition, I knew what to expect from the last time that I auditioned. When you get to an audition with the Piedmont Players, you fill out the application with your standard information and your measurements for wardrobe. You're given a number and are asked to sing and read lines of dialogue. This process normally happens for the first two days. By the second day the director, musical directors, choreographer, wardrobe and props managers gather the members of the cast and let them know that it's going to be an eight week process before the curtains go up on opening night.

I was selected into the cast and was given a good part, and was cast as Old Mister in the play. I wanted to do the lead for *The Color Purple*, but it didn't bother me that I wasn't selected for it. The lead had to do a lot of singing, and that wasn't so much my focused this time. I was happy that I had more lines than I did when I did *Dreamgirls*, and when it came time to do my biography for the program the people at Piedmont Players were gracious enough to allow me to do some free advertising with *Sign of the Times*. The actors were given their scripts and a CD of the soundtrack for the play. I try to make a habit of once I get the script to learn my lines as soon as possible, and if the director wants me to take the character in a different direction than do it the way that they want me to do it. When listening to the cd I loved the songs when I first heard them, but when it came to following it along with the script, I thought it was more like a modern day Gershwin version in the same realm of *Porgy and Bess*. I love that show as well, but I didn't want to do that for myself at this time. I made that commitment to the company and I wasn't going to turn my back on it.

Now that I was a member of the cast in *The Color Purple* I held my rehearsals for *Sign of the Times* only two days a week. I held them between the American Legion post on Thursday evenings and at the Rowan Public Library making use of the Stanback Auditorium and the Hurley Room there. Still not fully cast with my own production I wasn't too worried because I was hoping that I would've been able to acquire one of the cast members from *The Color Purple* who would've wanted to do some new ground breaking material. I was showing anyone who was a part of *The Color Purple* the script, but there weren't any takers. I knew that I was going to have to find someone, and I was leaving it in the hands of God. I did just about everything that I could do to get people there by advertising in the *Salisbury Post* in the weekend section for the arts and entertainment around town called time out."

By the time that we hit September, some things looked as if they were about to change for the better for me personally. During the day time I made a point of meeting Dee at the Goodwill Career center. I was beginning to be seen there more than I was seen around town or the library. One day Rosa, the woman who got the part-time position that I'd applied for, was now the site manager for that satellite office in less than six months. She asked me if I would be interested in doing an internship there. They made it reasonable for me to assist them at my convenience. This was also an outlet for me to use the computers to fine tune the marketing of *Sign of the Times*, and continue to hit the internet for job searches. I accepted their offer at Goodwill and took advantage of the resources that were afforded to me. This was an excellent opportunity for me to attempt to land a position with them, and to show them that I am fully competent of performing the job duties that were assigned for me to do.

I informed Keona, my case worker, that I had been hired to do an internship at the Career Center with Goodwill and that I wouldn't be able to make it back in time to have lunch at the soup kitchen. Keona told me that she was able to have the overnight staff provide a bag lunch for me to take with me so I didn't have to worry about trying to get back there before the soup kitchen closed. Keona also was instrumental in allowing me to receive a late plate from my rehearsal schedule in the evenings. She was also part of the stage crew and had her son who was a cast member for *the Color Purple*. Every night that he had to be at rehearsal she was there with him. I was busy to the point that I actually felt as if I was working for myself after many months of being unemployed.

For once this was a good feeling for myself, even if I had not made a dime. I was getting the feeling of doing something productive, and the people around me respected the work that I was doing. The employees who worked at the library would begin to address me with a title of Mr. Bennett whenever I came in there rehearsal. They were curious as to when my production would happen. I would post information about the upcoming show on Facebook, and many of my family and friends would also inquire about the production. Some went as far by addressing me by my initials as if I were an executive producing a very large scale production. I got a kick out of that when that started happening. Whenever I would enter into the shelter in the evening the residents would tell me that the wanted to see the finished product, and when I was going around the town trying to find sponsors the merchants and some of their customers would always have a word or encouragement. Finally I felt that doing the *Sign of the Times* was given me the recognition as a producer. My own director at the Piedmont Players Theatre was one of the most supportive individuals. I've explained to him when I went for the audition that I was in the middle of producing my own show. He didn't have a problem with it as long as it didn't interfere with the rehearsals for *The Color Purple* production that they were doing. More so than the recognition of being known as a producer, I was earning the respect of the people in this community. That was the most humbling part of doing the show. I didn't know how many people knew I was a homeless person, but doing all the things the way a person who is trying to run their own business made me feel blessed whether they knew my personal dilemma or not.

Now I'm juggling three different things at the same time. I was working an internship in the mornings at the Goodwill Career connections. I was working from eight in the morning, until noon. I was staying there for another two hours meeting with Dee to work on the marketing, sponsorship, and other things that involved the *Sign of the Times*. By two o'clock or shortly after, I would make my trek back to the Rowan Public Library. I would meet with the administrators there to make arrangements to reserve the Stanback Auditorium or the Hurley Conference Meeting room. The library was my office away from an office, and I did everything there that I needed to do. I met with sponsors, held meetings with the creative staff of Updaway Productions, auditioned performers, researched proposals, and a host of other things. The library took on a life of itself for me using all the resources that it had to offer. I would stay there from two thirty in the afternoon until six thirty in the evening. When I left there, I would go to rehearsal either at the Meroney Theatre for *The Color Purple*, or leave a little earlier to head over to the JC Price American Legion Post to rehearse with my group of performers on the *Sign of the Times*. One of the cast members April Bolder dubbed the company as "The Down Home Players." To me it only made sense to use that moniker, because the word Updaway came from my culture of living in East Orange, New Jersey. The North side of town was known as "Down the hill, or Down the way." The other side of town was simply known as Up the way. I remembered when Spike Lee produced the movie *Skool Dayz* and directed the music video for the group EU who had a hit song called "Da Butt." I felt that if I was going to be a director like Spike Lee or Tyler Perry then I better take notes and follow their examples. So instead of spelling out up the way the traditional way that I better do something that was eye catching so I added EU's and Spike Lee's touch and spelled it u-p-d-a-w-a-y, this way it will still sound phonetically correct.

I finally pieced together all the performers for *Sign of the Times*, as was getting closer to the opening of this show. While I was able to work at Goodwill, I was able to cast one of the people who was to portray the young man who this production had the plot about, and I was able to recruit three others who stayed at the shelter. Antonio Ingram was a student at Rowan Cabarrus Community College majoring in the performing arts and having him doing the role came at a perfect time. The three other people who I had performing that stayed at the shelter were Sharon, a woman who moved to Salisbury from the West Coast. She had some acting experience, and had even done a pilot for a television series that never aired. Marion was a young woman who lived at the shelter and had attended church from one of the volunteer churches that would also pick up people from there for Sunday school and service on Sunday morning. I heard her sing around the shelter, and in this production, there is a church choir singing in the opening of the play. I needed her, and I felt that she was strong enough to carry that part. Joseph was a disabled veteran who the Veterans Administration placed at the shelter until he was able to get into one of their programs that they have for disabled vets. Other members of my cast for Updaway Productions included Walter Brotherton, a local comedian who worked at A Little Sumthin' Sumthin' when they had open mic night. April Bolder and Tyeisha Campbell who was a spoken word performers. I cast Tyeisha as the lead for this, and April as her best friends. For the antagonist in the story, I cast Antonio Howell. A talented young performer, he fit the mold of what I needed perfectly. Antonio Howell could do anything as far as performing. He could play almost any musical instrument and he's a hell of an actor. Roosevelt Jenkins I met when his church came to the shelter to serve the residents dinner. I've met him several times and found out that he had done some commercial modeling when he lived in Detroit. I cast him as the reverend. For the lead male, I cast Chris Bolder. I met him while I was working at Goodwill when I was asked to go out on a recruiting trip with Eric the career connection specialist. Chris came along to help him and I told him about the play that I wrote. He showed interest and was willing to give it a try. Mesha was a member of the American Legion who I've known since my days of going to the Goodwill. We both were final candidates for the job at Goodwill, before I told her about the play. She was my inside contact to Mae Carroll in helping me secure the post as the venue. The young lady who I cast as the strong supporting actress was Yakiema. I met her when her church came to serve dinner at the shelter also. I heard her sing in church and was impressed, but she gave me my song for the show when I saw her sing at the local "Juneteenth" festival held on the west side of town in the city of Salisbury. I made a point of going to the church to ask her if she would be interested in doing the show. She agreed, and that was one of the easiest people to cast for the play.

Doing this was the blessing of not having to spend much time at the shelter. The only time that I was there was when I needed to come in for the evening to catch a late plate to eat, shower, and sleep. That was the routine for me during this time. I would do the things I mentioned, and by nine in the evening, I was headed into the shelter. I found a way to get away from the drama that the administration and the shelter residents would go through. I was considered by many who worked and stayed there to be the invisible man. I didn't do any duties of helping out in the laundry room after the shelter guest turned in their clothes to be cleaned because I was going nonstop for an average of about sixteen hours a day working between the internship, my production, and *The Color Purple* for the Piedmont Players. I don't know how I was going, but that I had to keep on going. I would fall asleep on the average around anytime between midnight and one o'clock in the morning only to get back up at five twenty and be back at the Goodwill career center at eight to do this routine for five days a week.

By now it's mid-October, and just about a week away from the opening for *The Color Purple*. Outside of the fact that I still didn't have a regular full-time position that was helping me to meet my bills, life wasn't too bad, considering the situation that I've put myself into. The people at Goodwill were pleased with the output of production work that I was doing for them, and I knew all the songs and lines that I needed to do for *the Color Purple* production. There were still some difficulty getting all of my cast members together for the *Sign of the times*, but Tyeisha and Antonio Ingram were the consummate professionals who knew their lines and just about everyone else's too! This was one of those rare incidents that I didn't worry about not working, because I was doing something constructive, and it appeared that it was about to take me to another level that I wanted to be. I had one rehearsal with all of my cast members for the *Sign of the Times* the following week. At that time I told them of the urgency that we all needed to get the scripts out of our hands. I needed them to do that, because the longer an actor holds on to their script the more of a crutch they depend on it. I wasn't going to have that performing taboo in my performing arts company. I was going to live as close to the company's credo as possible.

After that rehearsal I felt good about what it was happening with Updaway Productions. All of the pieces were fitting like a well-tailored suit, and the only thing I need was a model to put this suit on. When I arrived at the shelter, I told Keona that I wanted to have a meeting with the Executive Director of Rowan Helping Ministries Ms. Foster. I told her it was to invite her to the premiere of *Sign of the Times*. I also saw that this was an opportunity to attempt to have them come on as a sponsor of the play. Keona did as I asked her to do, and Ms. Foster agreed to meet with me. It was a couple of days after my request was received that I met with Ms. Foster. I informed her what I was doing by performing in the local production done by the Piedmont Players and that of my own for Updaway Production. I asked her if Rowan Helping Ministries would be interested in possibly sponsoring the show for *Sign of the Times*, but she told me that they wouldn't be able to do that because of their budget. I was fine with that and I invited her to the production. My intentions was to let her see for herself that there was something positive coming out of the shelter. Her own staff of case workers didn't actively recruit jobs for the residents who lived there, but I was a resident who was trying to creating a job for himself and others who performed at the show that resided there. I had the participation of five people who resided there that were participating in something that the administration and the staff didn't attempt to do for them. Although I wasn't sure if we were able to make money from the production, I was able to give the residents peace of mind. This play gave those who participants an outlet or a diversion from the stress and disappointments of being turned away from the jobs due to the fact that they were homeless.

Kyna was impressed and was willing to help me get some publicity for the show. I told her that I would be willing her to talk to the press about *Sign of the Times* if she could arrange for a writer of the *Salisbury Post* to do an interview. I inquired if I needed to sign a release clearing the shelter of all responsibilities to give them my consent. She told me that I didn't have to worry about that, because she's head in charge. We've talked about having a reporter meet with me so that I could be interviewed about the production of *Sign of the Times*. She agreed that we would make this happen. Within next few days, the cast of *The Color Purple* were fine tuning themselves before we had our dress rehearsal that was going to play for a private audience that was by invitation only. It catered to disabled senior citizens, disabled veterans, homeless people, and students from the school district. People who couldn't afford to pay to see the performance of a Broadway inspired production with all the frills included. Nothing was cut, and as a performer, we attempted to display a perfect performance.

The day before we gave the dress rehearsal performance the *Salisbury Post* gave a preview of the show. The writer was Deidre Parker-Smith who attempted to give the show a good review had several flaws in her column. One of them was stating that the woman who portrayed the role of Celie. She said that she was a great performer, and unlike the character she played who is described as being homely looking that in real life the performer was actually very pretty. She was right about that actress being a great performer. That actress won a Metrolina Theatre Award the equivalent to the Charlotte, North Carolina, metropolitan area's equivalent to the Tony Awards for the local community theatre. I saw that as a back handed compliment, and was thinking to myself is that it's theatre. Anybody who performs whether they're supposed to look glamorous or hideous is a performer that is doing a character. To me this writer was truly clueless, and didn't have any idea of what are the basic principles of theatre. The most disturbing thing about the article that Ms. Parker-Smith wrote was the fact that she disclaimed to the public that I was a resident of the shelter in the production.

I found out about the article when it appeared the next morning when I arrived to my internship at the Goodwill. Rosa had told me that I made the newspaper and it was about the preview that Ms. Parker-Smith had written. I read the article, and for the rest of the day, my demeanor changed. I went to work ready to do the work of what was expected of me with a good outlook, and I had to do my best acting role. I had to put on a face that showed that I didn't have a care in the world. Being in the newspaper wasn't a big deal to me, because as a performer, you want to see yourself there. You want to be seen in there the same reasons that business moguls and politicians want to be there, because of the recognition factor of doing the virtuous work of excelling at your craft. Deep inside I was furious, and I wanted to let everyone know it but I remained calm. I knew where the source of that information came from, and I was going to let Ms. Parker-Smith know that I didn't appreciate the slam job. I knew once that I let her know how I felt that she would relay this information back to Kyna. It wasn't hard to add one and one to find out the reason behind it. It didn't take long to figure it out, and it made perfectly good sense to me once I calmed myself down. Kyna told the writer about me being in the production of *The Color Purple* to use to her advantage. It made good sense to do this to me, because the more established Piedmont Players Theatre Company. If the people who donate to the shelter see this article then go to the show it allows the donors to look at positive impact of what's happening at the shelter, and gives the administration the leverage to ask the donors for more money seeing me as a resident there. It sends out a message that their case managers are doing their job helping the residents by directing them to do an avocation or vocation of the skills they are interested in. The plain simple fact is that the case managers didn't do anything but sit on their butts as they always do. They never direct or discover employment opportunities for the residents of the shelter. They don't look at ways or methods for interventions of the substance abuser, and their highest priority residents are the ones who are either receiving, or pending benefits from the Veteran Administration.

During that day at Goodwill, the usual people who use the center would read the *Salisbury Post* there or use the computers, or the copy that was delivered there daily. The people who used the center read it in between looking for jobs. Others who read the paper prior to coming into the career center came right up to me and congratulated me. There were a couple of regular people who came there that pulled me to the side and inquired about me being homeless. I told them, yes, the article is true, but I didn't shy away from the fact that my anonymity was now history. They expressed their compassion for my situation, and even offered me cash that I declined to take. I think that they felt embarrassed for me as much as I had for myself. When my working hours were over, I didn't do my usual routine with Dee. I called her and told her about the article and that I was fine after the insult of putting me out on front street for all to see. I told her that I just wanted to be alone, and that I'd see her tomorrow at the same time. I didn't go to the computer lab in the library like I normally do, but I picked up three big books and went upstairs to the research lab where most of the people use that facility to look up records and other things that deal with historical facts. I stayed there from one that afternoon until about quarter until five.

I left there to and brought my bag lunch with me to the Meroney Theatre and entered at the stage entrance. When I arrived there, I was there and the director was wardrobe director was there briefly to drop of the finishing touches on the outfit for the performance. Outside of that I was there by myself. I wanted to be, because I really wanted to find some peace in knowing that when I take the stage this evening that I was going to be on display for the whole world that read the article would know that I'm a homeless man. They didn't know that I'm also a product of Samuel and Dorothy Bennett who were educators and that I followed in their footsteps. That having a misdemeanor in Rowan County for an offense that happened almost twenty years ago means that I'm blacklisted here. That when I graduated from college I was in the top third in my class with a 3.27 grade point average none of that matter, but that the public will know that I'm just another person who came to Rowan County and added to their homeless population.

After having being there for almost three hours the cast, crew, and musicians were making their way into the theatre. All of the cast members came into the green room excited about the article that was written by Ms. Parker-Smith except me. When I saw my case manager Keona, I asked her what she thought of the article. She said it was good article what Ms. Parker-Smith wrote, and that this is going to help me with my own production. At that time when Keona came out of her mouth saying that I found out that she was clueless about working with the homeless population, and became a puppet whose strings could be easily pulled. At that point any and all respect that I had for her went out as quick as the words came out of her mouth. Here's a woman raised up in the nation's capital, known by many in the African American community as "Chocolate City," has this kind of thinking that it's all right to expose and degrade a person's anonymity. As bad as the homeless population is in the nation's capital, you thought that she would've known better than to come out and say what she did. That sealed it for me as far as her being a sellout for a position.

By that time, the director came in. He asked me if I was all right. I told him I was good, trying not to let on that I wasn't feeling too good about the article printed in the newspaper. He told me that he wasn't the one to disclose the information about me being homeless. I told him that I knew where the source of information came from, and I never thought that he would've done something like that. Although I didn't agree with some of the ways that he allowed the actors to get away with some liberties of performing standards he was a decent and compassionate individual. It was because of those things that he extended to them to me that I had gained a newfound respect for him. I thanked him for not telling the reporter about me, and embraced him with a hug because I needed it.

After everyone arrived, it was time to get into costume and makeup, and shortly afterward, it was time for us to do our vocal warm ups with the musical director. When that is over I went back into the dressing room to concentrate on my character. I knew that I had to block out everything that had transpired over the past twenty four hours. The closer it got to the time for the stage manager to make the cast meeting that took place minutes before the curtain call in the green room, I didn't know how I felt about going on stage. I put myself where I was totally engulfed in the character. When the stage manager did call all the actors to enter into the green room, I was still focused on delivering the best performance that I could. We all took our last minute instructions from the choreography, musical, and stage directors before we disassembled and were told to take our places.

For the first time since I've been performing, dating back when I was my elementary school's first black Santa Claus, I wasn't nervous but bordering on being petrified. I knew that there were a lot of people in that audience who saw the article. There were going to be people who would have their own notions and perceptions about me trying to do a performance. Normally when I perform, I try not to look out into the audience especially trying to recognize the faces. I have certain superstitions when I perform, and that helps keep me grounded and focused. It's the same as when someone say's good luck to an actor. I loathe it, because it's bad luck to say good luck to a performer before they go on stage. When someone say that to me, I tell them to say the showbiz term "break a leg" or "good blessings." As a Christian, I don't believe in luck, but I do believe in blessings, and as far as showbiz is concern, it's bad luck when you wish them good luck. Doing a performance should be considered a routine as breaking a leg, henceforth comes that term.

Now the stage director had called everyone for places. Just minutes before she did that I was already there getting my thoughts and my concentration together. If anything negative was going to come out of this than it was going to happen, and there was nothing that I could do about it. I was going to have to accept things as the way they are. In the opening of the show, I come out with the rest of the chorus portraying congregation members of the church. I made it a point of being the last member to hit the stage. Being that I am the tallest cast member when the dance numbers are performed, I am normally placed in the rear of those dance sequences. So by the time the opening number was over, I had the focus that I needed to do the show right. I guess my friend Frankie was truly with me the whole show. When I had to do my part of Old Mister, I was sharp and in character and didn't think about flubbing my lines. The timing was perfect and the rest of the show was good.

By the end of opening night's show, the cast sung the last number and the curtains closed. Once that happened we all got in too our positions to come out for our curtain calls to receive the applause from the audience. When it was my time to come out, my fear rose up again. There was nothing that I could do but do to it. When it was my time for me to come to the forefront of the stage, I didn't know what to expect, but when I did the people who I stayed with at the shelter came up to the lip of the stage and gave me the satisfaction that they enjoy the show. More so than than seeing the residents enjoy it was their applause and appreciation that validated the fact that I performed well. Next to the other people who portrayed the characters of Celie, Shug Avery, and Mister. I had one of the bigger applauses during the curtain call. When the curtain went down for the evening I went out to the audiences to seek them out specifically. I wanted to let them know that their acknowledgment of me was worth more to me than making a six-figure salary for doing something that I enjoy doing. When I greeted them and other audience members to thank them nothing was mentioned about the article written in the newspaper. I went to the dressing room to change, and go to the cast party, but stayed there briefly. I did that to show my face, but I wanted to get back to the shelter to thank them. I arrived and there were still people who were standing outside smoking cigarettes and talking before they entered in the shelter for the night. I notice that they didn't see me, and I'd asked them, "Hey, can someone let me bum a cigarette?" They clapped when I said that, and I was handed one. I told them don't clap, because didn't deliver them a line from the show. We all laughed and shot the breeze for about twenty minutes before I went to go to bed for the evening.

The Color Purple ran for another nine shows, and while this was going on I had to put my rehearsal plans for the *Sign of the Times* on hold. I told my actors what my circumstances were, and that I was involved with the show at the Meroney. I made a point of telling them that prior to taking them on as a cast member. I requested that they had to take on the responsibility of learning their lines, and when the run of *The Color Purple* was over that we would do rehearsals without the scripts. It would be only two weeks before the opening of *Sign of the Times* after *The Color Purple* production was done. I learn how to be a producer and director in a baptism by fire. My lead male Chris told me a couple weeks before *The Color Purple* opened that he couldn't keep the commitment to do the show. I wasn't able to find anyone who I felt comfortable to do the part so I took over the lead. I didn't want to do it, but my choices were limited. People around town who saw me perform in *Dreamgirls* and the Color Purple, and when I told them that I was doing my own original play that I've written, directed and produce they wanted to put a tag on me that I was the next Tyler Perry. I told the no, I'm the first Leroy F. Bennett. I didn't imagine that there would be more difficulties that lay ahead, but I was about to find out what a domino effect was when it concerned doing a show. My next obstacle was trying to replace my antagonist of the production. The most gifted and talented individual Antonio Howell stopped coming to rehearsals about the same time that Chris did, but he never let me know what was happening with him. I would see him and ask him but he said that he would be at the next rehearsal using that only as excuse. It got to the point that everyone made a couple of rehearsal, but him. A week before the Color Purple opened, I asked Brian Lewis if he would be interested in doing the part. Graciously, he agreed to do it. Brian was a performing arts major from Livingstone College and jumped at the idea of doing the production. It was a win-win situation for the both of us. It helped him get the work experience he needed for his practicum, and I was able to have him fill that role. Already I had to re-cast two roles, and this is only the beginning of my indoctrination into producing a theatrical production. Just when I thought that my troubles were over they were just beginning. The thing that I needed most was the cast members to make an attempt to commit their lines to memory. Tyeisha, Yakiema, Marion, Antonio Ingram, and Walter stuck it out and were true to the discipline of committing their lines to memory. Bryant was great because he came in and took ownership of the role I needed for him to do. My other cast of characters made it more difficult to make the transition from rehearsing to the performance. The other members of the Down Home Players had jobs, working off hours or attended school.

After weeks of rehearsals, the commander of the post wanted to know how the play was coming. She was curious because many of the nights she would be there to open the facility for the group to rehearse. There were nights that she was there and I would be blessed if I had three out of the twelve cast members there to run their lines and go over the blocking for the scenes they were in. I believe without the presence of the actors not being visibly present that there was concern for Updaway Productions. With just a week before the shows, Mae and I talked at length about maybe cancelling the show. Without everyone there to give her a preview of what the finished product was going to look like that I couldn't blame her. Here she is having to tell her board members that she was giving me an opportunity to put on a show at her establishment with the hopes of making money off of it, and the whole cast has been together only a few times, and that was in the infancy stage of the production. I assured her that she would have a show and that it would be good. I didn't tell her that the Legion Post would make money, but I did guarantee her that it would be entertaining.

On the next to last week of rehearsal things were starting to come together as I prayed that they would. Dee and I weren't successful in influencing any of the businesses or organizations into becoming sponsor, but we continued on getting other things together. We went to the clothing bank courtesy of Gethsemane Missionary Baptist church. They have an outreach house where they provide food and clothes for those who are in need of their assistance. On this day, I wasn't looking to try to get stuff to make a meal, but clothes to wardrobe my cast members. I was able to get most of the outfits for the adults there. I had already talked to Clifford Roseborough, my music arranger, and asked him to create a score of music to play for the show. I had only one request that he played "Safe in His Arms" at the opening of the show. Originally, I had another person as the music director who was going to get several members of a youth choir, which whom Yakiema was familiar singing with, but he never honored his end of the bargain.

That part of the production was a go, and slowly the pieces of the puzzles were starting to fit into place. I called on the assistance of Eric from the career center to help with the creation of the playbill to give the audience members. Eric told me that he received his associate's degree as a graphic artist, and asked what could he do to help move this production along smoothly? I was going to accept any and all the help if someone was willing to offer it for free, and I was going to give him a chance to display his talents. I asked him what he could do. He told me that he could post something like some street signs or something to that nature. I told him what the play synopsis was about and that I wanted to focus on the time frame. I wanted to focus on events that took place in 2003, because I needed to make reference to 9/11 since it's one of the critical parts of the play's production. I told him to give me figures, images of people and events that happened that timeline from 2001 to 2003. I told him I'll give him forty-eight hours to submit something to me. He` submitted something to me, and I was very disappointed with what he gave.

Coincidently, I got a message from my cousin in my Facebook inbox, and she told me to come over so that she could assist in the process of getting this marketing snowball going. Before I had rehearsal that evening, I stopped over her house to go over the bios for the playbill that she helped me edit, and then I showed her the submission of the playbill cover Eric gave to me. I won't disclaim what she actually said, but when I saw the playbill cover, my eleven-year-old granddaughter who didn't have a computer at that time could've done better. I told her what I was trying to do, and to bring it along with the timeframe. She worked on it for an evening and gave me the cover I needed for the playbill. That was another hurdle that Updaway was able to leap over. My crew consisted of two other brothers. From the shelter Zenobia and Stanley stayed there at the shelter also. I was able to make arrangements with the case manager to allow them to get in late in the evening and have the staff hold a plate for them. They each were known around town by a letter. Zenobia was better known as "Z," and Stanley was known as "Q." I'd given the instruction on how I wanted the stage set up for the scenes, lighting, and props included.

For once with a week left before the opening, it seemed as if it was all together for Updaway Productions. Since Mesha was a member of the post, she was in charge of handling the tickets and receipts, and she also started to get a better grip on mastering her speaking lines. My cousin sent out Internet flyers and did an excellent job of hyping up the event, and she, Dee, and I all worked together on the final edition of the playbill. Cliff and I had all the musical arrangements together, and together we had underscored the play where it needed to be done on certain scene sequences. My crew was finally in place and knew what to do when I needed to have the scene changes done. The wardrobe was in place and Dee doubled as the stage manager. I even got in touch with my friends who lived in Concord to see about getting the show videotaped. I'd given Mae the main things on the week of the show. I submitted a sample of the playbill, and tickets and I finally had a full cast and crew there for rehearsal to help ease any anxieties that she might had experienced. The final part of this of this puzzles that I had to succeed in was to get the cast running like a well-oiled machine.

Just a day before the actual show, we're holding dress rehearsal. This is a closed session where only the cast and crew are there. For once everyone was there and on time. Roosevelt was supposed to do the role of the reverend, but since he didn't give me any notification I rewrote his part into the dialogue for me to do. The beginning was going well, and Tyeisha, Antonio, Yakiema, and Mary were sharp. Their timing was good and on point and as close to flawless as a director would want. Walter was good to doing his lines well, but April didn't have any idea of when her cues were. It was obvious that she didn't study her script, but she was getting the lines fed to her on the last day of rehearsal before the show. We struggled by through the opening scene of the first act, but managed to get through it. The second scene was the strongest of all, because the performers who were in that scene made it obvious that they knew what they were doing. I didn't stop and continued to finish out the first act. The timing of it was very off, and it took longer to finish out that scene than the other two previous one combined. This time it was Yosef, Mesha, and April who didn't commit their lines to memory. These were important speaking roles that they had to perform. We finished out the first act, and took a five minute break before we resumed with the play.

The opening scene of act two was worse. We go to that point that I was wondering if I should cut my loses and tell the American Legion Post Commander that she was right to tell me to cancel the play. When actors didn't study their lines and attempt to do the dialogue it has to be precise, or it'll throw off the timing of the ones who did commit their lines and send them way out into left field. This scene was next to the closing one of the play, and before the cast could complete it, I gave the stage direction cut to cease all action. I asked everyone to come to the middle of the room and asked them did they think that we should continue. I asked them how they felt about the progress we were making with less than twenty four hours before the curtains go up. I wasn't pleased at all so I took this time to acknowledge the actors who could make to rehearsals and worked hard on doing all the right things. I also let them know my displeasure with the ones who didn't make the rehearsal because of their other commitments for work and school. I told them, "I cannot put a gun to your heads and threaten you, but you have to make sacrifices. I have made concessions for you to continue with your commitments, but you weren't willing to do the same for me. So at this very moment before I ask someone to spend their ten dollars of their hard earned income to come here to see a show of this poor quality, I would rather cancel the show than to have them to waste their money."

I did that to light a fire under them, because I knew they wanted to do the show then they knew that we had less than twenty-four hours to get it together. I don't know what I did, but Tyeisha, the lead actress and the hardest worker out of all the cast members, was very adamant about me cancelling the show. She was the one who got the rest of the cast fired up. They told me that there's still a way to pull it off, and that we were going to do the show. At this juncture in the production, I allowed them to find a way of us making this look right. The biggest problem was going to be April who didn't know any of her lines. So I asked Dee if she could use her cellphone Bluetooth so that she can feed her the lines off stage while April was on. I agreed maybe against my better judgment to go ahead and do the show, but I remembered the showbiz slogan that "the show must go on." We had one more run through for the evening, and I instructed the performers if they didn't know their lines that they needed to read them. I told them that I wasn't going to do a "readers theatre," and I didn't expect the public to pay ten dollars at the door.

If that was the case then I would've had a group of elementary or middle school students do the performance.

The last run through was successful. I told the cast that show time was seven thirty and that they needed to be here no later than six. The cast got together for our usual prayer and we dismissed for the evening. If ever there was a time that I needed a blessing from God it was now. This was the accumulation of all the hard work that I put in writing this play. This was my maiden venture going into this aspect of performing. It was my debut as a producer of a staged productions and also for my directing. I knew that along the way I was susceptible to making errors, and that I would learn from them. More importantly I was willing to go out of the way to make a name for myself, and the company Updaway Productions. When I got to the shelter that evening, I was thinking about the last-minute details that I needed to do. I took my shower, and I didn't eat the plate that was left for me, not because I didn't want to eat because I couldn't. After showering I dressed up the cot to sleep, and dropped to my knees to pray again. Most of the evening I didn't sleep, but that was fine. I told Rosa and Eric at the Career Center a week earlier that I had to get things together for the performance this evening. They understood, and allowed me to do what I needed to get done. First I got with my cousin to drop off the master of the playbills the printers, so that I can pick them up and ready for the event. Next was to confirm that my friends in Concord would be there to videotape the production by Carolina Execs. Then I needed to confirm what time Cliff would be there so that the band could do a run through and the last thing was to see that one of the cast member, Marion, would get with me before one o'clock so that I could have a stylist do something with her hair, and refit her for wardrobe. I was able to successfully do all but the final thing.

From the previous evening, Marion didn't come into the shelter. When the group disbanded for the evening, she went with her boyfriend. She was outside crying from what she stated that I was going to cancel the show. I attempted to reassure her that if I was that I wouldn't have had a final review of the play with all the characters. I had made it point to give her a call before I completed all of the main priorities that had to be done. I called her early in the morning since she didn't stay in the shelter the night before. I started my calls to her as early as nine thirty, and continued all the way until I finally able to hear contact her. Marion finally picked up the phone at four thirty that afternoon and told me that she couldn't do the show. I didn't beg her to come and do it, or even question her as to why. I knew that I had another hurdle that I had to jump. I immediately went to the computer in the library to contact those who were connect to Facebook so that I could let know the ones who could need to meet me at the American Legion Post at five thirty.

Dee and I got up there earlier than anyone else. Slowly the group started to filter in and I tried to wait for everyone before I told them the news about Marion, but I thought it was better for them to know what the situation was. By six o'clock, all the cast members had assembled downstairs in the dressing room. I had them all meet to let them know what the option was. I explained that after the previous night of rehearsal when we all agreed I didn't to pull our heads together to continue to do the performance. So I told them we have an hour and fifteen minutes in order to suture the scenes that had Marion in it. Much to their own credit they took on the undertaken like professionals omitting, rearranging and ad libbing if necessary. I left it into the hands of the performers, and just a little under the hour they had the script, and their parts right. Carolina Execs made it there to videotape the production, but the lighting at was being used at the American Legion Post wasn't adequate. So we had to scrap the video. Cliff and the band members were there and ready to perform. I let him know that the commander of the post that I would need her to cue the band when to start the program.

We had our own cast and crew meeting together in the dressing room fifteen minutes before it was time to call places. Dee made sure that April had the Bluetooth, and it was ready for use. I asked Mae Carroll if she could introduce the play, and if she would instruct the audience not to take pictures and turn off their cellphones. In our meeting, I told them that we've done all this just for tonight. I gave my best impression of my favorite director. I told them that we didn't have a perfect practice, but that didn't make a difference now. This performance that we're about to do was going to have to be perfect, and there's no turning back from this. I told them, "Let's give the audience a great show, but most of all, let's have fun doing this. When you're off stage pay attention to what's going on during the performance, 'cause if you don't, you'll lose focus that I will guarantee that you will miss your cue. So let's go out and break a leg."

It was now time for the actors to take their places, the band was playing and then Mae came out to introduce the play. The audience who attended wasn't large, but an intimate one who came to see the show. When it was time for curtains, the performers were ready. All of the actors gave a performance that was worth every penny that the audience paid to see. I was surprisingly pleased, and I thank God that things went as well as it did. When I thought of it, I was doing a lot of the things to help motivate the actors the same way that Charles Brooks had done when he had directed many of the productions that I worked with him. Sometimes you have to push some buttons in order to get the best out of your actors. Whatever I had to do in order to have them do the show and make it flow it worked. I know it wasn't me, but God who wanted this to work in me. When the show ended, Mae introduced the actors, and they all came out for a final bow during the final curtain call. I was pleased with the results, and everyone had a chance to meet and thank the audience for coming out. All the cast members were happy, and we did a second show the following night. I was happy because I was able to find some support from my fellow colleagues at the Piedmont Players Theatre who I acted with from the previous two productions there, and my sister and her friend drove up from Charlotte to experience the first play from Updaway Productions. That was the crowning achievement for me, because it reminded me of my parents coming to any function that was entertaining whenever any of their children would perform in an event or play sports. They were always there and my sister did that not only out of love, but she was taking her place as the family matriarch. Nothing else mattered to me but the affirmation of love that was displayed by her. I knew that my parents approved of not only my accomplishment, but her unyielding reassurance that everything that was is going to get better for me.

It was a week later when I finally felt like I could exhale when I had finished doing a play for my own production company when I was approached by a member of the Lee Street Theatre company. Robert who worked in the Library was also the president of that performing company. He or another member of that company view me in *The Color Purple* and inquired to me if I would be interested in doing a production of the Charles Dickens classic a *Christmas Carol.* I told him that I would, and inquire to him what was it that I needed to do? He gave me the name and phone number of the director of that play Justin Dionne. I got the number and gave him a call, but only got his voicemail. I left a message that I was interested in doing the show for him. He called me back and asked if I could meet him at the bookstore on South Main Street, and I told him that I would. I met with him and he told me that the next day they were going to have a rehearsal. I wasn't too sure how I was going to fit into this production, but I was willing to do it. He told me that this was a paying gig, and that it wasn't a lot of money, but in my mind any money that you can make as a homeless person looks as if you won the lottery. I went to the rehearsal and met him and the other players in the production.

This was my validation for doing the productions in town. With the recent successes from the productions of *The Color Purple* and the *Sign of the Times.* I was recognized by people in the performing arts community of Salisbury, and I wasn't going to turn down this opportunity to take advantage of doing this performance. This was a way of them telling me that you're accepted here, and you can do some good. I was ready to do whatever it takes to keep my name in the circle of performing artist in a positive way, and this play allowed me another opportunity of promoting Updaway Productions. Anything that I could do to build a group of actors who wanted to do material that was cutting edge, controversial, thought provoking or consciously progressive was going to be in my library of plays. I wanted people who wanted to work in that kind of forum.

The Lee Street Theatre players were rehearsing on the *Christmas Carol,* but it was going to be one with an unusual twist. This production was going to take place on the trolley cars that transport the people around the historic sites of Salisbury, and it was going to be done in the evening. The part that I was assigned was that of the ghost of Christmas yet to come. I was outfitted in an outfit that assimilated the grim reaper. It was complete with skeleton gloves for the hands, and I didn't have to say a single line, but just point. The rehearsal were held a week before Thanksgiving and I only had to come to the dress rehearsal.

The show started on Black Friday, and it was the last Salisbury Night Out of the year. Salisbury Night Out is done from March to November, and it's on a Friday evening to stimulate the local economy so that the merchants can extend their store hours for profit. Normally, the merchants would have musician playing outside their establishments to entice the potential patrons, and the city provides horse and carriage rides going throughout the historic district of the town. The trolley would go into the historic houses and businesses as it stopped for Scrooge to get the visits of the three ghost. At those stops Scrooge would get off the trolley to meet the characters for the appropriate times that are outlined in the story. All of the characters that played the roles of the ghost would get on the back of the trolley when the audience was unsuspecting before they made their entrances onto the trolley.

It was a clever way of promoting the historical places of the city, chamber of commerce, division of tourism, and the Lee Street Theatre. We averaged three shows a night on Friday and Saturdays. They began at six and would end at eight. This was done from Black Friday and ended the weekend before Christmas. This was a great gig, and I was getting paid to do it too. I love the fact that I was going to make some money to get my granddaughter a Christmas gift. I didn't want to have to rely on the generosity of my family members or friends to provide this for Shaylee. I felt it was my responsibility to do this, because she's just that, my responsibility. For once I didn't care about being at the shelter, because I was working. I may not have been making as much money as I needed to in order to move on, but still in all it was honest respectable work.

I continued to work for the first two weeks, and before I could continue to finish out the show for the last two weeks, I felt what I thought was a cramp in my foot around my toes. I was walking back from the library and the pain was getting worse. When I arrived in the shelter that evening, I asked the shelter aid on duty to please summons a taxi for me to go to the hospital so that I could have the doctors check out what was the cause of my discomfort. I found out after having my foot x-rayed that I had a stress fracture in my left foot. The doctor on duty told me that I needed to take it easy and had to be off of my foot from four to six weeks. This was a very big blow for me, because I wanted to get my granddaughter a digital camera and wanted to personally take it to her for Christmas. I wanted to see the joy on her face so that we could celebrate that moment together. The moment that I found out that I was immobilized I was crushed. I had to tell Justin about it, and I had to muster up everything in me not to cry over the phone. He understood, and he felt as bad for me as I felt for myself.

This incident couldn't happen at a more inopportune time, but what was I supposed to do? I knew that I wanted to get that camera for her even if I wasn't able to make it down to Columbia to see her. I called on my best friend Darren and explained to him the situation that I've been experiencing for over the past year. This was the first time that I told him about me being homeless. He wanted to know why I hadn't called him when it first happened about my situation becoming homeless. I told him to switch the roles, and if he was experiencing being homeless, would he want to tell anyone about it? He understood and asked what was it that he could do to help outside of the fact that I needed to get a camera to my granddaughter. I told him just pray that things get better, and that him doing this for me is going to help make this one of the best Christmas for Shaylee. Right now her happiness is the thing that is important to me. That disturbed him, but he did provide the Christmas gift that I wanted to see her have. Like many people he wanted to offer me money, but like many of the offers that I've received I turned it down. I don't want a hand out, but I want a hand.

In spite of the injury, I've been blessed to have the year has ended on a good note. I was able to establish a foothold in the arts community as a player who could bring something to the table. I made myself recognizable so that people in town will stop me to ask what's happening. Did I had another project that I was going to do? My job status and living arrangement is still the same, but I have to keep the faith that things are starting to look better for me. I don't doubt that my storm clouds are clearing up, and soon, I will enter into the season that the Lord see's for me to experience. My optimism is still good, and I'm glad to know that there are still people who care enough to go out of their way to help others. I'm hoping that 2013 will be better than what 2012 was. I'm going to do whatever I need to do to try to keep a positive attitude and pray that God is still working miracle on my behalf. I know that I was able to breakthrough that has his hand in it. Do I know when I will be out of here? No, God only knows when that's going to happen all I can do is wait on him.

CHAPTER 9

Smallsbury, Pillsbury, or Doonesbury?

The year 2013 came in without any fanfare and little celebration. I had another two weeks before I was able to resume my intern duties at the Goodwill Career center and also had an opportunity at researching new material to build on the reputation that I've started with Updaway Productions. The reality of continuing to live at the shelter started to hit me. I was unable to get around town because I was confined to using crutches. Since I wasn't working, I went to the county magistrate's office and was released on a personal reconnaissance bond. I served a year of probation, I had my vehicle confiscated, and my driving privileges stripped. I was operating a motor vehicle illegally without the car being registered, not having insurance on it as well. This was another reason why I knew that I remain unemployed.

The public transportation system in Rowan County consist of the North Carolina railroad system and Amtrak that have trains arriving and departing to the major cities in state of Greensboro, High Point, and Charlotte about eight trains traveling north and southbound daily. The city has its own bus line that has three buses that they keep simple by numbering them as 1, 2, 3 or the red, blue, and green lines. They ran from the Salisbury mall on the west side of town, back to where the county health department, and the department of social service to the on the eastside. Another bus ran by the VA hospital, Livingstone, and Catawba College's on the Westside. It would return to the depot and take people out to the small town of East Spencer on the eastside. The last transportation line would go from the city of Spencer also on the eastside and travel out to the unemployment office, the Goodwill Career Connection center, and the Rowan Cabarrus Community College on the westside. It wasn't like trying to get your way around the New York City subway system, but it was far from a complicated system and simple to follow when I first started using it. A shuttle bus system called the Rowan Express would take you from the smaller town of Rockwell and another shuttle that would go as far as go into Kannapolis, which was just north of Charlotte. Most of the buses and shuttle systems would shut down between five thirty and six thirty in the evening that the last ones would leave the depot. On weekends, the Rowan Express shuttles to the smaller city of Rockwell and the other larger city of Kannapolis wouldn't run at all. If you had to get out to either one of those cities, you had better have a ride or know someone who had one, and if not, you would have to walk a great distance to get there. The city bus that would normally go from Rowan Cabarrus College and Spencer wouldn't run at all, and the other two buses on the line would only run on Saturday from nine in the morning until four in the afternoon, and no bus service was available on Sunday at all.

Seeing how the operation with this transit system ran, I told a friend back home about it, and they told me that I must be in hell. Most places that I've visited that have a bus line have them available on the weekends, but here, the authorities who direct this system must not be making any money on it. They shut down the potentially busiest transit day for the vehicles to operate. Most of the other cities have a weekend schedule that ran on a modified hours of operation. This was to accommodate the people who lived in the areas that their buses and shuttles traveled through. When I found out that the system was ran as it did, I decided to give this town the nickname that many of the locals have. I decided to call it Smallsbury, and it was appropriately coined by the local residents.

It's really more of a village than that of city. It was founded in 1753 and hasn't grown very much since the three hundred and sixty years it was founded. A fine example of this is how the other true municipalities that have grown and have adapted to the economic adversities that they had to overcome. Cities that are as old as Salisbury and that aren't stuck solely on preserving the historical value of a society that has, for lack of a better term in an era, that's been gone with the wind. A good example of this is Winston-Salem, a town that is originally as old as Salisbury but has continued to build. The first part of that is the city of Salem, founded thirteen years later than Salisbury and has continued to grow. Since this is a tobacco road, Richard Joshua Reynolds, better known to the tobacco-loving public simply as R.J. Reynolds, built and opened his first tobacco-manufacturing factory in city of Winston in 1875. By 1913, the two cities had consolidated to form the city that we know it as today—Winston-Salem, North Carolina. Salisbury hasn't grown economically due in part of the great financial collapse of 2008. Once, this community was a thriving manufacturer of textiles, but when many of them found that it was cheaper to do business in another state or country, it devastated the economy.

Rowan County, along with Salisbury, has done little to attract any major commercial industrial companies because of their reluctance for change. Their main concerns goes back to preserving what has transpired in its past, holding on to the history of the city from the days of the civil war. Their present reluctance to change leaves very little incentive for the next generation to want to stay because of the current generation's opposition toward social progress. If you're ever in the city's downtown area, you can see the statue commissioned by the Daughters of the Confederacy of an embattled Confederate soldier being held up by an angel and several bronze-plated markers throughout the business district that commemorate and glorify some things that seem morally questionable. There are two such markers along with the statue that stand out to me more than any of the others.

The first commemorative marker glorifies a depression-era bank robber by the name of Otto Wood. Wood has been in and out of the penal system since he was a child. He's been credited with many crimes from theft, bootlegging, second-degree murder, and even had several successful jailbreaks. As a wanted man, he was spotted by a police officer in Salisbury and was killed on East Innes during a shootout. The other marker celebrates a political figurehead who served as the governor of North Carolina. John Willis Ellis was the governor at the time that North Carolina was the state voted to follow the other nine Confederate states to secede from the Union of the United States. As if that wasn't bad enough, as governor, he gave an executive order by President Abraham Lincoln to have his troops squash a skirmish among rebel soldiers. Ellis told the commander-in-chief, "I can be no party to this wicked violation of the laws of the country and to this war upon the liberties of a free people. You can get no troops from North Carolina." Both acts are viewed upon as treasonist, but in Salisbury, this is the place where the natives glorify the contrived acts of people who commit treason and murder. After living here over the past three years, it appears that the mentality remains stagnant by the natives and it has been in existence for over a hundred and fifty years.

If you move into Salisbury to start a business and attempt to present a way of having some fresh new ideas, concepts, or procedures, they are not encouraged. This is the way that things operates in just about every aspect of business and government here. The most disheartening part about that is the natives accept this as how it's supposed to be, and will always remain. For the reasons that I've just mentioned I have coined my own name for this town and have changed it for Smallsbury to Pillsbury. I call it Pillsbury because of the lack of dough that one will be able to make here. Salisbury's population is 33,596. In a study done by the University of North Carolina Charlotte Urban Institute had Salisbury listed as poverty stricken have populations between 25,000 and 45,000. The relatively small size of the ten cities named to the list probably helped them, to a certain extent "rise to the top" in the study, said Laura Simmons, a social research specialist with the Urban Institute. "Demographic changes tend to be more visible in smaller cities than large ones, especially over a short period of time," Simmons said. "In other words, it doesn't take as many additional people in poverty to alter the poverty rate in Salisbury as it does in Charlotte. Changes in the economy, like the loss of a major employer, have a bigger impact on a small city than a large one, Simmons said. That affects the poverty numbers as well, she said. According to the online article, Salisbury experienced a 12.4 percent increase in poverty from 2007–2009 to 2010–2012. Salisbury's poverty rate in 2010–2012 was 28.4 percent and median household income was $33,083, according to the article, which used poverty figures, home values, income and employment by industry from the U.S. Census Bureau's American Community Survey and six years of annual average unemployment figures from the U.S. Bureau of Labor Statistics

Since doing the three stage shows at the end of last year, it's the longest time I've spent at the shelter without a project. It's still the first of the year and I'm about a week away before I have to go back to working at my internship. I'm unable to perform my duties of the internship at the Goodwill Career Center so I was able to see more of activities that took place at the shelter. I would leave out of the shelter at the last possible minute before eight in the morning, because of the crutches. I wouldn't come back there sometimes for lunch to wait in the line for the soup kitchen to open. I would check in for the evening most nights at approximately at five thirty, because I was able to gain entry into the facility with the handicap that I possessed. I would be able to jump to the front of the line so that I could get a shower and dress my cot for the evening before most of the other guests with the exceptions of women with children and other people with disabilities.

During the winter months, the population of the shelter residents swelled. By law the Salisbury Fire Marshal posted that the maximum occupancy that allowed as many as fifty people in the sleeping quarters. It's not so much a fact, but it appears that on the coldest winter nights local residents in town would get into squabbles with their significant others and would find a way to get a reservation at the shelter. I don't know if they did that because they didn't have money to get a room at the hotel, or they didn't have a relative who would allow them to stay there. From January to mid-April the facility that was only supposed to accommodate fifty people was now hosting close to seventy people on a nightly basis. With the overflow of bodies came the problems among the residents that would escalate into arguments, and the conflict that is created when you have people living in extremely close quarters that could be volatile almost to the point of violence could erupt at any time.

Residents who have been there the longest are given a plastic tote box to store their possessions. Their most valuable possessions all of the residents would be locked in a separate cabinet in the laundry room. The shelter director didn't display any sympathy for the weather. The shelter director David was more concerned about running a shelter for homeless people more than the health and welfare of the people who resided there. There was another incident when he wanted to make it perfectly clear to anyone who was a resident there to know that he was the head man in charge. Case in point was when the shelter took in a man who had moved to Salisbury from Norfolk, Virginia. He was a young man in his late thirties and was extremely obese. Patrick is the man's name and was a person of good nature. He probably weighed anywhere from four hundred to five hundred pounds. He was so large that he couldn't sleep on the cot like the rest of the residents, but was given an air mattress to sleep on. Patrick was in the process of applying for his disability, but wasn't getting any of the assistance that he needed from his caseworker. Patrick had been a resident there since June of the previous year, and really didn't cause any trouble, but could go toe to toe playing the dozens with you until you either wanted to fight him or cry.

One evening, the facility was filled beyond the maximum capacity. Shelter guest were packed in there like sardines in a can and the tensions among the residents were high. Patrick was always willing to play the dozens with you if you were down for it. That evening he another guest started off this cultural custom of playing the dozens exchanging insults at each other. This exchange lead to someone not appreciating this craft and it got into a heated verbal squabble. I don't recall what exactly what the disagreement was about, but it was the only time that I do know of when two of the people who lived at the shelter had let a disagreement go beyond control. One thing lead to another, and shortly after that, fists started to fly between the two. When all was said and done, they had to have both of them dismissed from the shelter with a police escort. Patrick was accused of fighting like the other person, but they said that during the altercation that Patrick bit the other person during the fight. Both of them were asked to leave the shelter indefinitely, but they could appeal the decision by the shelter director.

Like anyone who was dismissed from the shelter, both people were given the opportunity to appeal the decision by David. The other person never bothered to appeal and had left town. Patrick had made his appeal immediately and heard of his decision from David a week later. By the time Patrick heard what the consequences of the result of his appeal, Patrick learned that he was on probation from the shelter for six month. When this decision was made, Patrick couldn't stay inside for the evening, go to the soup kitchen for lunch, but he could be on the property or visit the crisis center to come in for protection from the elements during the daytime hours. During the month of January and February just like in Newark, New Jersey, the evening temperatures would drop to the dangerously low marks where hypothermia would set in, and the high possibility of getting frostbite. Patrick would have to sleep outside most evenings behind the build of the shelter and would be in the sleeping under an old abandoned build by the train station. There was one night when the residents jumped on David, because the temperatures dipped below zero that he allowed Patrick to stay inside the facility of the shelter. This would be the only time that David would show that he was a compassionate human being, but this act of compassion was done because of the pressure from the residents or his fellow staffers.

When I finally was able to return to work the internship at the Goodwill. I went back to work there during the last week during the month to resume my duties with them. I decided that if I was going to continue to give them the services of the work that I was doing I needed to be compensated for it. I would still look for other job opportunities, but when the new year came in I made it my personal mission to find a job outside of Rowan county. I knew that I didn't want to work in Salisbury but that was easy because there weren't any opportunities in the whole county. My focus was working in one of the bigger cities in the state like Winston-Salem or Charlotte. I didn't have a play that I was thinking about producing, but working hard on getting out of this place. I would revisit looking at positions with the Goodwill, because of the fact that I've had several years' experience of working in the nonprofit sector of social services.

When the following week came I attend one of many meetings with the Rowan Business Advisory Committee that was held on the first Tuesday of every month at the Goodwill Career center. This committee was made up members from the local government of city, county, businesses, and community based organizations to meet at the Goodwill career center. The goal of this organization was to network so that the residents of Rowan county would be enlightened of the job openings, resources and services that are available to them. One of the community based organizations that were invited to attend the meetings was none other than the Rowan Helping Ministries. Since working my internship at Goodwill I had attended all of the meeting with the exception of January since October. At every one of these meetings extended an invitation to Rowan Helping Ministries had been sent. At every one of their meetings held at the Goodwill Career Connection, there hasn't been a single representative from Rowan Helping Ministries to attend one of them. The Rowan Business Advisory Committee have even extended an effort to do a food and clothing drive donation to Rowan Helping Ministries during the months of November and December that the shelter would graciously accept on behalf of the committee that donated the goods to them.

Since I was working there I thought that it was a great idea to fax over some of the job posting that were at the Goodwill over to my caseworker so that she could post them for anyone who was looking for a job, but hopefully that the residents of the shelter would benefit from it the most. I would take a few minutes out of the beginning of the week after Rosa would post the new job listings on their job board. I would make copies of the listings so that I would fax them to Keona. I noticed when I would return to the shelter I would look to see if the job listings had been posted on the bulletin board at the crisis network or somewhere in the shelter so that the residents could see them. Not much to my surprised the information that could have been helpful to the residents wasn't posted. I asked Keona if she received the information that I faxed over to her. She replied that she did get it, and thanked me for it. Once she received this information that I sent to her, and she thanked me for it I knew that she didn't really get it! I asked her how come she didn't post them so that the residents who needed to see what was available. She told me that they didn't have enough room on their bulletin boards to post them. I approached the shelter director with the same questions and got the same response. This didn't infuriate me, because I feel pretty resourceful having been able to acquire my degree from college but it really made me feel bad for the residents who weren't as blessed as I.

The residents didn't have a clue of just how bad that they were being subjected for the value of a dollar. This was a blatant form of oppression that is concealed to the shelter residents, and was done so that they were kept in the dark about how they were being used in order to acquire money on their misfortunes. The administration and the board of directors were pimping the residents who lived there, and the residents didn't know just how bad the agency was doing it to them. Rowan Helping Ministries was invited to a business networking session that if done for the purpose the Business Advisory Committee had intended it for, it would've informed the residents at the shelter that there were job openings. Still the administration of the shelter would ignore the invitation of the business advisory committee and accept donations of clothing and food from the committee. Personally this act by Rowan Helping Ministries sickened me deeply that I developed a deep disdain towards the administration, board members and anything associated with Rowan Helping Ministries. If there was someone who visited the Goodwill career center and asked for assistance on the services that Rowan Helping Ministries provided, I would refer the person who inquired about it and tell them where to get the assistance from another agency.

While I was at Goodwill I would not only check out the job board for the company that posted them with the agency, but checking out the jobs at the Goodwill of Northwest North Carolina as well.

When I returned to the internship I had missed a total of six weeks of work from early December until mid-January. When I returned I had looked at several job opportunities that were posted for the Goodwill agency. That really wasn't anything new, because I was looking at positions posted by Goodwill when they first asked me to work as an intern for them. Over the months that I worked for them I had applied for five job and wasn't being considered for a position with them. I noticed that whenever I looked at a position with them I wouldn't get a response from them or a reply from the people who asked me if I could do some intern work with them. When they would hold an agency wide training seminar I was invited to attend. The headquarters would hold a training seminar at one of the larger satellite offices, and would talk about techniques for servicing the public and following up on placements for those participants who use the resources of the agency.

When the delegates from the Salisbury office arrived there the administration of Goodwill was talking about how well the placement numbers came across from that office. One of my responsibilities was to do the follow up on the participants who utilized the equipment and other resources to help secure employment for themselves. I didn't do anything unique or unusual just used the skills from years of working in customer service and spoke to the people who I followed up on by speak to them with the respect that I'm sure that they wanted. I tried to treat each phone call of each participant with the reverence that I would like to get if the roles were reversed. Sheila Padrick the regional director of made it a point to let everyone know of the job that I did by getting the placement numbers up for the Salisbury office. In the process of getting the placement number up it made Eric look good and gave him an office away from the people in the main resource area with the participants using the computers, it was a feather in the cap of Rosa because it kept her from not having the data show that she was on top of the situation in her office and it justified a reason for the board members of Goodwill and administration to promote Sheila as the director of all of the Career Connection centers for Goodwill Industries of Northwest North Carolina.

While all of this good news was happening for everyone around me, but there was very little good news happening for Leroy. By the middle of February I had submitted seven applications with Goodwill without out a response. Since I've been doing this good work that I've been complimented for I felt that it was time for me to make a career move. I was hoping that this move would have been with the Goodwill industries of Northwest North Carolina. I made it clear after I submitted the last application that I had been with the agency as an intern for over the past six month. I acknowledged that I appreciate the opportunity work as an intern, but I was ready to move on. I informed them that I wanted to remain with the organization and of the previous applications that I've submitted without getting any response. I wasn't extended the courtesy as an intern to know if I was under qualified, over qualified or disqualified because of any previous conditions that the job may require. I was letting them know that I was ready to step my game up, and wanted to have a shot at the big leagues. I was appreciative of the opportunity to do the work of an intern, but now it was time for me to think about moving forward even if that meant doing outside of the agency. It wasn't as if I hadn't done any work like this before, and the result of getting the placement report completed ahead of schedule should've been an indication that I could bring something to the table.

I made a point of sending an e-mail to Sheila letting her know that I have been working for the agency as an intern. I wasn't abrupt or brash in the letter, but I did acknowledge that their complements were valued, but their compliments didn't do anything to help resolve my current living situation. I thought that it was unfair of them to expect me to deliver on projects that they assign for me without the possibility of the considering me for a position with the agency. I informed them that I've been with them over the past six month and applied for seven different positions that required my educational degree, and the experience. I had to let them know that I wanted to work for them, but if there wasn't a possibility of my working for the agency that I would need to use my time more constructively for the benefit of me.

Within a week of sending the e-mail to Sheila I received a reply for an interview in Winston-Salem at the headquarters for a mentoring position for high schoolers who were about to enter into a college program. I made a point of making sure that come hell or high water that I was going to make this interview. I only had a few dollars left after selling my food stamps, and I informed my caseworker that I was going up there for the interview. I borrowed some money from a friend to make sure that I was able to secure the transportation for the round trip. I called and secured the interview for a one o'clock interview. This allowed me plenty of time to get there, and have time to prep myself. I arrived in Winston-Salem after catching the train from Salisbury to High Point and then taking a bus from there into the interview. I had my bag lunch that I would normally take with me to the internship, and enough time so that I could eat it outside in the open picnic area at the Goodwill facility. When I went in I informed the receptionist that I had an interview scheduled for one o'clock that afternoon. I signed in so that I could use the resource center there so that I could hand deliver them a copy of my resume' and references. When I returned from the computer lab I had a little over an hour. As I was sitting in the waiting area of the lobby I saw Sheila and Reni Geiger leaving out of the building as if they were going to lunch or to a meeting. Both of the ladies looking surprised when I was sitting there, maybe not expecting me to make the interview. We spoke in passing and I told them that I was there to interview for a position that the agency had opened.

When the time came for my interview I felt pretty prepared. I had additional copies of my resume and reference for the interviewers. My appointment was with Devita Ewell, and I was ready to do this. This was one of the few times that I had my friend Frankie Fear visit me for the interview for it gave me little doubt, but this was some much needed confidence that I didn't feel in some of my previous interviews. When I arrived in the office of Ms. Ewell she escorted me to another office in the setting of where the duties of the job that I was applying for was going to be performed. When we arrived there we were met by another employee of Goodwill by the name of Anthony. I recall meeting him when we were at the agency training seminar that took place in the city of Statesville. I felt good about seeing him there but I attempted to remain cautious, because this is still an interview that I was on. I didn't want to get too comfortable with anyone because I must've given a good impression for the top brass I met in Statesville in order for them have two people to interview me.

Once the introductions of everyone was done it was time to get down to see if there was anything that was compatible for all the parties involved. The interviewers started out with the standard questions; "tell me about yourself", "what do you know about Goodwill" "what are your strengths and weaknesses", and "why do you think we should hire you"? Before I arrived in Devita's office I already said a prayer, and before I answered any of those questions I made sure that I inhaled a deep breath took my time to compose myself before I opened mouth. I felt pretty comfortable answering the questions before the next part of the interview came. The interviewers gave me an overview of the job, the responsibilities and expectations of how the duties that should be performed. Once that was explained I answered them by letting them know that I felt very comfortable about what the expectations were, and that I felt comfortable doing a job.

After that exchange my achilles heel was when I was asked about a question on the application that I filled out. The question is have you ever been arrested for a crime outside of a traffic ticket. It's something that I have to answer honestly, because if I don't disclaim it to secure the job then the agency will have every justifiable reason to terminate me for perjury. I answered it on the application, and thought that I've was very thorough with the explanation of what was the crime, charges and the sentence that I've faced. Still there was no getting around or trying to avoid the question so I told them that I was locked up for a simple assault charge which is a misdemeanor. I was taken to the Lexington County Department of Corrections where I served thirty three day and made restitution to the victim. It's a violent crime, and I explained that I am remorseful for ever having that part of my character happen. My mother always used to tell me that hindsight is twenty twenty vision.

The interviewers were winding down the interview by telling me about the benefit package that employees of Goodwill are eligible for, and the salary that the job is paying. They finished by asking me if I had any questions. I always try to make it a point of asking a question when it comes to the close of an interview. I asked them about the size of the class that I would be working with. They told me that it would be approximately between sixteen to twenty program participants that I would be responsible for. I inquired about the method of assessment that they use to measure the aptitude for entry into the program. Anthony explained that they would be using the Test for Adult Basic Education, the acronym used for this is called the TABE. It is used to measure the person's aptitude in the subjects of mathematics, reading, spelling, language and language mechanics. Participants would be accepted into the program is the can pass these components on a ninth grade competency level. I inform him that I was able to differentiate the TABE test, because of my familiarity using it as a measuring instrument from my days as the admissions director at the Urban League of Essex County. When I heard them mentioned that they were using the same testing method that I was using over twenty five years ago I just felt my confidence level elevate. I don't know if I showed any enthusiasm on my face or not, but I felt like the Pavlovian dog who was salivating at the possibility of getting what he wanted by working there for the Goodwill. I told them that I was familiar with the testing method because it was the same one that I used when I was employed at the Urban League of Essex County when I held the position as the Admissions and Recruitment Director there in Newark, New Jersey. The only other questions I had was how did this position become available? They told me that the person who was in the position was promoted to another position within the agency. When the meeting was over I shook their hands and thanked them for having me in for the interview.

On the way back I took some time to think about the possibility of what it would take to move to Winston-Salem. When I got to High Point I had to wait on the train that was going into Salisbury. I sat in isolation away from the other people who were waiting on the same train going towards that direction. I recalled that the pastor at my church was telling the congregation members that we need to take a minute during the day to go into a prayer closet. This is a way of a person communicating with the Lord, and be at peace. I heed the advice of the pastor and took to being alone so that I could communicate between just God and I. Taking this time to thank him for seeing to it that I had a safe passage to the interview and back. I was letting him know that I really wanted this job, and if it was his will to let me have it to please allow it. It was the first time that I felt good about an interview since being in Salisbury. I thought that it went well, but it's not up to me to make the final decision but the people who operate the agency at Goodwill who would have the last say if I was going to be a member of their staff. I never wanted anything this bad since I was a child when I asked my parents if I could get an action figure toy called Captain Action for Christmas.

The next day after returning from the Goodwill headquarters in Winston-Salem I went back to the duties that I had to do as an intern. At the beginning of the day before I did any work for the career center I made a point of taking the time out that morning to write a thank you letter to Devita. I wanted to display my interest in the position and by sending this email I was hoping that she and the other people who have the authority to hire would look the letter and put me into the position. I went back to my duties of doing follow up on the placement of the people who come there for assistance. I ran into Dee later that morning at the career center, and she inquire to me about doing another stage production. She was telling me about applying for grants to help do the production. She was working on getting her paperwork to reacquire her own non-profit agency status, and that she was willing to help me with putting on a production. Dee was telling me that she had reserved one of the private meeting room at the library that she blocked for several hours. She was using it to research grants to start up her agency, and invited me to join her to do the same for doing a stage show.

We met at the library for several days over the next couple of weeks taking the time to go through as many sources to find different foundations. We came across a grant application that was based locally in Salisbury. It was the Blanche and Julian Robinson

Foundations and it appeared to be one that we felt that we had a pretty good chance of acquiring it. Together she and I agreed that I would direct the production, and it would be under the wing of her nonprofit agency. We would get together and reserve the larger conference rooms for a day at a time. Using laptop computers to research for grants from foundations that were being offered locally, across the country and worldwide. There was also the use of the big reference books that are available at the library that had grants hidden from the public like a needle in a haystack. While researching for these grants I still didn't have a stage project that I wanted to do, but I knew that I wanted to do something that was going to get the attention of the people who lived in Salisbury and Rowan County.

The one project that I was very interested was in the format that I wasn't crazy about using, but the content of the play was an eye opener. It was a fresh new play that is produced in 2012 by the American Foundation for Equal Rights and Broadway Impact. The name of this new project that had my ears pointing straight up. The play is called "*8*", and was written by Academy Award Winning writer Dustin Lance Black. It is based on the California state trial of *Perry vs. Schwarzenegger* (now *Hollingsworth v. Perry*), the federal court case for marriage of gays and lesbian Americans. The words of the script are from the actual Perry court transcripts. "*8*" is the real life story story of Kris & Sandy and Jeff and Paul, two loving couples who want to get married but can't. Together with attorneys David Boies and Ted Olson and a host of expert witnesses, they take aim at proposition 8, a discriminatory law that took away the right for lesbian, gay, bisexual and transgender couples to marry in the state of California in 2008.

I found out that it was a reading presentation which is something that I'm not in favor of, but after reading over the synopsis I didn't have to think twice about not doing this. Every year in the city of Salisbury host a Gay Pride Festival in the community, and I thought that presenting this production during that time would allow me to build a following for Updaway Productions. I decided to solicit the help of my cousin and her husband along with Dee to recruit players and to market this for the pride festival. My cousin was adamant that she wouldn't help me with this, and her decision I could respect. It was because it displayed that I supported the acts of lesbian, gay, bisexual and transgender marriages. Dee was willing to help me do it, and I was given the impression that she viewed this occupation of same sex couple pretty much the same way that I did. I view the choices of gay couples not as pro-gay but pro-choice. The other part about doing this production that made it attractive to me was that there wasn't any royalty fees that had to be paid to the American Foundation for Equal Rights and Broadway Impact, but on the other hand there wasn't any profit to be made either. I was fine with the prospect of not making any money on it, but I wanted it to be known that Updaway Productions wasn't afraid to openly take on this socially impacting topic in a presentation. It's a non-fictional drama that is truly groundbreaking that goes into a very hot topic issue of the present. I went to some of the members of the Gay Pride organizing committee to present it to them, because I found that the more I wanted to put on this production with some of the people who call themselves actors that were either homophobic, or wouldn't do it due to their own convictions about same sex couples. I think that the thing the frustrated me most with the actors in this community wasn't the fact that this conflicted with their belief religiously, but there wasn't anything that required the physical act of intimacy or sexual acts of affection. I realized that not everyone will be as open minded as I. However a couple of the same sex couples decide to make their union isn't my personal concern, because it's not me who they would have to answer to but God when their judgement day comes that they have to be accountable for their actions.

Just when I happen to look for a performance project to direct, the performance project happened to find me. Later during the time that Dee and I were researching grants for the new play, a project happened to fall into my hands. I received a call from one of my co-stars from the play I directed Sign of The Times. Linda White Deyo was a last minute understudy who did a good job in a bit role of the play. One night at the shelter, she and members of her church were serving dinner to the guest. She told me that she had written a play, and that she would like for me to get the Down Home Players to perform. I told her that I would look at it and have to read it before I can considered it. She was happy that I would consider doing it, but at that moment I was happy to be presented with a project that someone wanted to entrust me to take over as a director.

I asked her to meet me at the at the Koco Java coffee house on South Main Street the following afternoon. She had to get off her job from the Rowan Salisbury School System before she could meet me there. At that meeting I found out that there was a lot of common interest that we had. I found out that she graduated high school with my cousin in the city that I was born in Orange, New Jersey, and that she also worked at the Veterans Hospital in down the street from where I used to live in East Orange, New Jersey. She had co-written the play she presented to me called *"The Verdict: The Beginning or The End."* This fictional drama embraced the struggles, complexity and the beauty of the African American community. It is based on the history, trials and liberation of the African-American race as it chronicles the people from the ancient kingdoms of the motherland into the 1990s. The subject matter of *"The Verdict: The Beginning or The End."* engages and expands the knowledge of African American social consciousness and the history of the culture. This play was originally written for a African American History program while she was still employed at the Veterans Hospital.

After reading the script I thought that it was worthy of presenting it to the public in Rowan County. I also had Dee read a copy of it, and suggested that we try to see how you can acquire funding so that we could have a submission of the production ready for The Atlanta Black Theatre Festival in October. We were looking at several grant opportunities, but concentrated on one grant at a time. We looked at the Blanche and Julian Robertson Foundation Grant as the first source of securing the funding for the project. The next grant submission was to the Rowan Arts Council by applying for the Arts and Cultural Development Grant first, and later would apply for the Grassroots Grant that we would have to secure matching funds. Our efforts hadn't ceased there with just the county of Rowan in North Carolina, but applications were also placed with the Brown Foundation, The Heinz Endowment Foundation, The Andrew W.

Mellon Foundation, The National Theatre Project and a host of others. It was helpful that we were able to find out a lot about the eligibility requirements from the online source of the *Non Profit Times*.

Once all the applications that were found to be the most compatible with what we were trying to establish, the next thing was to secure what is the second hardest aspect for me as a producer in securing the venue for the performance. The current timeframe is now February so trying to do as a African American History program was out of the question. So for the next biggest event that would be centered around an Afrocentric theme would have to take place during the month of June for the "Juneteenth" celebration. This event is when the African American community holds a weekend festivities commemorating the Emancipation of slave from the bondage of their former slave masters. These festivities would be held on the west side of town at Kelsey Scott Park. That would've been alright, but it would be better if we were to get an audience that wouldn't just cater to one specific group of people, but we needed to find a venue where it would be accessible for a wide range of diverse people to see this event. The J C Price American Legion Post was possibility, but it was hard to attract a diverse audience to see this production there. If Updaway Productions was truly going to be recognize as a major player in the local theatre industry it needed to be seen where the majority of people in town can be at during a major event sponsored by the town.

I thought about it, and the idea came to mind that the local chamber of commerce sponsors an event on a Friday every month from March to November called the Salisbury Friday Night Out. When they hold these events the residents and visitors patronize the local businesses in the downtown area until nine o'clock in the evening. Salisbury has a couple of parks that were build that have an amphitheatre design that I haven't seen used for any kind of entertainment event. The one place that stood out more than the other is the Eastern Gateway Park. It stood out because of the location on East Innes street and had a large fountain that used to be placed in the center of downtown. It is centrally located, and accessible to the public for anyone who would walk by to stop by view the performance. Parking was great, because it was adjacent to the local bus depot and the train station was just across the street.

About a week later Dee, Linda and I met in the library to discuss the plans for putting on the production. I told Linda that I like the play and that we should focus our efforts on presenting it to an audience that would be able to see it. I suggested that we should use the park and presented right on the heels of the Juneteenth festival. The open date that the chamber of commerce had in June was on the twenty first. I informed her that I wouldn't be doing any acting, and I was going to take over the directing and producing the production. I was bringing her on as a consultant and as an actor. Dee was going to handle the marketing, and Dee and I would work together on getting the funding for the production. With the new project being in place reinvigorated me to make this the best project yet. My main focus was to secure the venue by meeting and going to the Chamber of Commerce, and the Tourism Division of to confirm the date for the Friday Night Out. I met with Melissa who I knew from previously working with her when the division of Tourism, the Chamber of Commerce and the Lee Street Theatre did the *Christmas Carol* trolley play. She directed me to go to the city's parks and recreation department to see about getting a permit. I did that and made an appointment to meet with them.

About a week later, I met with one of their representatives and a member of the Salisbury Police Department outlining what the requirements would be to host a show at the park. They informed me that they would've preferred that I use the old farmers' market area or the parking lot across the street from the library to conduct the event. One of the reasons that they wanted me to do it at those other places was because the park is closed when dusk hits. This was a fact that I already knew, and that was one of the reasons why I chose the date of June twenty first, because that's the longest day of the year, and there are more hours of natural sunlight during that day than any other in the northern hemisphere. I informed them about this fact, and it was agreeable by all parties that this would be acceptable. I was informed about what the conditions of the terms should be. I would need to contract a security firm that is registered with the state or pay the city for police service and I would have to get a million-dollar insurance policy for the day. I wouldn't be able to charge anyone who wanted to see the program, but would be allowed to pass around a hat for donations. I found this to be a fair deal, and the terms seemed to be reasonable. The security for the police was just fifty dollars for an armed officer, but the insurance was the objective that I would have to overcome. The price of the insurance was steep at four hundred dollars for a day. Now if I had a home, I could've had my agent underwrite that under my homeowner's policy. Since I didn't own a home, and was still living at the shelter the next thing for me to do was to get sponsors.

This is during the month of March, and I still had several things in my favor. I had gathered a cast that I'd advertised for auditions, and by this time, they were pretty much dedicated to the schedule of rehearsal and much more disciplined than the previous cast members from *Sign of the Times.* My time working the internship at Goodwill was done when I received the e-mail from Devita stating that Goodwill decided to go in another direction by hiring another person. I was still living at the shelter, and the conditions weren't getting any better for the residents who stayed there. I used this time to engulf myself into the work of putting on a production that was going to use some of the residents of the shelter as players in the upcoming production of "*The Verdict.*" I was still hopeful that one if not both of the grant applications from the Robertson Foundation or the Rowan County Arts Commission would be approved. My main thought was trying to find money for the production to go on without a hitch. The other thing that I was hoping for was that I could've had this together so that Updaway Productions would've been able to submit it for the Atlanta Black Theatre Festival in October, because I didn't have all the principles in place I wasn't able to get the application in before the deadline.

One of the worst things that I like to do as a performer is doing a show for the public that is only going to take place as a "one night only" performance. The reason why that is, it doesn't allow the actors very much room for error, and if there are any, then that's what the audience will remember more than the good points of the performance. With that being done as a one-night-only show, everybody would have to be on their marks, and I knew that I was working with. I had only three people who had done some live theatre that realized what it required to do a show like this, and the magnitude that it could have on the audience allowing them to leave the performance with their dissatisfaction of the performance or having them wanting more. Even though this was my second effort as a director, I wanted this one to be much better than what happened in the *Sign of the Times*. I was able to see what were the flaws that I had with that, and I was going to alter whatever it took to make the necessary corrections to make *The Verdict* a better production from a performance standard.

During the first week of April, I was on my grind hitting the pavement pounding on doors making appointments to meet with business and others who would allow me to visit them and present to them my plans for the play that was going to take place during the Salisbury Friday Night Out. Dee was doing her part working the research on the grants, and using her contacts to get anything that she could from them. Just a couple of days away from my birthday with still a couple of month away from the performance, I wondered how this was going to be pulled off. I started to worry about that for the first time since doing this. Just a month earlier the Lee Street Theatre had done their groundbreaking ceremony that I attended. They were moving out of the Black Box Theatre and into their own building, creating a new venue to rival that of the Meroney and the Norvell theatres. At the end of rehearsal that day, I went back to the shelter thinking what I needed to do was to get Updaway Productions into becoming financially solvent. After my shower and a dinner, I made my cot to lay down for the evening.

I didn't sleep too well that night, because for once as a producer, I was feeling the pressure of delivering on the show that I've hyped up. I knew that if I didn't deliver than I would be known in this town as a great hype man who didn't come through. It seemed that by the time I finally fell asleep it was time to hear the shelter aide Austin do the five twenty wake-up call. For once that morning I got up early, because I knew what lie ahead of me for the day. I walked into the bathroom not fully awake when someone had left some folding chairs in the walkway going toward that stalls where the urinal and toilets are. I hit my foot against it, and it happened to be the same foot that I had the stress fracture injured. At that time I had decide to go ballistic. Earlier in the month David had stated that there were too many obstacles that were being left in the men's bathroom, and that they shouldn't be left in there. When it felt like that I had re-injured my foot, and when I had so many things pressing my mind, I'd lost it. In the restroom there were three folding chairs that were blocking that stalls to the urinal and the two toilets. I was in a lot of pain, and I asked the two other guys that were in there to move out of the way because I didn't want them to get hurt. I picked up each of the chairs one at a time and threw each of them at the wall headed toward the door. The guys obliged my request and moved out of the way while I was using them the same way that an Olympic athlete uses the hammer throw. I knew deep inside what I was doing was wrong, but it felt good to get all of my built up frustrations released by throwing those chairs as hard as I could. Although doing this was just a temporary euphoric expression, it felt as if I had gotten rid of a year's' worth of disappointments and frustrations. I even found out that I broke one of the chairs.

When the shelter aide Austin heard the noise, he came into the bathroom and asked me what happened, and I told him that I tossed the chairs because hurt my foot. He told me to get myself dress, get my things, and leave. I told him that I would, but I was going to leave after I got dressed, and if he had to call the police, then go ahead and do it. I was going to be kicked out, but I wasn't going to rush to get out of there. I finished washing up, and went back to my cot to finish getting my things together, and shortly after that, two officers from the Salisbury Police Department arrived. One of the officers approached me and asked me about the situation and I explained what I did. While I was explaining to him, I was getting myself and my things together so that I could leave without any further incident. I finally got my stuff together, and I was escorted out of the doors by the two officers.

I went outside and was smoking a cigarette before some of the other shelter residents started to make their way outside asking me what happened. When they did that, I told them and that I knew that I was going to have a pending suspension from the shelter. At that point it didn't matter to me. I was tired of feeling like a caged animal without the liberties that I was accustomed to having. I didn't have any right to state the wrong that was occurring at the shelter, and when I did, it was always replied with "we'll look into that situation." When the dawn broke, I made my trek to the library and I didn't bother worry about doing the business for Updaway Productions. I stayed there until it closed and then I went over my cousin's house and explained to she and her husband what happened. They asked why I did it, and I told them that I simply cracked because of the pain in my foot and that I had to let them know that I couldn't take the treatment of what the administration and the staff. I asked them if it were possible for me to stay there for three days, because I thought that's how long I would be kicked out for. They agreed and allowed me to do that. When I did this reaction that caused me to get kicked out of the shelter, I viewed that living in Salisbury was more like living in the Gary Trudeau comic strip of Doonesbury. This town and it's people are very much epitomize the name of the popular comic strip. The name "Doonesbury" is a combination of the word done (a prep school slang for someone who is clueless, inattentive, or careless), and I took the surname when I thought about the city of Salisbury, North Carolina.

The next day, I went to the shelter before I'd gone to the library to see what the punishment would be. I waited in the lobby to see my case manager, Keona, or the shelter director, David. After being there from eight that morning until nine forty-five, Keona finally called me back into her office and gave me a letter on their letterhead notifying me that I was kicked out of the shelter indefinitely. I wasn't allowed to be on the grounds of the shelter, I couldn't go to the soup kitchen to get a lunch, or use the shower like they would allow for anyone who isn't a resident of the facility. I was told that I could appeal the decision within three days for the time of the incident. So I immediately appealed the decision right then. I wasn't going to procrastinate and not have anywhere to sleep and I was trying to get back in there as quick as possible. I was given an appeal date for a week later.

For the next couple of days I kept the routine of going to the library and stay at my cousins. I told Dee that I was kicked out of the facility, but that I was appealing it. We had a rehearsal on the last night that I was staying at my cousin's, and at the end of the rehearsal, I told Linda the same about my situation. Linda offered me an opportunity to come and stay with her while I was waiting to find out the decision on my appeal. I told her that I wouldn't take her up on it, unless they suspended me for more than ten days. We had a couple more rehearsals before I found myself sleeping on the bench at the city bus depot. I felt pretty safe being there. The cops would drive by and wouldn't bother me and once in a while you could find a Good Samaritan who would just give me cash anywhere from five to ten dollars at a time. I would talk to Patrick who was already sleeping outside for close to three months, and he would always say that he would eat better than the people who lived inside the shelter. He wasn't lying about that either, because the majority of the people who knew that I was staying out of the shelter would offer me a plate or to take me out to get a bite. I would be embarrassed to know that someone would extend themselves to a stranger. That had to be my most humbling experience since being homeless.

When my week was up and it was time to do my appeal, I went back to the shelter to meet with David and Keona to plead my case to be readmitted as a resident of the shelter. I told them that I was remorseful for the actions that I took and that I was hurt when the chairs that were left in the bathroom caused me to re-injured my stress fracture in my foot I had. Neither Keona and David had anything to say about the incident or the date in question. The only thing that David said is that I need to call back in three days to get the decision that the executive director Ms. Foster would determine. I felt that I was going to get screwed on this deal, and it had to do with the letter that I sent to Deirdre Parker-Smith of the *Salisbury Post*. My suspicions were right and I was about to get screwed. Once I met with the people who I submitted my appeal to Ms. Foster I had been out of the shelter for ten days already I was to hear back from Ms. Foster the following day, but she was out of the office. I called back the following day and was told that she was sick, and I didn't hear from her for another week. By the time that I received the decision it was already thirteen days before that happen to find out that I was persona non grata from the shelter for a thirty day period.

This was something that I thought was an extreme act on behalf of the shelter. I didn't act out any further, but I could always express my displeasure by speaking to them with words that were above the heads of those who I allowed to make a decision for me when I broke one folding chair and tossed two others. I contacted Linda to ask her if the offer for me to stay over her place was still valid. She told me that it was and that I could come over to stay starting that evening. I had her meet at the bus depot for her to pick me up. I was very grateful for she and her family letting me stay with them. I stayed with her for the next three days, but I never truly felt comfortable staying there so what I did one day when she dropped me off at the library I went to Rowan Regional Medical Center and checked myself into the psychiatric unit called LifeWorks. At this point in my life, I knew that I was facing depression. For once in my life, more than I hurt myself, I knew that I wanted others to feel the pain of not being able to do the work you've invested four years of your life to do. I now knew that this was truly hell that I've gotten myself into. When I arrived at the hospital, I e-mailed my cast and Dee told them that rehearsal have been postponed indefinitely. I didn't leave any explanation as to why they were, but that they were until further notice. I knew that I was going to have to get some help other than from the people who I was asking to do the play and the family members who asked me to leave their house in the first place. Depression was setting into my life, and I knew that I needed to get some help quickly before I would get myself into some trouble that I would have had a hard time trying to get myself out of. Shortly after Linda dropped me off, I was at the library trying to continue the work on the play, but I couldn't devote myself to concentrate. So after a few hours there knowing that I wasn't accomplishing what I need to, I took the time to walk from the library to the hospital and admit myself in the psychiatric unit at the Rowan Regional Medical Center. This unit was called Lifeworks, and when I checked myself into Lifeworks, I didn't know what exactly to expect. I knew that it was going to serve a purpose even if was a short-term fix of getting me off the streets. Doing this wasn't going to be easy, and I felt as if anything and everything that I was working towards was starting to collapse around me. I almost felt as if I was going into a pit of quicksand, and that the more that I tried to succeed the more I was failing. I was sinking deeper into becoming an introvert and losing more of my outgoing extroverted personality. This admission into the psychiatric was my way of asking for help outside of the support network that I thought that was going to be there for me. Family was there, but I was too embarrassed to be a burden to them. I didn't get the support from the people at Rowan Helping Ministries, and now this was going to be my last chance to try to rebound.

CHAPTER 10

Life Doesn't Suck, Situations Do!

I was experiencing a serious bout of depression when I admitted myself into the psychiatric unit at Rowan Regional Medical Center. Here I was, just turned fifty-two years old, with a college degree, and haven't truly lived up to the potential or promise that I displayed as a non-traditional honor student at Benedict College. For once, more than feeling homicidal or suicidal, I was feeling like the past fifty-two years of my life was nothing more than just a failure. When I admitted myself into the care of the psychiatric professionals, truly there weren't any feelings of suicidal thoughts. I knew in order for me to get off the streets, I had to play the role of someone who was capable of hurting himself more than he would hurt others. I admitted myself as a suicidal, homicidal patient who was ready and capable to hurt anyone who would get on my last nerve.

Before I was admitted there as a patient, I could see myself becoming withdrawn from a few of those people who cared about me the most. The once-outgoing, extroverted personality that I was known to express has now turned inward to the point that I became somewhat of a recluse. Hopelessness was replacing my friend of fear. I had to do some soul searching from within to find a way of getting myself back on track and refocusing to get my eyes back on the prize. I was at my last end of trying to deal with being patient of letting things fall into place. I had thirteen months of frustration from giving my best efforts to anything that I attempted to do or accomplish and seeming not to get anywhere with those efforts. There was only so much of this disappointment that I could stand that in my own haste, I acted out by throwing the chairs in the bathroom of the shelter. I was on a hamster wheel trying to go somewhere fast, but was staying in the same place. All during this time I've been reaching out, asking for and not receiving help until it came to a head. When I felt that this was the only way for me to get the help I've been asking for was to show my ass and become a patient of the mental ward. It wasn't until after I was admitted into Life Works that the medical community, the social services agencies, and some of the faith-based ministries were willing to help me.

I found when I moved to North Carolina that it was no better, or even worse than when I was living in South Carolina. The prejudice that I experienced in North Carolina was more open, blunt, and direct as opposed to that of some of the racist views of the people of whom I may have encountered in South Carolina. When I was living in South Carolina, I was able to work as a program coordinator with the Columbia Urban League for a year and as a permanent substitute teacher for a year and as a teacher's assistant over a three-year period with the Richland County School District One. I recalled when I was a basketball-playing scholar athlete at Allen University, we came to Salisbury to play in a series of games at Catawba College. The coaches and players didn't receive the very courteous treatment as regular-paying customers. This occurrence happened at two separate places when we came into Rowan County to play at a tournament at Catawba.

The first incident happened while my coach was in the middle of confirming the hotel reservations at the Holiday Inn on Jake Alexander Boulevard. The desk clerk had the audacity of attempting to belittle him and speaking with a bad attitude. Here was a man from an accredited college that was patronizing their establishment and the business that Allen University was using at their hotel but he was condemned by the employees of the Holiday Inn. During the same visit, when the team had a pregame meal at the local Pizza Hut, the employees at that establishment treated us like we did something wrong and came across very rude to the people who were patronizing their establishment. After going through those experiences, I should've known better than to think that the environment in this small town had changed.

When I was there at Life Works, the first couple of days I didn't have any sense of pride. I didn't bother to wash my clothes and made any attempt not to go into the group therapy meetings with the other patients who were there. The only time that I would get out of the room was to enter into the dining area to have my meals. It wasn't until the third day, when I met with the caseworkers and the other mental health professionals, that I decided to get myself out of my room and stop feeling sorry for myself. I haven't contacted anyone outside of the walls of the psyche ward. I was notorious for being on Facebook when I wasn't looking for a job, so when I was admitted there, all of those actions ceased. It wasn't until I contacted my sister and my oldest brother when I began the process of recovery. When my brother thought that I was going through a pity party, he told me that I was at the shelter first because I wanted to be there. That truly bothered me, because I never wanted to be at the shelter. For him to tell me that hurt me more than any of the job rejections that I've been turned down.

When I met with the psychiatric assessment team of doctors and social workers, it was to assess my situation and to get on a plan for recovery. While they were asking me questions as to what led me to come into their program, I told them about the events that transpired prior to admitting myself in there. I made sure I let them hear the anger and frustration in my voice of what led me to them, and that I was very much capable of hurting myself as well as someone else. At one time I could've done something that was going to get me into trouble or to the point that could get me incarcerated. I didn't want to do that, because it was hard enough for me to get a position in this state with just a misdemeanor assault charge that happen almost twenty years ago in another state. It wasn't until afterward when I mentioned that I was kicked out of the shelter for the actions that I did that was when the psychiatric team seemed to get it. When happened, they were more understanding what my dilemma was. The professionals appeared to be more compassionate to my experience and found it ethical to allow me to stay there for the remainder of the time before I returned to the shelter.

While being a patient at Life Works, I noticed that there were several others who were there from the shelter, and other local Salisbury residents who would hang around the shelter were patients also. One of the locals who would hang around the shelter was a guy who I would talk trash to about his favorite pro football team named Joe. He was a young guy who would be around the shelter, because his girlfriend was a resident there. He admitted himself there shortly after me and, like myself, found out that he was suffering from depression. After his first couple of days, he was coming back to being the person that I have come to know. Joe's stay was a short one, and before he left, I asked him not to tell anyone at the shelter that I was admitted there. He told me that he wouldn't and I took him at his word. Another person who admitted himself into Life Works was a person who was in the bathroom at the time that I lost it who went by the name of Big Ed.

He slept at the cot in front of mine when we were both guests at the shelter. Big Ed was an illiterate six foot six-inch tall man that weighs about three hundred pounds. While he and I were there, we would talk about what happened at the shelter prior to the both of us coming to Life Works. He was a product of the Rowan Salisbury School System, and by the time Ed reached high school, he excelled in football and basketball. The closer it got time for him to go into his senior year of high school, Ed decided to drop out of school. When he left school, he was the muscle for some of the local the drug dealers who needed to have an enforcer to hurt a regular customer if they didn't pay up their debts. He told me a little more about his past while we were at Life Works. The big guy told me that he had done some time in prison for being an accomplice in a bank robbery. He did federal time in jail after they found him in a hotel room in Florida with the money. Ed was one of the nicest guys who you would like to know, but people would take advantage of the fact that he was educationally challenged. If you ever got on his bad side, he was capable of seriously hurting you. Receiving this information made me look at the situation of just how bad the flaws are in the education system was for him and others in the Rowan Salisbury School District. Knowing that he was a peer of mine and that he knew the street code of ethics, I asked him too if he wouldn't say a word to any of the other residents of the shelter on my whereabouts. He told me that he'd take it to the grave.

One of the other people who I grew a fondness for was a young lady by the name of Shotzie. She wasn't a regular visitor who frequented the shelter or a guest who lived there. Shotzie was the type of person when you saw her, you would assume that she didn't belong at a place like Life Works. She was a smart young woman who had her own business and lived outside of Salisbury in a well-to-do neighboring town. She was a quiet woman who kept to herself the first day, but opened up on the second when everyone attended group therapy. When she came in, she was having her own struggles with being bipolar. During our time in group therapy, she didn't open up to many, but when we were outside of group, she was able to communicate comfortably with me. We exchanged our feelings about why we were in there and what our plans were individually when we got released. She told me that she was going back to resume working her business and looked forward to moving into a new place. She also told me about the love of her life who wasn't just her soul mate, but he showed her the business that they worked together. I explained to her that staying in Salisbury wasn't the best thing for me. I've been there going on three years, and had very little success in what I was trying to do. I figure that I'd try to give it one more shot. I wanted to go back to direct the play I was working on before I admitted myself into Life Works. Before Shotzie left Life Works, I met her boyfriend. Whenever there was a visitor who would come to see on a patient, the other patients would give them the respect to try and give their guest some space. When I met her boyfriend, she introduced us. He thanked me for being kind to her while we were there together. I didn't think that I did anything special, but he felt as if I did. She left there just a few day before I was released from the psyche unit. We made sure that we kept in touch through Facebook and have been in touch since.

Just a few days before my release from Life Works, I was somewhat apprehensive about returning to the life that I left at the shelter. I knew that nothing was going to change, and definitely not the personnel who worked there. I knew when I left Life Works that I had to get a grip of myself and check my emotions before I re-entered into the shelter. If there was going to be another tirade of an emotional outburst, I knew that I was subject to being prohibited from staying at the shelter indefinitely.

When I arrived there, I there was a new person who I have never saw there before. He was a new resident who was in there for a couple of days before he was heading out of town. I don't know why he was there, but he let it known to me that he thought that he had some of his valuables missing. I don't recall what his name was, but he wanted to get in there to get the remainder of his possession out of the facility. This guy wasn't happy about how he was treated and disclaimed that, if any of his stuff was missing from there, that he was packing a gun and would not hesitate to use it if his possessions were missing. For the first time since I was staying there, I experienced something that I hadn't since the days that I was living in South Carolina. I knew that someone had possession of a concealed weapon. Before I was allowed to enter as a resident of the shelter again, I had to meet with my case manager Kiona to get clearance. Once I met with her to get confirmation, I went back to wait at the entrance for the residents. When I got back there the man who was fired up was just going into the building. The shelter aide on duty that evening asked me if I was going into the building. I told him that I was going to smoke a cigarette before I come in. What I was really doing was waiting until that guy either started to shoot his piece off in the building so that I had time to get away, or wait for him to come out without any shots going off. If he was to leave without any shots going off, then I was going to get my butt in that building as soon as he left. After the man received his personal items, I went into the screening area where the shelter aides would make you take out all of your valuables before they would wand you with the metal detector. I was told that I had to turn in my locker key that stored all my valuables that were still in there, because it was assigned to another person as was my cot. I was given a newly assigned cot and a plastic shoe box so that my valuables were locked away in the office where the shelter aides do the laundry. The third shift evening crew of shelter aides would normally consisted of Will and Willie working during the weekday evenings.

On my first night back at the shelter, I forgot just how long when Will and Willie were when they working the entry for the resident to gain entrance for the evening at the shelter. They were so slow that I coined them "Slow and Slower" as a parody to the 1994 hit film that featured Jim Carrey and Jeff Daniels. Will was the lazier of the two aides whenever he and Willie would work. Will was an educated man that graduated from the University of North Carolina-Charlotte and who attended Salisbury High School with one of my former church members who was an openly gay male. When my church member found out that I was a resident of the shelter, he had told me that he knew Will and that they were once the lovers. At one time Will had worn his hair in the loc style that my former church member said that he used to be the person that re-twisted his hair. When Will would work, he tried to do as little of the manual labor as possible. Will would spend the majority of the time staying in the office on the computer, perpetrating like he was processing the paperwork for the shelter. Most of the time he was playing on the computer, procrastinating in order to get out of doing any manual labor that needed to be done.

Willie, on the other hand, was more laidback and easygoing. He was a retired vet and started working at the shelter as a part-time gig when he was employed at one of the local mills. When the mills closed down, he managed to get himself employed as a full-time shelter aide. Willie was a cool man who loved listening to his smooth jazz music while he was working and was more extroverted too. He was the kind of guy who reminded me of the round-the-way brothers who I grew up with from East Orange that wouldn't mind taking a shot at playing the dozens with you. He was good at it also, and part of the reason why he was so good was due to the fact that he was an ex-army man. See he's been around the world as a service man and has been exposed to many diverse cultures so for him to go a round of playing the dozens wasn't a big deal to him.

The one thing that hindered Willie was that he is a diabetic, and he wasn't able to do certain things because of his diabetes. After the volunteers would leave, Willie would do the majority of the laundry while Will would do the majority of the paperwork in the office. When the shelter guest would volunteer, they would do more than their equal share of the work without the pay, or the benefit of sleeping an extra few minutes later in the morning. I lost the privilege of working in the evenings assisting the shelter aides with the laundry, which I never really considered it a privilege, because I could enter into the facility early to take a shower and make my cot up before the majority of the other residents who stayed there. That was the pro of working in the laundry room in the evening. The con was that the shelter would have volunteers from various churches, civic groups and community based organizations. They would come there to serve food and assist the shelter aides with the laundry service. The volunteers would come there every night and would stay there most of the evening until about 9:00 p.m. After that time, the shelter aides would be responsible for completing the clothes being washed and dried before the morning. The aides would solicit the help of the shelter guest who were on a list that they could have them assist in the completion of the laundry service. When I was assisting the shelter aides, I would go in at five fifteen in the evening and would help them until midnight if I wanted to. The con of doing the laundry service was that if you were working in the laundry room, you couldn't get to sleep a little later because of the help that you gave the shelter aides. Just like any other guest at the shelter, you would be required to get up when the first shift of shelter aides would tell you to do so at five twenty in the morning. So not doing the laundry wasn't a big lost to me either. No, I wasn't able to gain an early entry into the shelter and catch a shower before the majority of the guest, but I was able to come into the facility for the evening and I could to go to bed before nine in the evening if I wanted to.

Before I went to my newly assigned bed, I entered from the screening area where all the residents are scanned down with a wand to help detect dangerous objects from being smuggled in, and another device that the residents had to breath into detect for alcohol consumption. There were a pamphlet taped to the glass showing the plans for what appeared to be a blueprint a new shelter facility. The biggest irony of when I arrived back for my first night at the shelter, the director David was conducting his monthly shelter meeting. It would just happened that I was returning on the first Thursday during the month of May. I hated having to sit to listen to the broken promises of the administration, of plans that would be implemented but always fell short, and of the rules that were always changed like child changes the rules of a game being played. The thing that David and others in the administration did not realize was that this wasn't a game, and that they were dealing with the welfare of other people's lives. Whether or not they would like to admit it, the administration and board members look at the number of guests for the sole purpose as a way of finding the loopholes in the tax laws as a source of fattening up their own pocket under the pretense of doing missionary work for local faith-based community of Salisbury and Rowan counties.

After dinner and shortly after the volunteers from the local churches have left for the evening, David would ask that all the men and women who stayed at the shelter to assemble in the dining area for the shelter meeting. The only major complaint that David had about the residents was that they were putting in more than the required amount of clothes in their laundry, but the majority of the meeting didn't talk too much about any of the old rules that may have needed to be amended. David announced that the board of directors have approved the plans to build a new shelter. He told us that the board had purchased up to eighty percent of the land that encompassed the square block that is on East Liberty, North Long, East Council, and North Shaver streets. There weren't very many residential properties in that area, and it was only across the street that most of it was a grove of pecan trees from where the current shelter and crisis network is.

During the meeting David was trying to put the emphasis on what were the plans for the new facility. David informed the residents that the new facility would have more room to house more people who were in need of receiving the temporary housing assistance. He elaborated that the facility would also be able to accommodate the residents so that they wouldn't have to leave during the days when inclement weather happened. At the current facility, the residents were required to get out of the sleeping quarters by eight o'clock in the morning, because that was the same area shared for the noon-day soup kitchen and the dining area in the evening for the shelter quest. The new shelter would have an area where the residents could stay and not be required to leave in the case of inclimate weather. Not only would the residents of the shelter would be moving there, but the administrative offices and the crisis assistance network were to be housed at the new facility. At the old shelter would remain the facility for the food pantry, the noon-day soup kitchen, and the clothing donation and distribution center would be housed in the old building.

David informed the guest during the meeting that there would be visitors coming into the facility to examine the current structure and the system on how it's being ran. He let us know that they would possibly come to inspect and ask questions of the guests who stayed there. He also proposed that the administration would take several guest out to have dinner for an inquisition about the shelter's current state, and what was it that the administration could do to help make it a better place for the people who lived there. The moment that he opened his mouth with that last statement, I knew that event of taking out a selected few residents wasn't going to happen. I wanted to believe that there was an ounce of compassion that the administration had for people who were less fortunate than themselves, but I know that deep in my own conscience that they didn't have it in them to follow through on what he just said. Only time will tell if he ever does bring to the table what he said he was going to do.

A few days after the announcement of the new shelter, several people toured the facility when the majority of the guests were there having dinner. Naturally David was the brown noser giving them the tour while Kyna made it a point not to be close to the shelter population. Most of the people who were given the tour were men and a few women were also present. The visitors toured the dining facility and the sleeping quarters of both the men's and women's area of the shelter. Few of the visitor who asked the guest some questions about the shelter itself, and one of the women saw that a shelter resident had taken a pair of blue jeans and was folding them so that they could have a crease in them, put the jeans in between the cot and the mat that went on top of it. She noticed this and got the attention of another visitor who was evaluating the place and showed him another person who was doing the same thing and told him, "This is how they press off their clothes." When I heard that I felt like a caged animal in a zoo being put on display for the humans to critique the behavior of the animals that they came to view. This had to be one of the low points of my stay at the shelter.

There was a written rule that the residents at the shelter could not speak anything negative to the volunteers who came to work at the shelter. After all, they were the people who donated their time, money, and efforts to support the shelter and the residents. Some of the religious groups who would come to volunteer their time were condescending to the residents. This one group in particular was an example of being very narrow-minded when it came to the residents. I can't recall what religious denomination they were, but the women in this church dressed like Mormon women. The majority of them had long hair that were covered under hair scarves and wore long dresses. There were usually more of the women who would be there than the men who were with them. They would serve the dinner, and they would also bring an ensemble of singers with guitars and electric piano performing hymns and giving testimonies during the dinner.

During one of their visits, I noticed that they had a former resident of the shelter who joined their church. Amy was a woman who stayed in the shelter with her newborn child. One time when the weather was hot, she left the care of her child with another resident who didn't know how to care for the infant. While in the care of the person that she left her child with, the infant suffered a severe sunburn so bad that they had to admit the child into the hospital for a couple of days. After several months, the child was taken out of her custody, and one of the church members of the group who looked like Mormons received custody. A couple of months after Amy lost her child, she became a member of the church and came back with them when they were to serve the dinner for the shelter guests. While she was serving the dinner and during the time they were singing their hymns, the leader of the chorus from the church asked Amy to give her testimony of how God is working in her life. She gave a very moving story of how she moved off of drugs, and how God had guided her to join the church reuniting her to see her child on a constant basis.

The next time when this same church came back to serve dinner and fellowship with the shelter residents, I noticed that Amy wasn't with them. I thought that maybe she wasn't feeling good and just didn't come. I never gave it a second thought until the leader of the chorus stated in front of all the shelter guests that Amy chose to leave that church. He said that she found the ways of the world more appealing than what the church and God can do for her. Personally, I thought that what he said was uncalled for. If the church had an issue with Amy, then they should've consulted Amy about the issue. I didn't like the fact that they made an issue disclosing her information to the public. Another incident happened when they were giving their testimony during the fellowship at the dinner hour. They had one of the younger member of their chorus trying to do his best to give his testimony. When he delivered it, he made the mistake of calling the residents of the shelter "these people." Many of the residents, including myself, took offense to that term. The people who reside at the shelter had a hard enough time dealing with the everyday experience of living in this town. Unless we had a place of employment, the options of having a place to go to for leisure are minimal. When he called the residents "these people," it was an example of what he was conditioned to think of the residents. These people were normally your substance abusers, prostitutes, delinquents, street hustlers, and other low-life forms that weren't very complimentary to an ultra-conservative society that Rowan County and Salisbury is ready to accept let alone give any assistance to get off the street. When that happened, I decided that when this particular church was serving, I would not indulge in their food or their fellowship.

While all this was happening at the shelter, I knew that I needed to get myself focused on trying to resume the show that I started working on with the Down Home Players. When I was in the psyche ward, the only people who I kept in contact outside of my family members were Linda and Dee from the show. When I got out they were the first two people who I contacted about resuming the show. I returned from the hospital in early May, my original plans for trying to make the performance happen in July had to be pushed back. I knew that I wouldn't have enough time to try to find any sponsors who would want to invest in the project with that short of time.

All three of us met at our usual place in the study room at the library. We knew that we needed to come up with some capital because the grants that were applied for were turned down. We found out that many of the foundations that we've applied for grants were not very willing to give their money to new and unknown agencies that don't have a track record of having previous experience of receiving grant money. One of the actors who I've worked with previously that performed with me at the Piedmont Players Theatre Malcolm told me about trying to see about soliciting the funds from the social media fundraising website Kickstarter. He didn't have to twist my arm to try to sell me on using the website as another tool to acquire money for the production. What was still as happening is that we're in the process of restructuring the creative team. Linda was the main consultant since she was the co-author of the play. Dee was still in charge of marketing since she had the business connections with quite a few people in the African American community in this town and I bought Malcolm on board because he showed that he was an excellent visual artist that was truly the best for this area.

The first order of business was to go out to recruit some businesses and individual who would be interested invested in sponsoring the play. Everyone in the creative team was going to attempt to try to find an individual business who would possibly be interested coming on board to sponsor the show. The next thing that we needed to do was to secure a venue to host where the Down Home Players would be performing the play. Everything would have to change from the original venue. We would be moving from an open outdoor venue that was acceptable to the public where we would have to pass around the hat for donations, to and enclosed indoor theatre where we could charge at the door to make some profit. The one place that came to mind was an intimate theatre setting that wasn't too far from the shelter and in the art's district. It was a nice place that the Lee Street Theatre company used called the Black Box Theatre. I asked Justin from Lee Street Theatre about it, and he directed me to meet with the manager Brian. I made an appointment to meet with Brian and he set the time so that we could take a tour of the facility. I notified the members of the creative team that I made the appointment to meet with Brian so that we could take a look at the venue and find out about the availability of dates and cost. Malcolm couldn't be there because he wasn't off from work and couldn't get back into town from Charlotte by three thirty that afternoon. It was up to Linda, Dee, and myself to meet with the gentleman to get the specific.

Dee and I were the first to arrive at the location. Brian gave us a tour of the theatre as he showed us the stage door entrance, dressing rooms, lighting, sound equipment, and everything that's included in renting the property for nice four-show run in three nights. There were several positive things looking at performing at the Black Box Theatre. The best part about it was to do this in an enclosed environment opposed to doing it outside and we would save beaucoup dollars on the insurance policy alone. If we were to spend the amount of money that we were quoted to do the performance at Eastern Gateway Park that would've cover the performance for one night. If we paid the same money to do it on the discounted days, we could've five shows in four nights. Linda arrived late but was able to take the tour when she arrived, and we were giving the prices for the days that we wanted it for. Looking to do the performance at the Black Box would have allowed us get the word out that there was going to be a new independent production company and build credibility by having a venue with the stage amenities that other local performing arts companies have.

Phase three of getting the word out was to get our Internet fundraising campaign up and running on the Kickstarter website.

When Malcolm told me about trying to do the Kickstarter Internet fundraiser program, I knew that I had to find a source of getting money to put on the show. He told me that it was a way of receiving donations by posting your project online, and getting the donors from around the country to see what your project was online. Once you posted the site, you give the donors and incentive to make their contribution. The donors could give as little as a dollar and you can set the limits as to how much more that you can receive from the donors. Doing this was a good idea and a way to let the people know what was happening with the play. I had drafted a letter and asked the creative team to send it to everyone they had in their email contacts, and that they shouldn't leave anyone in those contacts out.

The letter read:

> Hello, friends of the performing arts. I have launched my online fundraising program with the assistance of Amazon.com. This campaign will run from now until July 30, 2013. I have over fourteen hundred Facebook friends who I am requesting your assistance so that I can put on a production of the newest stage play from Updaway Productions. The goal of this production is to develop cultural diversity outreach opportunities, to promote community outreach, and to facilitate an interchange of cultural ideas/ experiences and acknowledge the social issues of the African-American and minority communities. The writer's theme challenges their audience to leave the theatre with a renewed sense of dignity. The subject matter of "*The Verdict: The Beginning or The End?*" engages and expands the knowledge of African American social consciousness and the history of the culture. If I was able to receive a $1.50 from each of my friends, then the production would go off without a hitch. Please go to the link view the video and contribute a donation if you wouldn't mind. Donations start

as low as a dollar, and you may contribute if you're able to do so up to five hundred dollars. Please go to the web link listed below and you will see a green sign that says "Back This Project." Click on it and follow the instructions for payment. If you are unable to contribute a financial contribution, then I ask that you please repost the link listed below at the bottom to your pages so that others who are able to assist have the opportunity to do so. Thank you all for taking the time to read my plea, and for showing me the love. Sincerely,

Leroy F. Bennett.

I did every contact out of all the e-mail address websites and made it a point of contacting every one of them. Malcolm had also made it a point of me networking with an expert who has an Internet radio program promoting businesses who were doing project using the Kickstarter system. Abdullah was the brother's name who had he Internet radio show, and he also consulted people who were submitting their projects. I called Abdullah and he guided me on the do and don'ts to make this a very attractive package by having graphics and a video included in the presentation.

The final phase of the project was to make the public of Salisbury and Rowan County knowledgeable of the show that we wanted to do. Malcolm and Dee were the main people from the creative team that took control of this aspect of it. Malcolm was added onto the team because he was a computer wizard creating graphic design, and knew what graphics would catch the attention of the public. I remembered when I was doing *Sign of the Times*, and I was looking for an actor to take the lead male role, I approached him to do it. He wasn't able to do it, because he had previous commitments. He and I are members of the same church. One day, after service, he inquired to me to see if I was doing another stage project. I told him about *The Verdict*, and originally I had my cast in place. He took me out to eat an early Sunday dinner after church services were out. I agreed, and we rendezvous about an hour later in front of my office away from an office the library.

An hour later, we met at the library and he asked me where I would like to go for dinner. Since he was treating, I wasn't going to ask him to put on the Ritz. I was fine by stopping into McDonald's or Burger King, because I knew that those places had Wi-Fi services for us to use our laptops. Malcolm suggested that we eat at a real restaurant with great food. Originally he wanted to eat at the soul food café in town called Grits, but they had a Sunday buffet that kept the place crowded. So he settled to going to the Thai restaurant called Bangkok Downtown. Malcolm showed me things for advertising the show that would've been good enough for the executives on Madison Avenue in New York if he were to take his graphic artist skills there.

Originally, I was more impressed with his ability to make attractive works of art than I was his acting, but I knew that Malcolm was capable of giving a solid performance and delivering the lines from the script. Apprehensive was I about adding Malcolm as part of the cast initially because I remembered that he wasn't very disciplined when it came to committing his lines to memory. Working with him on stage was a pleasure because he caught onto the blocking quickly, but when it came to remembering his lines, he had given me the impression that he could fake it until he got it. That was one of my biggest taboos to work with an actor who drags on a scene because they don't know their lines. When he accepted the role of the lead male in this production I told him like I did the rest of the cast of what I expected of him. In order to have a truly successful stage production, you need to get the cast off the script as soon as possible. That was my biggest mistake that I did when the Down Home Players were doing *Sign of the Times*. I didn't want to have history repeat itself. Going from the script is fine when you do it during rehearsal in the early stages. Getting off it shows your discipline to remember the lines and makes it easier for the director to work on the delivery of the lines, blocking, and the motivation of the actors. It's not about having practice to make it perfect, but having a perfect practice to make for a perfect performance. I expect that from myself, the cast and crew, but more importantly, the paying audience expects to get a perfect performance if they're handing over their hard earned money.

All the phases getting the play together were in place, but opening up the account for Kickstarter was my most difficult drawback that I had to overcome. I had to wait until late in the month of June before I was able to open up a checking account so that I could subsequently open the Kickstarter account. Kickstarter was set up by Amazon.com and went through the PayPal system. Eventually we were able to run the Kickstarter campaign for only a thirty days instead of the original forty-five–day period we intended on doing.

Now there is a serious urgency to find one business that would be willing to be a sponsor. One person who came to mind was the owner of the Hairston Funeral Home, Tommy Hairston. I had the pleasure of meeting with Mr. Hairston when my church was holding a dinner theatre after a Sunday service. One of the members who knew that I was about to launch a new play directed me to see him about sponsoring our play, *The Verdict*. At the end of the program, I introduced myself to him and asked him if I could get a business card to make an appointment to meet with him. Tommy agreed, gave me a card, and told me to call to make an appointment. I saw Dee the next day at the career center and told her of my encounter with Mr. Hairston. Like many the people in a small town she grew up in, Dee knew him, and she was our best angle in trying to get him to commit to sponsoring the performance.

There were others who we encountered including the local barber shops, beauty and barber supply stores, restaurants, and other businesses that could be potential sponsors that wouldn't commit. We attempted to use any and all of our resources that were available. One example of utilizing the resources that didn't require any out-of-pocket expense was to create a flyer to pass out at a local event when we knew that there would be a lot of people around. The creative team got together several days before the original date of when we were supposed to do the production in the park. We let the public know that there was going to be a new production company that was going to put on a show. Dee, Malcolm, and myself decided to meet at McDonald's to become creative in producing a flyer in the shape of what appeared to be a courthouse. Linda was informed about what we were doing, but she had another commitment and was not able to attend. What was produced was a clever marketing tool that sprung up interest by the people. Collectively, we made a figure of courthouse with the name of the play *The Verdict*, along with the venue and show dates on the flyer.

This was executed on the town's friday night out that we completed it and started passing out the flyers to the public. In the process of passing out the flyers Malcolm ran into an artist who had a gallery in the downtown area that wanted to know more about Updaway Productions. Whitney Peckham, along with her husband, Syed, were the owners of the East Square Artworks Gallery downtown in Salisbury, and she gave Malcolm her number for him to have me call her. Whitney and I got in touch a few days later and met over at her gallery. She expressed an interest not in becoming a paying sponsor, but one who was willing to allow Updaway Productions to utilize the space in the gallery for rehearsals and performances. In return she didn't ask for a percentage of the gate, but wanted the space to be used since she and her husband were going to leave town for an extended period of time. It was a win-win situation for the both of us. It allowed Updaway Productions to gain a venue, and it gave the East Square Artworks Gallery free advertisement and exposure. I was thinking finally this was the thing that I've been wanting to do for the longest. I was receiving my opportunity to have a venue at my disposal, but there were a few problems that I would have to overcome. There wasn't a central air system there and I would've had to use a heavy-duty fan in order to cool down the facility. This production was going to take place in August, and being inside with the fans blowing would've made it hard for the audience to hear the actors without a wireless sound system. There was more than adequate room to do the performance, but it would've required extensive work to build a stage and set. The last objective would have been required was having a dressing area for the women to be separate from the men. It was still a good thing, because if all the efforts to do it at the Black Box Theatre failed, then the play could ultimately be performed at the gallery. I told Whitney that I loved the idea of doing the production there, and I told her the reasons why we wouldn't be able to do it there. Together we mutually agreed that it would be a great place for us to do the rehearsals, and during the month of August, Updaway Productions would patronize the establishment for the last two weeks prior to the premiere of the show.

The kickstarter campaign was the priority that we needed to address as soon as possible. There was an urgency to get that out, because of the timetable that was set for the program. Due to the fact that I had to open up a checking account and didn't have the money to do so immediately, that reduced the amount of time we had to run the online donation campaign. All the paperwork to get approved by Amazon.com to run the campaign was complete, but the main selling point was to produce a video for the campaign.

It was one of the few times that we got all the members of the creative team together to brainstorm how the presentation of the video was going to be done. Everyone was there, and for the first time, everyone was putting out their input collectively. I recruited a woman who stayed at the shelter by the name of Crystal to do the videotape and editing the video for the submittal of the online campaign. Linda, Dee, Malcolm, Crystal, and myself were also there. We all met in one of the largest meeting room at the library and stayed there over the two hours at we were allotted. The people who were scheduled to have the room for the next two hours never came so this was a blessing. By the end of this meeting, we all agreed that Linda and I would be the representatives to do the video promoting the project. One segment of the video was to have me going to the staging area of the Stanback Auditorium in the library to promote the play while Linda was to use the old Rowan County Courthouse that is now the county museum. We were all on the same accord and had scheduled to do it within the next couple of days because of the work schedule of Linda. I felt stressed that time to produce the video was of the essence, because of our window to get the online donation campaign running. When the time came to work on the video, Linda wasn't around and an unforeseen incident arose. I felt that it was in the best interest to forego her part of the video and do it without her.

Crystal and I were in the library at the time when I decided to proceed with the production of the video. All the previous plans that I made were scrapped. Linda wasn't available, and time was starting to go against us. I noticed that one of the meeting rooms that I used had a picture of the old Rowan County Courthouse. Crystal and I both thought that it would make for an appropriate backdrop, because of the fact that the title of the play is *The Verdict*, and it does deal with a fictitious trial. By the time that we did six takes, I didn't feel great about the job that I did on the video, but it was a video that was completed from the filming point of view. In order to increase the interest of the play, I had given Crystal some videos of the rehearsal that I recorded. I would record the rehearsals after I saw Dee do it one day. I would later do it as a way of critiquing the actors on their performance during the rehearsal. Once they could see it, then they can make the necessary adjustment for the next rehearsal, and by showtime, it would allow them to a near flawless presentation by showtime.

It took Crystal another couple of days to edit the video for the presentation before we could post it on the Kickstarter website. Once it was completed, I immediately posted it and shared it with all of the cast and crew members so that they could do the same on their own social media pages. The online campaign that was supposed to run for a forty-five–day period was now only going to run for a twenty-eight instead of a thirty-day period. A day after it was posted, Linda was upset because she wasn't in the video. I had to explain the reasons for me not putting her into the video was due mainly to the fact that the time constraints of trying to get it posted to receive funds from donors. The need to get it posted along with the vital information for the Kickstarter campaign needed to be posted as soon as possible, and I attempted to reassure her that this would be better if we had this on the website for the purposes of making our production visible to the public. She accepted it, but never really bought into the video. You could see a change in her enthusiasm in doing the play, and there wasn't the drive she displayed from the earlier rehearsals.

It was she that asked me to produce and direct her production that she had written with a colleague of hers when she was living in New Jersey. I was grateful that she considered me to do the project for her, but it wouldn't have been my first choice as a project that I felt strong about doing. I took on this production because it was an original piece of work that I wanted to produce. Another reason I did it was because it had some good parts that would allow for some cultural diversity in the casting of this production. When Updaway Productions started, I wanted to produce shows that displayed and elaborated on the stories of African American life. These stories could be fictional or nonfictional, but the main emphasis on the stories had to have some social substance that would have the audiences leaving the auditorium talking about it as to say wow that was deep. The one flaw that I did see in this script was that it didn't have an antagonist, or an enemy combatant to the storyline. The timeline on it being written was a good one, and it made a lot of valid points. It didn't have enough of the hate, or disdain in this character for me.

One of the things that I try to do when I'm directing a project is to allow my actors to do some improvisational acting if I see that it fits the script and the scenes that we're doing. One day at rehearsal, one of the actresses, Mary Jane, brought to my attention that she wanted to try something different with the part that she was doing as a member of the jury. She wanted to portray herself as a Jewish woman who was impartial to the argument by the defense attorney who represented the positive aspect of the African Americans. The one thing that she brought to my attention was that the six-member panel who represented the jurors all had affirmative views that were in favor of the defense. There wasn't any members of the jury that appeared to have any objectionable arguments to the defense attorney, and all of them sided with the prosecuting attorney. I allowed her to bring something to the table so that I could view what she wanted to show me. She came with the perfect Jewish accent and a demeanor of a juror who didn't want to be on duty, but more partial to the prosecuting attorney's argument.

When we started to do the scene when the jury was deliberating, I told Mary and only her to go for it. I allowed her to improvise the scene, but instructed her to stay close to the script so that she wouldn't throw any of the other players off their cues. This would allow the others to come in to do their lines on cue. It was a somewhat awkward situation, because all of them knew when they were to come in to deliver their spiels. Mary Jane deviated just enough to give her character the appearance that she didn't want to be on jury duty, and that she didn't like the company of a majority African-American jury. There was a point in her dialogue of her character that she was talking about her late husband that didn't have any significance. At the end of rehearsing that scene, I told her that she would have to lose the husband in her dialogue, but outside of that she really nailed! It was so good that I had to do the task of assigning two other characters the duties of being partial to the prosecuting attorney's view as opposed to the views of the defense attorney.

It's still just a few weeks away before we're scheduled for the curtain to open for the production of *The Verdict*. We still didn't have any sponsors for the show and the Kickstarter campaign wasn't going the way that we hoped for. There were several efforts to contact Tommy Hairston to get him to commit. I was successful in contacting his wife on one occasion and delivered my sales pitch to her. She was open to the idea of listening to what I had to tell her. While I was talking to her, I attempted to find what I needed to do in order to find what would trigger her interest in sponsoring the show. I was able to find out that she was a graduate of Livingstone College, and that she was also from Paterson, New Jersey. I tried to use that angle to my advantage, by talking about the show that were put on at the Paper Mill Playhouse in Short Hills, New Jersey. Mrs. Hairston liked the idea of doing theatre here in Salisbury, but told me that it would have to be a decision that had to be done collectively with her husband. Weeks earlier, Mr. Hairston told me that he would view the information from the media package I left him and that he would have to discuss it with his wife. At this point I didn't know how to feel, but I knew that I gave a pretty good presentation. I let them know that they would have a full page ad on the playbill and that we would flood the social media websites mentioning that they were the sponsors of the show. Days later, I contacted Mr. Hairston again. At that time he told me that he wasn't able to sponsor the show.

Since living in Salisbury, disappointment has been one of my biggest comrade, but I was too determined to give up on this project.

I knew we had to get some business that would put their name out there to do the show. There was one other person who I talked to who told me that they would commit to sponsoring verbally. I went to the owner of the store who sold oils and incense earlier just before we began the online campaign. Rick was the owner of a shop called the Smell Factory. I met him when my cousin had her boutique next door to his shop. I left him a media package and he told me to get back to him, and I did. Shortly after being rejected by the Hairston Funeral Home, Rick made a donation to put his name on the inside of the playbill. It would be the only business from Salisbury or Rowan County that would go out of their way to do any kind of sponsorship for the production.

The online campaign wasn't working as well as we wanted it to. Updaway Productions had only received sixteen dollars and fifty cents toward the goal of fifteen hundred that we set for ourselves. We only had another nine days in order to meet our goal or make other arrangements to do the show at the East Square Artworks Gallery. My demeanor as a director had changed. I was being more meticulous to the detail of the actors, and I demanded that they get off their scripts. There were more supporting actors coming in and I was requesting that we became a more disciplined performing company. Unless it was something that was work related, I needed everyone to start being there on time, and to be prepared to perform their roles. We needed to go through the plays with all the characters in place so that we could suture the areas of the play that were weak. After weeks of rehearsing, I already knew what areas of the production were weak, because I was videotaping the performers as we were performing the acts and scenes.

The opening scene of the first act was the weakest. The sharpest actors in that first act where the prosecutor and the bailiff. The judge and the defense attorney were the weakest. I had gotten to the point that I told Malcolm who portrayed the defense attorney that if he didn't commit his lines to memory, I was going to replace him with myself. The witness for the defense wasn't as strong as I had needed her to be, but she made her character more believable the more we rehearsed the scene. The second act when the jurors were deliberating was, without a doubt, the strongest. All the jurors knew their lines and their blocking assignments. I had to do very little with them outside of the motivation to give them the impression of being a hung jury. The closing scene was almost as strong. It would've been as strong or stronger if the writer Linda didn't add a four-year-old child into the mix of having the closing line in the production. She was a cute little four-year-old, but she didn't have any experience. There were times in the rehearsal that she wouldn't say her line on cue, and there were too few times that she would. Giving the audience who had just viewed the play that wow factor of man that was a good production, I really want to see that play again. Most of the times this child was shy and introverted and wouldn't say the line at all. I gained a new respect for W.C. Fields who didn't like to work with children and animal acts. Now I knew why he felt that way. Those kinds of acts can either upstage or upset you as a director.

With less than a week to go on our online fundraising campaign, it appeared that I was going to have to make the arrangements to contact Whitney to use the art gallery as the venue. My normal routine in the mornings was to focus on working as a producer for the play. I would go into the library and check my emails, update the websites that I created for the production, edit any script revisions that needed to be done, review the contributions that we may have received in Kickstarter, and check my Facebook page. By the time I finished doing all of the previously mentioned things when I got to my Facebook page, I received a tagged message from the writer, Linda. She was informing me that she has the publishing and copyrights of the play and that she wasn't pleased with the way that things were going. Linda was pulling out of doing the play. This was a major surprise to me, but I should have expected to see this coming. She went on to her Facebook page telling everyone that she knew that she didn't feel what I was doing as a producer and director was right.

This was the message she posted to on her Facebook page:

> Ummmm, What's on my mind? Well a play I wrote/ Co-wrote in 1994 (*The Verdict, the beginning or the end.* stored safely away in my file cabinet for 19 years is about to go back into my

archives. I don't play games and I don't chase any-body around, I don't have to. Due to unprofessionalism I have decided after much thought and prayer to remove my play from Leroy F Bennett & Updaway Productions also Ainavad Jhett and Dee, only because she is a Board member and have a vested interest in updaway productions, it is my desire to abandon this project, I have no hard feelings, I just don't feel this company holds my best interest at heart, I don't like not being informed of changes in cast, changes in performance dates and financial reports, also unreturned telephone calls. As a member of the "Board" & writer of *the verdict*, I was entitled to all information regarding my project, after careful consideration and consultation with my attorney, I hereby dissolve this collaboration and any ties to Updaway productions/ Ainavad Jhett in connection to *"THE VERDICT* "the beginning or the end.* To the actors, I enjoyed working with you, you are a special and very talented bunch of people and I will miss you, if you need to speak with me inbox me (actors & actresses, Dee) As per the confidentiality agreement signed by Leroy F Bennett & Updaway productions & Ainavad Jhett AKA Dee, and myself. *The Verdict* and no part or similarity can be used in any production or reproduction of "The *Verdict"* the beginning or the end.* Just as a reminder. And as a result of this action, It is with great regret that I must also severe production ties with my buddy Dee, an outstanding woman, someone I will always respect. Thanks for who you truly are. Kickstarter.com should be shut down immediately and no funds pass this point shall be collected on behalf of *"THE VERDICT"* *the beginning or the end."*

Needless to say, when I kept seeing all of the replies that she was getting, I stopped following the post. Personally, she could have sent me an inbox message to display her professionalism, but the way of putting it out there publicly was so immature, but that was her choice. I knew that I had to bounce back from this experience, but the question for me was how was I going to do it this time? At this time, it was definitely one of the lowest point of my decision of moving to North Carolina. Efforts were made to hype up this production by making interviews on the Internet radio markets, posting this event on Facebook, Twitter, and networking throughout Rowan County. For once since I've been living in Salisbury, I felt as if I was a bust. I decided that I wasn't going to do any theatre for the rest of the year. I wasn't going to take a look at any material, and I was going to isolate myself away from the people who come at me with the pretense of wanting to help me when in turn they were using me for their own personal gain.

When this incident happened, I became withdrawn again, but I started to close my circle of people who I associated with in Salisbury. The one person who I stayed in contact with during this period was Dee. It was as much a shock to her as it was to me. It hurt her, because it was under her non-profit organization that the production of this play was going to be performed. Dee and her non-profit were still in my corner, and for that I truly know that I had a friend who has stayed with me during the best of time as well as the worst of them. What this experience was was a teaching instrument. Updaway Productions and the writer each had our own contracts that were signed, but I didn't want to take the opportunity to put out a lawsuit. The main reason was that I didn't have the financial backing to do so. My father always told me that experience is the best teacher. This was a lesson that I had to learn from the school of hard knocks. It reminded me of a line from the play in *Dreamgirls*, when the character of Curtis Taylor tells the girls that "showbiz is rough biz." I knew that sooner or later, I will get back into performing, directing, or producing another play. I was going to have to let some of the hype machine that I built up die down before I would try my hand at another production.

This was the time for me to stand still, weigh out my options, and think about beginning a new plan of execution to attempt to resume a life that is considered to be normal. There wasn't time to dwell on what happened that was negative, but to use the accomplishments of what good came out of this experience to use as a springboard for the next project. It wasn't time to try to jump into something new as far as putting on or being in a stage production. It was time for me to review where the mistakes were made and to rejoice in the achievements that were accomplished. The mistakes that I made was that I needed to have total autonomy of the production. The control for the order of the production should be my top priority and to work with a smaller cast especially when they had little to no experience being on stage. The achievements of finding a new network of people who were willing to let me do a production at a venue was a key part of business, and personal development at this time. Knowing that I still had someone who was with me from the first production that Updaway did and stuck by me through the worst of time was the other blessing that I received.

Living in Salisbury was starting to give me the impression that I was living in a black hole like the ones that are in outer space. A black hole has a gravitational pull that is so dense that nothing can escape it, not even light. I often think and wonder sometimes if I'll ever get out of this place. Will I be stuck in this twilight zone forever? All that I know is that I'll have to depend on the new network of contacts that I was able to acquire when I was shopping the play around. My true belief is that I felt that I was on the verge of a breakthrough and that giving up wasn't an option that will be too easy. There were still many people that want me to produce a show for them, after I told them that I wasn't going to be a part of the play called *The Verdict*. That was very encouraging. The one thing that I know is that God has a bigger plan in mind for me, and I had to keep the belief that he's working harder than me. That I had to wait on him. I realized that the word "wait" has a twofold definition to it also. The first meaning is to serve the Lord, and the other is to remain patient. I've been patient, and now it's time to do his will, not mine!

CHAPTER 11

Renovations At the Inn

Now there weren't any shows for me to look forward to audition for, and the only thing left for me to do was to find a way to get out of this hellhole that the residents called the Hotel California. The shelter director David was following the direction that the board member of Rowan Helping Ministries on getting things together for the new shelter. When the board was able to come up with the funds to get the groundbreaking done, they gave David the autonomy to implement the rules they already had in place and the ability to make up some new ones on the fly as he felt necessary. Still the situation hasn't improved for me personally, and they seem to start to get on the decline at the shelter. David was very adamant about enforcing the policy of people who were couples, either married or not, when it came down to showing personal display of affection. The irony about that was he didn't want the guests to display their affection on the grounds of the shelter, but when there were a lesbian couple who needed to stay there, they were allowed to sleep in the area of the facility that was designated for families. One such couple were in fact a family where one of the two females had her children with her when they all were admitted into the shelter. Another lesbian couple didn't have the family unit, but the case managers allowed them to sleep in the area that was designated for the family also.

The administration was always looking to keep the facility full. They would concentrate on keeping the place stocked with veterans from the service. When they came in, the shelter would receive a subsidy from the Veteran Administration. Placing them into the facility was a good business practice, because it paid for some of the overhead. Most of the veterans who were admitted were applying to receive their disability, and some were already eligible, but others were waiting to receive some housing assistance from the VA. There were others who were admitted there with some serious mental handicaps that could be questioned as to why the administration would allow them entrance into the shelter.

There were several incidents where veteran were included into the general population with the regular shelter residents. Sometimes putting the lives of the guests in Jeopardy. For instance, there was one guy who was a veteran trying to get his disability. He was very much a loner and rarely spoke to others at the shelter. I can't recall his name, but I can remember some of the things that he would do. He stayed in with the general population for about a month and a half. He would walk down the street to the store and would shadow box for a distance, and other times he would sit on a bench outside of the building talking to himself. After being in the shelter for the time that he was, an opening became available in the Eagle's Nest housing for a veteran to move in. He moved into his new dwelling, but that became short lived. David would have the caseworkers and the shelter aide staff do periodical checks of the people who resided in the Eagle's Nest. About two weeks after he was admitted into his place, the shelter aides were doing their bi-weekly room checks. When they went into the room of this vet, they found that he was gone from the facility and had left a pot of water boiling on the eye of the burner and a can of lye opened next to the boiling pot. When they saw that they immediately packed his possessions and brought him back into the general population with the rest of the shelter guests. He would stay at the shelter until they were able to get him admitted into the mental ward of the VA. While he was at the shelter, he had a problem taking his shower before coming into the dining area. He was physically able to take his shower, but didn't want to do it. One time just before he was admitted into the mental ward of the VA, he went to take a shower. Now the showers in the shelter were open without any dividers between the showerheads. They're set up like the showers that you take at the YMCA so privacy was nonexistent. One day this guy got into the shower and brought a bottle of hot sauce, a can of dog food, and potato chips and started to eat them in the nude. When this occurrence happened, it sent shock waves throughout the male population of the shelter, and many of the guys demanded that the administration try to place him in another facility immediately. One reason was because the guest didn't know what this man was capable of doing. The possibility of this man going off was high, and the majority of the people were concerned for their safety when it involved being around this guy.

This was one of the few times that the administration of the shelter had respected the wishes of the residents who lived there. This wasn't always the case when the residents wanted to try to get changes made. While getting ready for the new shelter still about a year away from opening its doors, the administration made changes of their own.

Changes were being rumored on what the criteria for entrance into the new facility, and they're going to start implementing these changes immediately at the old facility. There was a new policy for residents of the shelter. They would now have to show their shelter guest pass every evening in order to gain entrance into the shelter. Discontinued was the policy of showing your pass once a week, and if you were on the grounds of the shelter and crisis center after five in the evenings, you needed to have the pass to be there or you were considered to be trespassing. David was given the authority to notify the Salisbury Police Department to have anyone that doesn't have a guest pass to have them removed from the premises or arrested if they resisted. This was implemented for the interest of public safety for the shelter guest.

That wasn't always the case. One of my biggest concerns when I first moved into the shelter was how careful would the administrators screened the people who came in there for assistance in their living arrangements. I do not recall having to go through any kind of extensive background screening process, or I would have to go through a waiting period before I was able to gain entrance to accommodate myself as a guest there. This was a concern of mine, because some of the women who had to stay there have children, and for my own personal safety was a major concern. Often I thought what it would've been like if I had my own granddaughter staying there with me if I had custody of her. I wouldn't want her, or any child for this matter to ever have to experience the life of living in a shelter. My concerns became valid when a resident who didn't associate himself with anyone there came to stay for a brief period. He was a white male that didn't gravitate towards anyone, and rarely spoke. He didn't smoke cigarettes, and when the staff dismissed the guests that lived there in the mornings for the day, he wasn't seen around town. He would come in during the evenings most of the time when the majority of the residents had their dinner and it was close to the time for lights out, but still he was obedient to the rules that were mandated by the administration.

One early morning in July, I was given the task of mopping the kitchen area. When I was finished, I needed to take the dirty water outside to dump it. I didn't mind doing that, because it allowed me to catch a couple of cigarettes before I had to get my possessions that I need to take with me for the rest of the day. Once being able to get outside in the early morning, it gives one a brief moment to feel as if they've been released from the zoo inside the walls of the building. After doing that I was headed back inside to get my things before leaving the shelter for the day. Before I returned inside the building, there were several cars that sped into the parking lot they had their lights flashing. Undercover officers circled around this unassuming white man who pretty much disassociated himself with all the residents who stayed there. The law enforcement officers got out of their vehicles with their handguns drawn upon him. They instructed the man to drop to his knees with his hands on his head. He obeyed their directions, and several of the officers came to him and cuffed him. There weren't any children outside in the area thank God, but there was a good many people from the shelter, and others who like to arrive at the crisis assistance network before the doors opened who were there to witness the events that took place.

It wasn't until the next day that the residents and other witnesses were able to find out about the events that took place in the parking lot. It was reported in the *Salisbury Post* that the person who they took away is Waylon Vernon Russell who came to the shelter. He was a fugitive on the run that was accused of murdering his father that occurred eleven years earlier in Georgia. He's accused in the violent murder of Ronald Wilbur Russell on October 26, 2002. Waylon Russell allegedly stabbed Ronald Russell in the neck and then set him on fire, a U.S. Marshals Service news release said. He was arrested at the request of the U.S. Marshals Southeast Regional Fugitive Task Force. A detective supervisor with the Georgia Bureau of Investigation said Ronald Russell was Waylon Russell's father. Ronald Russell's body was found on the bank of the Satilla River in Wayne County and had been unidentified until recently. He was identified earlier this month through DNA comparison conducted by the Georgia Bureau of Investigation, officials with the Wayne County Sheriff's Office said in a statement. Waylon Russell was charged with murder and additional charges were possible, the agency said. Waylon Russell was believed to be homeless, authorities said. Officials at Rowan Helping Ministries said they could not comment on whether Russell had been a client.

The DNA evidence that the authorities had was the nail in Waylon's coffin, and for a period of eleven years he was able to evade the police until he was caught in the parking lot on the premises of the Rowan Helping Ministries property. With about a quarter of the population who was staying at the shelter who witnessed the event. According to the NBC television affiliate in Charlotte they reported that the U.S. Marshals Office says a wanted violent criminal was arrested in Salisbury Friday morning. Around 9:30, the U.S. Marshals Joint Fugitive Task Force arrested forty-two-year-old Waylon Vernon Russell in the 300 block of East Liberty Street in Salisbury. Both of the news sources got the story wrong, because the events happened approximately between seven thirty and seven forty five that morning. It wasn't on the three hundred block of Liberty Street, because that's across the street from where the shelter is at the intersection where the new building is going up. This was done to save the face of the administration. Giving a denial or not disclosing the information was for the benefit of Rowan Helping Ministries. It didn't do anything for the benefit of the residents of the shelter, but it did put all of the residents of the shelter in danger of hurting someone there seriously.

Now since I didn't have a stage performance project to work on there had to be another way for me to focus on getting myself out of there. Most of the days I would revert to going back to the career center, but spent the majority of my days at the library. Many of the people that lived at the shelter would spend most of their days there, because it was local and convenient to get to. For many of them to go to the career center was a couple of miles away. Many days when I did go to the career center I would walk there. I would continuing to look at job opportunities, but now make my focus on positions that would be on securing a position anywhere but in the southern region of this country. This time I wasn't sending out applications to job opening anyplace south of Washington DC.

There were times when I was in the library I would do some research on a play that hasn't been exposed to the Piedmont region, but the only thing I was doing was looking for some way of getting out of this place that reminded me of a cross between Peyton Place and the Twilight Zone. Here in this town that has a population just under thirty-four thousand people many of them wanting to know just about every time that you blink your eyes. Now that's not everyone who lives in this town, but just the ones who you will allow to get close to you. If you happened to get yourself exposed in the local press it can be a blessing or a curse depending on how the story is printed. If the press wanted to defame your character, they could do it, with very little opposition to refute them. When those situations would happen many of the townspeople would approach you to question what the circumstances were. Others would talk negative about you when your back was turned to them. That was a learning experience for me, and from that point if the press would ask me about any comments I refused to give them one.

One incident that the press slept on broke shortly after the groundbreaking ceremony for the new shelter. The groundbreaking ceremony for the new shelter facility that took place it was a big deal. Taking place during the festivities was the town's who's who in every facet of business, non-profit agencies, city and county government officials. This was the most talked about event of the summer. The local paper gave it the top coverage, and it came with all the pomp and circumstance that would be normally associated with a major corporation moving into the town. Just days after the groundbreaking of the new shelter took place the *Salisbury Post* broke the story of a missing thirteen year old girl from the county. Missing teens isn't anything new, but the unusual thing about this story is the fact the she has been missing for almost two years before it was reported by her adoptive parents. Erica Parsons was a thirteen-year-old white girl that is fifteen years old when the story breaks.

She has been missing since November 19, 2011, and was reported missing July 30, 2013, by her older brother, James Parsons, 20. James Parsons told law enforcement his sister was either missing or he didn't know her current location, Capt. John Sifford said. Parsons said he'd moved out of his family's Miller Chapel Road home two months ago. Casey Parsons, the teen's mother, referred questions to attorney Carlyle Sherrill, of Salisbury. Sherrill said Casey and husband Sandy came to his office after they'd been questioned by law enforcement for two days. He said the couple felt intimidated by law enforcement and contacted him after their interviews. Sherrill said the Parsons couple had some indication that Erica, who they adopted as a baby, was in Asheville. He confirmed the Parsons do not have any relatives in Asheville, but he said the connection to Asheville was through the girl's birth mother.

After this story broke it was continuously in the local news. Television stations and newspapers from Charlotte and the Triad area of North Carolina flood the courthouse when members of the family were subpoenaed to appear in court. Between North Main and East Council streets you could see the media setting up to speak with the lawyers of the adoptive parents, and always doing their reports from in front of the court house. What concerned me most when this story broke was the fact that this was a child that's a native who resides in Rowan County that's been missing for the last couple of years. It wouldn't mean a thing to these authorities if I were to get into a confrontation with someone that I disagreed with, but if I were to suddenly become missing I perish the thought about it. An African American missing in Rowan County wouldn't make any news unless it was to get exposure in Charlotte or the Triad areas.

Shortly after this story reached the *Salisbury Post*, billboards with the picture of Erica Parsons were set up throughout the state. A month later in August the adoptive parents appeared on the *Dr. Phil* show. This included them being interviewed and submitted themselves to a polygraph test. A polygraph expert says Sandy Parsons, the adoptive father of missing teen Erica Parsons, was "strongly deceptive" to questions he asked the father during a taping of the *"Dr. Phil"* show which aired later that day. Sandy Parsons and his wife Casey taped the show along with their attorney Carlyle Sherrill last week in California. Casey Parsons reportedly did not take a lie detector test. The polygraph expert, Jack Trimarco, said he asked Sandy Parsons two questions and fully explained the questions. Trimarco told Dr. Phil he considered the father deceptive to both questions. Trimarco asked Sandy Parsons if he deliberately caused Erica's disappearance and if he had a plan to cause her disappearance.

By now it was the latter part of the summer. I knew that longer that I stay here the more that I put myself in the way of something dangerous happening. It appeared that as the summer months were winding down that more people in the community were coming to find refuge into residing at the shelter. With the recent developments concerning safety, there wasn't any other options to find contentment in trying to reside at the shelter. I needed to get out and I need to do it like yesterday.

The conditions at the current facility are deteriorating rapidly. There were two times that the residents had to be evacuated from there because the clothes dryer had caught on fire. The first time it happened was just before the residents were about to enter the shelter for the evening. When we entered into the shelter, we were instructed by the shelter aides that there wouldn't be any laundry service for the evening. Also instructed that we would need to hold on to our scrubs that we use as pajamas, because they didn't know just how long it would take for the administration to get the machine fixed or replaced. It took ten days that the residents had to make other arrangements to have their laundry services. What that did for me was to take a good portion of the money that I had to use the Laundromat down the street from the shelter. What the administration did was to get the dryer fixed, but the incident of it catching on fire occurred again in the evening after it was time for lights out a little after ten that night a month later. We were asked to get out of the place while we were in our scrubs. The good thing about it was that nobody was injured during the process, and that the weather was at a bearable climate outside of the shelter during that time of the evening.

The other conditions that were deteriorating at a rapid pace was the development of black mold was building up in the restroom facilities. You could see it develop on a daily basis if you had to use the men's restroom and showers. There was black mold that was building on the ceilings above the wash basins, on the wall and the showers. During the season changes, there were more cases of individuals who get sick displaying symptoms of coughing, wheezing, and other respiratory effects. When the residents who got sick to the point that they had chronic coughing spell sounding to the point I was wondering if they had whooping cough, I took notice and decided to record what was the public didn't have access to see. It's been document in the journal of *Environmental Health Perspectives* that evidence from epidemiologic studies and meta-analyses showed indoor dampness or mold to be associated consistently with increased asthma development and exacerbation, current and ever diagnosis of asthma, dyspnea, wheeze, cough, respiratory infections, bronchitis, allergic rhinitis, eczema, and upper respiratory tract symptoms. Associations were found in allergic and non-allergic individuals. Evidence strongly suggested causation of asthma exacerbation in children. Suggestive evidence was available for only a few specific measured microbiologic factors and was in part equivocal, suggesting both adverse and protective associations with health.

It was time to make an effort to let the people, churches, and other community based organizations know what their financial contributions weren't being used to assist the homeless population that they contributed to. What I did was to take the pictures of the facility with my camera. When I would come in at night everyone was ordered to give up their cellphones, but if you had your laptop or any other electronic devices, you could have them over at your bed area, but it was your own responsibility if anything was missing. I waited until the shelter aides call for lights out that evening at ten to go into the men's restroom area to get pictures of the mold on the ceiling, walls and in the shower area. There wasn't an operable exhaust fan that was working in the men's room. When the weather was hot outside and if some of the nastiest men who stayed in the shelter didn't clean up after themselves, it was unbearable to stay in the bathroom for any extended period of time. The restroom was damp, musty and the mold is building up. The smell of it was so pungent that the fumes would probably give you the impression that there was methane that accumulated from the lack of cleanliness and ventilation. This could've been one of the possible reasons for the buildup of the black mold there. I wasn't going to let this go undocumented, so I made sure to take still pictures and videotape a brief narrative of the facility.

The next evening I was able to solicit the help of a woman Jean, to do the same for the women's restroom facility. Their facility appeared to be worse off than the one of the men. The really sad part about that was is that the children who happened to stay in the shelter also had to use the showers on the women's side. I had my friend Jean to take still shots and a video of the conditions in the two restroom areas that the women and children use. What I saw was the same thing that I noticed in the men's room. They had mold that developed on the walls and the ceiling around the showers. One of the showers had shower curtains, and there was mold that had developed on the insides of the shower curtain. The other shower had a Plexiglass door that had soap scum and mold on the tile. This was especially unhealthy for the children who happen to stay there, because we had a couple them that did have mild to strong cases of asthma. Also stated in the journal article was evident dampness or mold had consistent positive associations with multiple allergic and respiratory effects. Thus, prevention and remediation of indoor dampness and mold are likely to reduce health risks.

The ceiling in the dining area had large water stains on it from where it appear that there was a water leaking into the area. There was one big water spot that was just over the area in the sleeping quarters where the men would sleep, and it cover an area large enough to affect two of the cots that were set up if it were to come down. There was a problem with a large amount of flies in the dining and kitchen areas during the warmer months of the year. When the volunteer would come in the evening to serve the residents their meals they were informed by the staff to remove the Plexiglass sneeze guards from the serving counter. This was a serious concern for me personally. I didn't like the fact that some of the residents would get in line and would cough or sneeze without covering their faces. The other factors that concerned me was when the sneeze guard that is set up to protect the food from incidents like that was removed when it came to serving the residents who lived at the shelter, but at lunchtime when the soup kitchen was open the sneeze guards up for the entire time of the volunteers serving lunch. The people who were serving the food didn't wear any hairnets or hats while they were serving, and they didn't have any latex or plastic gloves on their hands. So when it came down to the state mandated required health recommendations none of those procedures were followed at all. The administration did spend any of the money to see to it that the volunteer followed those rules.

My intent was to bring the practiced improprieties to the attention of the public, government authorities, and the press. The first thing that I did was to notify the Rowan County Health department. I called the county health department to let them know that there was some possible violations that were happening at the facility. They directed me to call the state office in Raleigh to report the happenings at Rowan Helping Ministries. When I called the state officials in Raleigh, they referred me to call back to the county office. I could see that this wasn't going anywhere, and there had to be something that could be done. They were putting me on a hamster wheel. I thought about doing the *Salisbury Post*, but after what they had done with the slanderous and defamatory allegations against myself and others that I knew, I thought better about it. That was nothing but a pipeline back to the administrators at the shelter.

The next thing that I thought of was to bring it into the television news media so that they could report on it. I made contact with the people at the ABC network affiliate in Charlotte to notify them. I've sent them a letter explaining about the situation. They looked at the letter and the videos I've sent to them, but weren't willing to send their whistle blowing news team to investigate since the shelter was in the process of building a new facility. I didn't feel bad about it them not doing anything, because I exhausted all the local and government resources that could to help bring the attention about the living conditions. When I did what I needed to do, then I didn't feel bad about the situation. I knew that this wasn't going to be a good fit for me staying in this facility.

Some other things that the administration had the staff and residents do was to sell the products that were being donated from some of the merchants for the shelter guests. The staff members had set up some tables in front of a vacant store on the corner of East Innes street and Old Concord road. This was done on a Saturday when the crisis center and the shelter were closed from the public. The administration would use this as an opportunity for a fundraising venture. What would transpire was the staff would set up some tables to put out some items that were donated to them by the local CVS pharmacy. Another staff member would bring out their enormous grill just like the ones that you would see at a football tailgating parties and cook hamburgers and hot dogs for sale along with non-alcoholic drinks. Some of the items would include toiletry products, soap, toothpaste, battery-powered toothbrushes, deodorant, mouthwash, and other products. They would also sell some of the electronic equipment, battery operated digital clocks, battery-operated toothbrushes, radios, foot massagers, headphones, disposable cameras, soap, colognes, body scents, and other items.

Whenever the shelter held those fundraising efforts, it was normally a successful function. The items that they had for sale would be purchased by the public, and the shelter would have anywhere from two thirds to three quarter of the merchandise items sold. I do believe that there was a need to do the fundraising, but why wasn't some of these goods offered to the residents who stayed at the shelter. Since I was a resident there, at no time was any of these items offered to the guest. The soap, deodorant, and toothpaste have been provided to the guest, but the battery operated clocks and radios weren't. The executive director, Kyna Foster, and David never disclosed to the residents about much anyway. By keeping a tight lip about the progress of the new shelter, they must have felt that the priority in the current place that the people are living in now takes a back seat to the new building that was being erected. This gives many of the residents who live at the current building the impression that Kyna supports the job that David is doing and there is the probability of someone in the administration that is misusing funds for the residents at the current facility.

Between August to November, nothing much of anything was happening when it came down to job opportunities. The only increase that I was able to see was the number of applications and resumes that I submitted nearly doubled, as well as the population that was staying at the shelter. The weather was getting cooler, and more people were looking for a place to come to. Some of the people would come there if they had a domestic dispute at their homes, avoiding some kind of internal family situation with their spouse or significant other. This was a refuge for those who wanted to come to the shelter. Some of the people who would come there to use the shelter as if it were a summer or winter vacation home. The only thing that I had going for me at this time was the peace of mind knowing that when nine o'clock in the morning came that I had an outlet of being away from the shelter by going to the library. The only times that I was there was to stop in at the soup kitchen for lunch, other than that I was only going in there to lay my head down in the evening say my prayers and hope that tomorrow was going to be better for me than today was.

At this time period the shelter director, David appeared to be on a mission. He stepped up the random drug testing of the residents. Testing that once was done sparingly was now being done three out of the four weeks of the month. Residents who were caught having dirty urine samples were given ten days out for the first offense as opposed to the three days out initially. I was tested four times while I resided there. The first time was when I was kicked out of the shelter for the chair-breaking incident. Before I could regain entrance back into the shelter, I was tested for controlled substances. My caseworker Keona asked me was I using any drug, and naturally I responded with a resounding no. I was asked if they could swabbed my mouth. I agreed and let them do the results, and it came back negative for the use of drugs. The second time was during the early part of autumn. My number came up and it was time for me to be tested. This time they issued a urine test. I gave them a sample, and again it was negative. The last two times came in the month of November, a week apart from each other, and they were negative. By this time I was figuratively pissed off and asked both my caseworker and David what else did they want from me, the blood of my first-born child?

I suspected that this was an effort to try to get me out of the facility permanently. What their reasons for testing me so often was a mystery. Before the chair breaking incident happened, I was a resident volunteer who assisted their staff with laundry service from eight in the evening until midnight. I got along well with the staff and had nothing more that few verbal incidents with the other residents of the shelter. Although I don't have any proof. I do believe that it may have been someone from the county health department that may have tipped off someone in the administration that I was about to drop the bomb on the shelter, and the fact that they didn't hold up the facility that if they came in on a random inspection it wouldn't make it to the health code. My belief is that the administration and David in particularly wanted me out of the shelter was that they viewed me as an intelligent threat to their system of oppression of the less fortunate. Even though I wasn't working in the capacity of a case or social worker, there were things that I saw that just wasn't right with the operations of the shelter morally or ethically.

This was an organization that went under the premise of using the name of a ministry, but in actuality, it was a business. They invited churches, civic and other community-based organizations to volunteer their time and services for the betterment of the homeless community.

It's actually a network in the city and county that would try to find ways to manipulate anyone or anything that was willing to change within the legal limit the way that things have been done. When the administration was abusing the resources of the businesses, churches, and other private donors who gave their time, efforts and money toward assisting the shelter residents. The administration wouldn't account on how those resources were being used. I once asked my caseworker if she could provide a contact for the board member of the administration. I was told that I would have to look at the website of the organization to get it. I did, but when I went to the website, I only saw the names. There wasn't any contact information or anything about the current member from their businesses or affiliations that the board members has outside of the Rowan Helping Ministries agency.

The administration and staff members treat the residents of the shelter as livestock and try to dehumanize them by having the residents wear hospital scrubs when they already had pajamas that were suitable to wear. What was their reason for taking away the pajamas to the residents? When I asked, they didn't give a reason. It cost them more money to buy hospital scrub than to use the stock of pajamas that they already had. This is an attempt to institutionalize the shelter like that of a county jail. The only thing that was missing from the scrubs that were given to the residents to wear were the black letter painted on the back of them with RHM for Rowan Helping Ministries. That was one of the most degrading things that I had to experience.

Some caseworkers spoke down to the residents as if they weren't able to comprehend. One time before she left her position as the caseworker, Linda Hunt had Joe the artist as her client. Joe was attending school at Rowan Cabarrus Community College, and was taking the time after so many years to acquire his high school equivalency diploma. Now in the interim, when Joe hadn't been going to school he would use his time constructively. After classes, he would hustle up some work by doing some portrait sketches of people on campus or around town. His caseworker Linda told him that he needed to start keeping a record of his job searching activities. He explained to her that he was in school and that he was doing his hustle of making quick sketches for pedestrians off the street. Linda then told Joe that he needed to open a bank account so that they can monitor where his money is going. If he failed to do so within month that he would be subjected for a non-compliance order by his caseworker and that could lead to a dismissal from the shelter.

Part of a case plan when I came to the shelter was to be enrolled into a school as a means of a plan of action to reenter into the work society. Resident guests could be enrolled at one of the four colleges in the area: Livingstone, Catawba, Rowan Cabarrus Community College, or Pfeiffer University. This was a plan of action for self-betterment, and it's an acceptable means by the administration. If you weren't enrolled in one of the previously mentioned school, you needed to show your caseworker documented proof that you've been actively looking for employment with at least three contacts a week. If you weren't doing either of the two, then they had a program for people to go to called New Tomorrows.

New Tomorrows is a faith-based program under the wing of Rowan Helping Ministries. Its mission is to give the people who are lacking in social and employability skills to help inspire them. The staff assisted the resident trainees with job search skill applications that include; resume preparations, job application skills and interviewing techniques. They also bring in guest presenters to assist with that. Another aspect of the program comes from the arts community in Salisbury where the trainees who attend learn how to do artistic crafts such as painting and making a birdhouse or feeder from scratch. The final part of the New Tomorrows program is where the faith based community visits to give the holy word to the trainees. Other parts of the program to assist them into mainstreaming back into the employment and other social issue are; clinical psychologist, social workers and substance abuse counselors that test and inform the trainees. One week there may be a person coming in to inform and test the trainees about HIV/AIDS. Another week there may be another to inform them about the Affordable Healthcare Act.

New Tomorrows has a good idea, and some of the information that the trainees receives is helpful, but quite a bit of it I was familiar about because of my previous background and employment training. Working as a pregnancy prevention counselor when I instructed teens regarding the best practice methods to prevent pregnancy, HIV/AIDS and other sexually transmitted diseases. Even though I haven't been working for the past two years the one thing that I try to take advantage of is the use of the internet and the library. I was pretty much ahead of the curve when the reforms in the Affordable Healthcare Act was passed into law, because I tried to keep my ears free to hear about what was going on and read on it as it evolved.

The residents who were required to attend these sessions at New Tomorrow didn't like it. I inquired to some of them who attended and asked them what it was like. They stated that they didn't like to attend because of various reasons. Some felt as if they were required to go there when they weren't religiously grounded. Others felt that most of the time during their discussion group that the staff didn't have topics that address their situation, or anything worth talking about. The one thing that stood out more than anything was that they staff would have employers come in to give seminars to the trainees about doing their job searches correctly. The quest speakers would come from different companies ranging from the major corporations in Rowan County to a mom-and-pop store. The trainees would do exercises in filling out sample job application, resumes and working on their mock interviewing techniques. The most disheartening aspect for the trainees was the employer would only do the exercises. None of the guest presenter from the employment sector would take this opportunity to screen the trainees for employment opportunities.

A person who's been unemployed over an extended period of time, the trainees thought of it as a slap in the face. Many of the residents who are told that if they don't attend the sessions at New Tomorrows that they are subject to having their privileges suspended of staying at the shelter. I don't blame the employers so much as I blame the shelter's administration for not doing their jobs. As a former worker in the social service field, it's the responsibility of the case manager to network and help create a job opportunities so that potential candidates can meet and be screened by potential employers so that both sides can secure employment. Don't get me wrong, but if you're only completing one phase of an employment-inclusion program for the residents to re-enter into the workforce, it needs to be completed. By not completing all the phases of the program the rate for recidivism increases for the most of the trainees without the proper employability skills is very likely to happen.

The trainees were given the impression that they were working toward the betterment of their future by acquiring employment using the skills that they learned, without a return on their investment the time and efforts. They were hoping that they would be placed by the companies that were counseling them. The residents want those employment representatives who had the authority to hire them as workers for their companies. That was one thing that never happened. When the employers came to counsel the trainees, they never screened any of the applicants. They never attempted to qualify any of the trainees to see if they were eligible, or a potential candidate to work for any of those companies that came in. The trainees were truly deceived by the administration. The same administration that told them that they needed to be looking for a job, but overtly mandated these trainees to attend the sessions at New Tomorrow so that the administration could cash in on the grant that paid for their deceptive training. The same administration that wouldn't give the trainees any promise of an interview from one employer who came to do a presentation on how to apply for a job. This program was nothing more like what a car salesman would do when a person didn't qualify to buy a car that the buyer desired, but the salesperson wanted the commission so bad that they would switch the buyer into a purchasing a lower-model car in the old "bait and switch" technique. The administration was only looking at one thing and one thing only. How can they get the dollars for the residents to participate in their program at New Tomorrows? The trainees who attended New Tomorrows had coined a new catchphrase, "New Tomorrows means no future."

CHAPTER 12

Shay's Letter

Meanwhile the administration kept on with their agenda of getting the new facility built. At this point, it seemed not to matter to them about putting any more money to make the conditions better for the residents at the current building. Things had gotten to the point that the job prospects didn't matter as much to me. I was still looking, but I didn't care too much to look for jobs the way that I had in the past. Now that the autumn of 2013 is here the season of the year wasn't the only thing that was changing in the area. The staff of the administration changed with the resignation of Linda stepping down from her position of being the evening case manager. With that event happening, the staff roster of the shelter administration shifted. This is the time that you have to keep a scorecard to track the lineup changes of the staff at the shelter. Teresa Vinson who accepted the position of manager at New Tomorrows when Keona was promoted to the shelter case manager, was now promoted to the shelter advocate for the Veterans Administration and Transitional Housing Coordinator. That was another one of the duties that David was doing when he was promoted to the shelter director. New to come aboard the program were Willie McCoy. He replace Linda as the night time case manager on duty, and Sheena was brought on board to replace Teresa as the manager at New Tomorrows.

Willie was a local young guy who recently graduated from East Carolina University. I recalled seeing him in the mornings coming in with the other staff members who worked inside the crisis network. He was a volunteer that would come to serve the community there. Sheena was a young lady who came there after the shelter had posted the position in the paper. I don't recall what school that she graduated from, but I do know that she was continuing her education pursuing her master's degree. Both of Sheena and Willie were in the process of pursuing their graduate degrees.

On the day that I was assigned Willie as my case manager I saw Keona who was my current case manager at that time. I went to her to renew my shelter pass so that I could re-enter into the shelter. She was the one who informed me that he would be the one to do my case management. That evening he introduced himself to me calling me Mr. Leroy. He told me that he would be my new case manager and that he and I would have to talk. I told him, "What do we need to talk about? You're my case manager. You have records and everything that you need to know about me is in my folder. I'm an unemployed educated man who had one mistake in my lifetime of a misdemeanor assault. I have my bachelor's degree and I can't get a job in my field of concentration because of the assault record." He said, "Okay, we still have to talk. I didn't think twice about it and kept thing moving."

With the change of climate, it also came the new infusion of people moving into the shelter. The current place that housed fifty people to stay in the overnight shelter was slowly increasing the population on a weekly basis. The increase jumped from fifty to sixty, sixty-seven, and even reaching a high of seventy-seven people figuratively sleeping on top of each other. Monday through Friday the doors to the crisis assistance network were open, and the people who needed a place for warmth could go inside for comfort. On Saturday's the majority of the shelter residents could be seen at the library. The blessing of the library being open on Saturday was that it closed at five in the evening. That gave you just an hour before the shelter aides allowed the residents in. The downside of it closing at five on Saturday was that you would have to endure the elements if the weather was inclimate.

One of the things that I happened to notice was the football schedule of the Carolina Panthers. I saw that they were playing both of the teams from New York, my beloved New York Jets and the only team I hate worse than the New England Patriots is the New York Giants. Since I wasn't working, I had too much time on my hands. I continued to look for job at the career center and the library, but it seemed that professional football was an outlet to temporarily put the stressful things of the week away.

A lot of the stress that I felt would came from not being employed, and the fact that I was still living at the shelter approaching a year and a half in September. When I was at the shelter, David would continue to have his monthly meetings on the first Thursday of the month. He once told the residence at a meeting during the month of August, when the board of directors decided to approve the construction of the new building that he, the executive director Kyna, and a case manager would take several of the residents out for a dinner at a real restaurant. David stated that this was an effort for the administration and staff to find out what the residents would want the administration could do to help make the conditions at the new facility better for the residents.

Another thing that he was extremely adamant about was the PDA rule on the grounds of the shelter. He took it one step farther. One day when some of the residents left the facility for the day three of the residents went to a place in the business district called "Easy Street." I was a place that was located behind the main offices of the F&M Bank on north Main St. The place wasn't so much secluded, but it wasn't used by the employee who worked in the vicinity. One day three of the residents went over there on a nice clear day when the weather was nice. A man named Mike, his girlfriend Marlene, and Jim left the shelter that morning wound up there on Easy Street in their patio area. That patio area has a couple of patio tables and some chairs located there. It's a place that is peaceful and some electrical outlets so that you could charge your phones or other electrical devices.

On this day the three of them were sitting there not making any kind of fuss, drinking soda, listening to music from the playlist of their computers and smoking cigarettes. The music wasn't loud enough that would cause anyone to notify the law. In fact there was a county law enforcement officer parked in the lot adjacent to the patio. David drove over from the shelter to that area to ask the three of them what they were doing there. Jim told him that they were there because it less congested than the shelter or library and peaceful there. David told them that they had to leave. They asked him why? He said that area was off limits to people who resided at the shelter. Jim stated that they weren't breaking any laws and there weren't any signs posted stating no loitering. David told them that he wasn't going to argue about it, if they continued to stay there that they would be given three nights out from staying in the shelter. All three of the residents got their possessions and left Easy Street.

Things like that caused the stress and tension level to remain high for the residents who lived at the shelter. You didn't know what to expect from day to day. It appeared that the administration would change the rule on the codes of conduct from day to day, minute by minute. What you could do the day before you were unable to the very next day. Another example of this is when I would iron my clothes the night before. I never wanted to look like a homeless person. The majority of my clothes that I had while I lived at the shelter were business attire. I would request to use the iron at around one o'clock in the morning. It was convenient for me to do it at that time, and the majority of the shelter residents were already in bed or asleep. Residents that lived there and worked outside the shelter would come in after nine in the evening. The last person would enter the shelter for the evening about eleven. Where I could use the iron and ironing board was over by the entrance where the shelter guests would enter. The next day without notice David told the shelter aides that the ironing needed to be done before eleven thirty.

The fact that there are surveillance cameras located in every room with two to three angles made me feel as if I was in a maximum-security prison. It didn't give me a feeling of security, but a feeling of discomfort. Trust me when I say this, that there is nothing at the shelter that I want besides a bed and a shower. I am grateful for the food that I received there, but I really didn't want it most of the times. When you would go to have lunch at the soup kitchen, or if they didn't have a group to bring in their own food the stuff that was served was outdated. Sometimes the food served was so old that it was eligible to apply for its own social security benefits. Being that this is a culture that is raised on pork I passed. I hadn't indulged in pork for twenty years at this point in my life. When I entered into the shelter my weight was at one hundred eighty-five pounds. Over the year and a half being there, I ballooned up to two hundred and fifteen pounds.

David continued to hold his monthly meetings, and from August to November, a day or two before they were being held he found a way to clean house. This was normally done by him doing the random drug testing of the resident. It was easy to find the one who did it, because the residents who were working at the shelter that stayed in the transitional housing complex called the Eagle's nest would drop a dime to David and the case managers on who were on duty knew exactly who was doing what, when and where. I'm not too sure if they were dropping dimes on the others so that they could avoid the attracting the attention from themselves. I recall in the month of October the staff hit the jackpot. They tested the residents for three successive weeks and were able to get thirteen residential guest time out of the shelter for substance abuse. The reasons why the residents left because they were charged with illegal substances that ranged from marijuana to oxycodone and cocaine when they were tested.

During that October meeting David informed the residents that they wouldn't be able to request a night out unless they did it within a twenty-four–hour period prior to leaving the facility policy was in the past. The residents had to notify their case managers for a seven day period ahead of time. With the only exceptions would happen during the upcoming holidays, and family emergencies. He also told the guest that there would be more changes the closer that they are to completing the new building. He also took some questions from the residents at the end of what he informed everyone about the changes.

JP inquired if the new facility was going to have Wi-Fi capability. David said that there wasn't any way for the shelter to allow the guest to get Wi-Fi without the residents going on any unauthorized websites, meaning going to sites that had pornography or how to make a bomb. I tried to explain to David that their internet tech can do the settings so that it can block people from going on the websites that they want it to. Then he said that his internet tech told him that it couldn't be done, and I told him respectfully, "That's bull." I said that the county offices and the library put blocks on certain websites, and that their tech told them a lie. David replied saying that he wasn't going to get into an argument about something that he didn't know about. I replied, defense rest!

Just as the meeting was ending all of the residents were afraid that I was going to be kicked out of the shelter. I told them that I shouldn't, because I didn't raise my voice or said anything that was disrespectful to the director. I didn't mind telling them that there were injustices in the system that they were implementing. When I spoke out on them the David and the administration knew that I was knowledgeable, because of my training and education. Resident looked at me as a person who didn't mind looking out for their welfare. It was about looking out for the welfare of them as well as for me too. I wasn't accustomed to living is the condition where mold, disease and infestation of insects and mice could be seen in areas of where some of the food was being stored and outside of the building by the large trash container.

Talking to the residents there wasn't too many things that we had in common, but I refused to remain ignorant that I have a lot more in common with them now than I did before I took refuge into the shelter. The thing that I had to learn more than anything I ever had to learn in life was how to conform to the standards that the residents have to endure. The one thing that I wasn't going to do was to be treated like an animal. If the staff and administration wanted to receive respect from me, then I expected the same in return from them. During autumn the one thing that eighty five percent of the people who lived there had in common was their love for the game of football.

In the south, life is a different culture that may be view as strange. Honestly, it is unique to the point that it was described on a plague of a sports themed restaurant in town called Uncle Buck All-American Pub and Grub. This establishment had the same kind of atmosphere as an Applebee's or TGI Friday's, but it was strictly a hometown restaurant. The plaque define the south as; the south the place where tea is sweet and accents are sweeter, summer starts in April, macaroni and cheese is a vegetable, y'all is the only proper noun, front porches are wide and words are long, pecan pie is a staple, chicken is fried and biscuits come with gravy, everything is darling, someone's sweetheart is always being blessed and where football is king."

College football is definitely king, and pro football takes a back seat to the college game. Not for me! I would do all my trash talking about the pro game, and I wouldn't let anyone out talk me about my love for the New York Jets. My best friend's younger brother Eric who lived in New Jersey would be the biggest trash talker when football season came. We keep in touch on Facebook when I was going through the down time of not finding a job, and it was quite often. Eric connected me to a friend who was able to get me tickets to the see the Jets when they played the Carolina Panthers. His friend introduced me to a former New York Jets linebacker who was an All-American when he played his college ball. This player who I shall remain to leave nameless had befriended me, and was kind enough to see that he had some tickets left for me at the will call window. This was a much needed stress reliever.

When I found out that I was going to get tickets to the game, I went to see my case manager Willie to notify him that I would need to return late in the evening when the game was over, because it was an afternoon game and the train wouldn't arrive into Salisbury until after the hours that the shelter is closed. It is mandatory the shelter residents have to let the management know when they're going to need to enter into the shelter after the specified hours due to travel, work or an unforeseen circumstance. I did this because I wanted to make sure that I remain in good standing with the authorities.

Willie told me that it was all right for me to go to the game, and that I should be back to the shelter before midnight. Although he was new, Willie appeared to be the best of all the case managers who knew the ethics of the profession. He was only working there for six hours a day during the week, but he would do more things in those six hours than the others weren't willing to do all week in the forty plus hours they put in. He posted jobs listings, helped residents move into transitional housing, recommended residents to go to the clinic and other social services that they may needed. More than having a passion for the job, Willie had compassion for the clients that he had to do the service.

Willie approved for me and my friend Jean to attend the game in December, but he was concerned about my progress for finding employment. I informed him that I was singing the tune of the Talking Heads singing the lyric from the song "Once in a Lifetime." I replied, "Same as it ever was" to Willie. He chuckled for a brief moment, and told me that I'm going to need to take any job that I can take. I told him that I was willing to do that if someone would offer me a position to work for. I've been to every fast food restaurant in the area. I applied to work at mom-and-pop store, and anything for anyone who would offer me employment. I explained to him that I did an internship at Goodwill during a six month period applied for six positions with them. The best results that I had an interview and an e-mail telling me that they chose to go with another applicant.

Willie informed me that the new changes the administration were doing was going to require me to start attending the sessions that were being conducted at New Tomorrows if I didn't secure a job soon. David was on him about having me attend the sessions there. It was David's way of playing the role of an oppressor. It didn't make any sense to me. Here I am a man with a degree that made an offer to the shelter for one of the positions that they had opened that I was qualified to fulfill the job. For the shelter's administration to have someone that they could've taken full advantage of the knowledge, expertise, and skills of the job was a riddle that I couldn't crack.

For a good half hour Willie and I debated on the pros and cons of me attending the sessions at New Tomorrows. It came down to me telling Willie that if they were to put me into that program that I may have to leave the shelter, not on the terms that I was hoping for. Willie was asking me where would I go, what would I do to support myself. I didn't have a clue, because as far I knew Rowan Helping Ministries was the only shelter in the county, or to the best of my knowledge. I knew that going to New Tomorrows wouldn't benefit me at all.

Willie told me that he would do everything to help me find a position, and that he would try to do everything to keep David from putting me in the program at New Tomorrows. Out of all the people who ever worked that as my case manager, Willie was the only one that I felt comfortable with. He knew the responsibilities of the position, and was thorough when it came to performing his duties. More than anything else Willie was compassionate about people. He may have been fresh out of college, but he worked as if he had experience from working in the profession for years. I knew that he was a man of his word, because I witnessed him in action. He was only a part time employee there, but I can say that for the short time that he started that he was able to place shelter guest into better situation for employment and housing.

I was given the okay to go into Charlotte to see the game. I asked my friend Jean to come with me, and she agreed. The game wasn't until December, and now it was late October. Having tickets to see the Jets was probably the best thing to happen to me during this time of living at the shelter. It allowed me some bragging rights among the sea of Carolina Panther fans who haven't been to Charlotte to see their own team play. Trash talking was a recreational outlet for me, and the other people who love the game of football. It gave us something to look forward to, and it took away some of the stresses of living at the shelter.

A week after receiving the okay to go to the football game, I went to see Willie to get my shelter pass renewed. He informed me that me and several of the residents were going to be required to attend a class on self-esteem. I questioned him as to why did I need to attend. He told me that the administration retained a woman from a funded program that was instructing this six-week class and that it was mandatory for me to attend. If I didn't attend the class that I would be subjected to being put out of the shelter indefinitely.

At first I wanted to be resistant to attend, but the sessions only met once a week. I did that all the way until the classes were done.

By the time that the class sessions were over I was asked by the director of the Lee Street Theatre group to do the Scrooge Christmas trolley show for the holidays again. I accepted it, because it would afford me the opportunity to see my granddaughter in Columbia. The shows started on Black Friday, and the day after on Saturday. The show ran from November 28 until December 21, and the best part about this show it was a paying gig just like they did last year. Not only would I be able to make enough money to go down to the game and back, but have enough to buy a Christmas gift for my granddaughter for her.

When it came time to go to the game, Jean and I caught the train from Salisbury to Charlotte that morning. It was a four o'clock afternoon game so we had plenty of time to pick up our tickets at the will call window. We got down there in time to get something to eat before the kickoff. We had a good time. We had the chance to go to Bank of America stadium to watch her Panthers beat my beloved New York Jets. By the time that the game was over we made it to the train station way ahead of time before the scheduled train was to arrive in Charlotte. I go to the gas station down the street to get something to eat because we have another three hours before our train arrives to get us back into Salisbury. Once I returned from the store, Jean informed me that the train won't be arriving until three o'clock in the morning going north. I called the staff at the shelter to inform them of the situation, and that they didn't need to hold a plate of food for either of us since the train won't be getting into town until almost 4:00 p.m.

We had a longer than expected layover in Charlotte, but when the train departed, it was at three forty-five in the morning. By the time that we arrived back in Salisbury, it was four twenty. To walk just a block away to the shelter from the train station wasn't a task, but it happened by chance that David the director was working that morning. He was there to allow Jean and I into the facility. He told us that we couldn't get a plate, because it was only an hour before the staff would wake up the residents. I was cool with that because that meant that breakfast would be served at six. Then David also said that we couldn't get a shower either. I asked him could we come back in the afternoon after the soup kitchen closed to get a shower. It has been the policy of the shelter to allow anyone, who's homeless off of the street to come in and take a shower from two thirty to three thirty during the week. David replied with a resounding no.

I knew the policy when it came down to allowing people to take a shower and I didn't want to take a chance on arguing with him. By the time that I knew that David made this his personal agenda to humiliate me. David didn't like it when someone in the shelter that had any knowledge of the policies, procedures of what social workers were required to do. The policy of allowing people who came off of the street that wanted to take a shower was that they could do that after the staff had cleaned up the facility when the soup kitchen was over. For example, if you got off of the two o'clock train coming from Charlotte and you wanted take a shower, you could see the case manager on duty and they would allow you to bathe if you needed to do so.

This frustrated me so much that I was going to report it to the management of the shelter. This isn't the first time that David had humiliated someone intentionally. One other time, when the residents were out on a Sunday afternoon a woman caught a case of diarrhea. I was with her and gave her my windbreaker jacket to cover up the mishap. This was a rarity, the mishap of the young lady, and a bigger rarity of David being there working on a Sunday afternoon. We ranged the bell to the office, which was on the other side of the entrance where the residents would enter. David answered the door and asked what the problem was. She explained that she needed to enter into the shelter to take a shower because of the mishap. He told her that she had to enter at the entrance where the residents would enter for the evening. He gave her no other alternative, but to bring herself in front of the other residents to get the brunt of embarrassment among her peers.

That action was uncalled for as well as the present action of not allowing me to get a shower that afternoon. I was going to let the administration know my displeasure, and this time I was going to go over the head of the executive director this time. I sent an email to Kyna and made sure that I did a carbon copy to David, my case manager Willie, and a board member, Chris Bradshaw, as well. My letter to them read;

Hello everyone!

I hope by the time that this message reaches you that it will find you in good spirits. I'm writing to acknowledge that I had went to see the NY Jets vs. Carolina Panthers football game yesterday. I was blessed to receive tickets to go to it and it was a late afternoon game that started at 4:00 p.m. I called the shelter aides to let them know that I and Ms. Jean Williams were going to be late. We were to catch the 1:45 a.m. train leaving Charlotte and return into Salisbury this morning at approximately 2:30.a.m. The northbound train coming back was delayed and was to arrive into the Charlotte station at 3:00.a.m., but it was delayed again and didn't depart Charlotte for Salisbury until 4:00 a.m. I've called twice to let the aides know that we were delayed. When we arrived in Salisbury at 4:50 a.m., we were informed by Austin that we wouldn't be allowed to take a shower or get our laundry done. We understood and accepted that. I asked him if it were possible to come back in the afternoon so that I could shower after the soup kitchen was closed. I was informed that I couldn't take a shower. The aides on duty who witnessed this act were Austin and Vickie. I need to get a thorough understanding of this, if you wouldn't mind verifying this for me. I know for a FACT that there are and have been people who weren't residential guests who were allowed to come into the shelter after the soup kitchen closed to shower. I am a

guest who has gone through all the proper channels and protocol of letting the staff know that I
was going to be late, and I was denied the right to
take care of my own personal hygiene. I'm writing all of you to state my displeasure with this
decision. Anyone who wants to get a shower can
come off the street and do so, but the guest who
follows the correct procedures isn't allowed to do
it. Rowan Helping Ministries is supposed to be a
ministry. A ministry is one that serves as a means;
an instrumentality. If this is the means of being
discretionary to whom and whatever you want it
to do then the work you're doing is hypocritical.
I will be in there this evening to get a shower, and
I pray that you will continued to be blessed. No
one should ever have to go around feeling unclean
when there is a resource for them to cleanse the
dirt and stench from their bodies. Thank you for
taking the time to read my request. Sincerely,

Leroy F. Bennett.

Kyna replied back to me telling me that there would be an investigation to the fact of what transpired. I found out the next morning
when I woke up that the shelter aide Austin was questioned by his
supervisor David what happened. He said that David told me that
he wouldn't allow me to take the shower. There was no other inquiry
by any other member of the staff to Austin as to what happened the
morning of December 16. Kyna replied back to me stating that the
actions of David were appropriate, because he didn't need to allow
me to come into the shelter that hour. She didn't understand why
I wasn't allowed to take a shower, because they allow anyone who
wants to receive a shower to get one at the end of the soup kitchen.

This truly had me wanting to explode, but it took everything
in my own good nature from not going off. I knew that this was
bullshit, and they knew it was bullshit too. This was the turning
point for me, and I knew, sooner or later, I was going to get out of

the shelter one way or the other. I was going to leave on my terms or theirs. I was praying that it going to be on mine. The reason that I felt that David had to try to make an example of me was because I was questioning him and the administration about their operations during their monthly meetings for the residents. I never came out of my mouth telling them off, cursing or disrespecting them. They find it disrespectful when an intelligent person questions their motives. Also when you're a tall, imposing figure like myself some of them use a Napoleonic complex, so they have to display their authority in order to try to keep you in your place.

When the weekend was approaching, I received my pay from the Lee Street Theatre Company, and I went to the Big Lots department store to get my Christmas gift for my granddaughter. Christmas was just three days away so I was going to the Ace Check Cashing store to purchase my bus ticket and making my reservations to go to the train station to get to Columbia. I hadn't seen her since she had graduated from elementary school, and I had to try to make this a better Christmas this year than it was the year before. This was my chance to try to catch up on three years of time that's been missed because of my own hasty actions of moving prematurely.

Once I had all my ducks in a row, it was Christmas Eve. I took the train to Charlotte and waited until the next morning to catch the Greyhound to Columbia. While I was in Charlotte, I had my laptop chronicling my trek to see my granddaughter. My high school classmate Rochelle that lived in Charlotte saw this and was chatting with me. It was great to chatting to her for the brief minutes that we did. So I decided to call her while I was at the bus station. She and her husband offered me to come over to wait at her place until my bus came, but I refused. My sister and her son were on their way to the station to drop off my Christmas gift for me. When they arrived she crocheted me a winter skull cap in the colors of my football team the New York Jets. It reminded me of the crocheted items that my mom would make me. One of the last items that my mom made me was a scarf that if you were to stretch it from end to end it would measure close to nine feet long. That's the one item that I still have from my mother that I keep. I cherish that item above anything else, because she made it with her own hands out of the love that she had for me.

Throughout the night, I stayed in the terminal until it was time for the bus to leave early the next morning. When I arrived in Columbia, I called my granddaughter's mother to pick me up, and she came within an hour. When I arrived at their house my granddaughter was up already, and had just got finished eating their breakfast. Her siblings and other grandmother was there also. This wasn't my ex-wife, but her mother's mother. I had my camera with me, and I was taking picture of my granddaughter. I caught her off guard because she was still in her pajamas, and her hair wasn't done.

This was a far cry from the days when she was a child of two years old coming from her mother's house to mine on Christmas day. Shaylee had a fever on that Christmas day that year. As she walked from the door, she came right to me into my lap so that she could fall asleep in my arms before I could take her to bed. Now this was a thirteen-year-old who was maturing. She was more concerned about having something pink in her attire for whatever she was going to wear for the day, because that's her favorite color. I had bought a bag filled with candy to let the kids all share among themselves. I collected and saved it from various times when the volunteers who came to serve dinner. They would give the guest who stayed at the shelter what I called a goody package that included; gloves, socks, skull caps, toiletry items and candy. When the excitement of granddad being there settled in for her some of her friends came by to meet me, but I told her to go to be with them. I went to rest in her room, because I realized that I was more tired than I thought.

It wasn't a big deal to me, because I had another day that I could be with her. So by the time that she returned I woke up about an hour after she came back. We talked about everything that I could think of. I didn't realize how much of that time that I really missed with her. I was talking to her about her studies, and I found out that my former colleague that I worked with was her physical education teacher. I found out that she received a C grade for her interim. Now I know that she's a good athlete, and I let her know of my disappointment in that grade. It was then at that time that I told her the reason that I don't come to visit her.

I told her that I haven't been living in a house going on two years. I let her know that I was homeless. She asked me, "Weren't you living with your cousin? What happened?" I didn't lie to her, and with her being as old as she was, I wasn't going to start now. I told her that there was a misunderstanding between my cousin and I so I was asked to leave her house. I told her that it was complicated, but I didn't want her to worry about me that I am in good health. She questioned me about me being in the hospital, and I told her that I was there because I was upset about being homeless.

She tried to hold a strong front, and I told her that something is going to break through, but we can't let it break our spirits. I told her when she goes to bed at night say a special prayer so that I can be working, and that we could resume our weekends together. She promised that she would, and that she will remain strong. I told her that I am in the process of writing about this experience. She was like really, and I asked her if she wanted to read what I wrote so far. She started reading it, and could only read the first three pages. I asked her what was wrong, and she told me that she couldn't read anymore, because she didn't want to start crying. I grabbed her to embrace her to let her know that Granddad is going to get past this.

I asked her if she would do me a favor. I wanted her to write down her feelings about how she felt about this situation. I wasn't going to criticize her for her candor, because this didn't only affect me but her too. She agreed and started typing in my computer. When she put down her thoughts this, and this is how she feels. She wrote, "Living like I'm in jail. I can't take a shower without you looking. Gotta be inside before dark. Follow the rules or you'll sleep in the streets. Dang! Dang! Dang! See what choices get you? When you move from good to better, but better is worst. When somebody say they are going to help you but when you stay for a little longer, they put you out, and now you stay in a shelter. How FUN is that? That's not really FUN, is it? I know, right? Never ever thought that it would ever come out to be like this. People always say also that the good one always are the one to suffer, or the choice you make is the type of life you will live. My grandfather is the one who gives me when he don't have it. The one who tries his best to make me happy when he can't afford it. So why can't God just give him the life he ask for? I've been thinking that God send him this way because he just needed to see how it feels, or he just didn't give a homeless man a dollar when he had it. I think that's why God hasn't answered his prayers, because I think there was a homeless person that have asked my granddaddy for a dollar and he didn't give it to him and I gave him one of my dollars. My granddaddy also told me that he wanted to be there. I also hear that from my grandmother and mother. I always wondered even though he didn't give it to him, why didn't God give him a chance? But now I think he knows how he feel. But you know what? My God is an awesome God, so he does things for a reason. So I have no reason to question him."

When I read this, I was truly overwhelmed. Over the past four years, I had to witness the maturation of my granddaughter as an outsider. When she wrote this, I knew that she grew up without me. Her mother was doing a great job of raising her and keeping her grounded so that she doesn't get into any serious trouble. I am so grateful that her mother and other relatives have kept her into the church. For her to know just how good that God is and knowing that this season of my life will pass, she understood it fully and didn't feel the need to question God. The other part of that comes from her father.

One of the few times that I've written him since I've moved to Salisbury, I told him about me living at the shelter over the past couple of years. He's been incarcerated before he was able to see the face of his daughter. He wrote me back to remind me that I was not as bad off as I think I am. I was reminded that he's been locked up for the past thirteen years, and that there are worse circumstances that I could have. When I read the letter that he wrote, it was a reality check. I found that I was having a pity party, and it was time for me to get out of it. It was time to suck it up and continue on this journey.

On the last day there with my granddaughter was one that we spent together, and we took full advantage of our time together. We talked about everything under the sun. We talked about how much she loved her Gigi, my mother, and how she missed her. She told me that I needed to send her my resume. I asked her why, and she told me that she was going to send it out to a job search engine online for me. She wanted to help me get a job so that I can move back to Columbia. I e-mailed her a copy, because it would've been better being closer to her than being so distant. We both talked about how much we missed spending our weekends together. Being there for the three days was the highlight of my holidays for 2013. This was a time that I didn't want to end, but the reality settled in that evening when I had to pack my bag to return to Salisbury.

The next morning I woke up early. She and her stepsister were already in the kitchen cooking breakfast for me before they had to drop me off at the bus station. When we got in the car, I shared the pictures that were taken from the previous days as we looked at them on the computer. When we arrived at the station, I told the children and their mother good-bye. My granddaughter, who was truly a big girl now, got out of the car and had some last words for me. She gave me a nice tight hug before they left, and then shortly afterward, the clerk announced over the loudspeaker that my bus was arriving at gate two. I had my ticket, and I told them to go ahead. When they left I could see she and her siblings looking out the back window as they were driving away. This was a time that I could forget about the stresses.

When I returned in the early evening to the shelter on the twenty-seventh, I was feeling great. I had the opportunity to visit my granddaughter to make up some valuable family time with her. I had a good feeling that 2014 was going to be a better year than the previous ones that I had endured here before. For the next couple of days, I had a focus that I didn't channel into like never before. I found a renewed source of committing myself on getting out of the hell hole that I put myself into. By the time that Monday morning came around, I didn't have a morning chore to do so I left the shelter early to stop at the McDonald's to get a cup of coffee and a steak bagel.

I concentrated on looking for new job opportunities, and I saw one that caught my attention in an email I received that morning. It was a position for a sales manager trainee for United Rentals and

WELCOME TO THE HOTEL CALIFORNIA

it was located in Charlotte. This looked like something promising, because it was a job position that was sent to me by the Career Builders search engine. They based it on my qualifications on my resume in their database. I filled out that application and proceeded to go on with my day like I normally do. I left the restaurant before the library opened to go there, and did my normal job searches for the day.

I stayed there all day before it was time to return to the shelter for the evening. Shortly after I arrived in the shelter, my case manager, Willie, asked to talk to me. We walked into his office together, and waiting in there to meet me was David. They were there to inform me that I've had my case plan restructured to go into the New Tomorrows program. I asked them why and didn't get a rational explanation as to why, but was told that if I didn't participate, I was subjected to being put out of the shelter indefinitely. I didn't have a leg to stand on. I was told that I had to start attending the session at New Tomorrow on the sixth of the new year. I left the office without any argument or fanfare, but I was going to let them know of my disagreement with their decision.

I wrote another letter to the same people that I did when I saw the wrong that David had done when I came back from the football game. I wrote a letter trying to state the benefits of me not going to the New Tomorrow program. It said:

> Hello Everyone!
>
> I hope by the time that this message reaches you, that it'll find you all in good spirits. I am writing you because I do not agree with the prescription for the case plan that has been assigned to me. This has come about because of a recent complaint that I made against Mr. David Holston. To refresh your memories, I submitted a complaint against Mr. Holston stating that I requested to him when I returned from a football game if I could come into the shelter during the afternoon hours to get a shower. He denied me, by hav-

ing the shelter aide Austin tell me so. I asked Mr.
Holston in front of Austin and Vicky if I could
get an afternoon shower and he told me no. Once
I've told you of this impropriety, Mr. Holston was
in charge of the investigation. Biased as that was,
I accepted your ruling that there wasn't anything
inappropriate of Mr. Holston's actions. I am
requesting that I do not have to go to the New
Tomorrow's Program from 8:00 a.m. to noon. I
am a very well-educated individual who holds a
bachelors of science degree. I've worked at two
different Urban League affiliates and have taught
individual on how to produce a resume, cover
letter, and interviewing techniques. I understand
best practice modules and for me to go through a
remedial program is a waste of time when I could
be doing something more constructive. For you
to put me into this program doesn't make a bit of
sense. If you are doing this because you receive
funding, then I suggest that there are several
other shelter guests that make for better candidates than I. I spend the better time of my day at
the library or the Goodwill Career Connection
doing job searches. I have put several applications for your own agency, and because I am a
shelter guest it has been stated that I fall under
the ineligibility for employment with you. The
one reason I'm not working is because I've had
an assault charge in 1994. This is supposed to
be a ministry again. I was taught that only God
can judge, but I was wrong. God has forgiven me
for what has transpired twenty years ago. I was
wrong, given the authority that some of the people at the shelter have been empowered that they
have a God complex. I am submitting to you my
current resume and a sample cover letter and ask

that you reconsider your decision on me attending the sessions at New Tomorrows. Thank you for taking the time to read this request. Sincerely,

Leroy F. Bennett.

I included a copy of my resume and a sample of a cover letter, but it all fell on deaf ears. This wasn't the way that I wanted to bring in 2014, but I knew that the clock was ticking. I was going to do my damned best to get out on my own terms, and not theirs. I had to get control of my life at any and all cost.

CHAPTER 13

Don't Overstay Your Welcome

Another new year has entered into my life with no changes, but hope springs eternal. After returning back from visiting my granddaughter, some of the changes that the shelter's administration did was starting to take its effect on me. Now I was being subjected against my will to continue my job search and ordered to attend a self-esteem classes. The one thing that I didn't lack was having a low self-esteem, but the thing that I was lacking is a source of income that I was accustomed to having prior to moving to North Carolina. Since seeing my granddaughter, my focus seemed to be better than it was before. When she asked me to give her my resume, I was so overwhelmed with emotions that I decided to consider moving back to Columbia, South Carolina. If this child was going to take the time to make it possible for me to find a job back where she lives, then I wasn't going to ignore what she was doing for her grandfather.

I was only thinking in one direction. My disdain for the environment, culture, and attitudes of the people that are stagnant in their thinking now had to take a backseat because of the love that my granddaughter had displayed toward me. That was more important to me than wanting to be more of the man that she needed in her life. I didn't totally give up my attempts of moving back to my own home state of New Jersey, but if an opportunity opened itself up to move back to be closer to Shaylee, then I was going to take that opportunity and run with it.

Now this year begun with a higher hurdle that I have to leap over in order to achieve my goal of trying to secure employment while having to attend these self-esteem classes. I go there on the first day, and the moment that I get there, the participants weren't enthused about being there. The young woman, Sheena, expected all of the participants to be there in their seats of the study or day room of the local church up the street from the church. We could drink coffee, but we had to go outside if we bought a snack to eat. That was all good, because the setting is taking place at the New Beginnings Baptist Church on Park Avenue.

On the first day she performed her duties like a teacher. She welcomed me into the group and told me the ground rules of what was expected of me while I had to attend the sessions. I understood it, but I didn't suppress my disappointment about having to go to the classes. When the day started on that Monday, she asked the group did we attend church service, and if we did what was the topic that the preacher taught. Some of the members of the group told her that they didn't attend service; others who attended service didn't recall what the sermon was about. I told her about the service that I attended and that it spoke about waiting on God to send a blessing your way. If being there at New Tomorrows was a blessing, I found it hard to understand. How it could be? Someone once told me that if you wanted to make God laugh tell him your plans.

Being there wasn't one of the easiest things that I had to go through. I had to go through remedial session regarding self-esteem. When Sheena inquired about my feelings at one point in the session, I didn't hold back. It was like being in a gunfight, and she gave me an opportunity to voice my opinion. I came at her very respectfully without using any profanity. I had the barrels blazing, and it was like I kept shooting until I didn't hear another word from her. Once I got finished talking, the room was silent. Sheena took a moment before she addressed me. She told me that she felt bad for the situation that not just I was going through, but all of the members of the group, and that attending these sessions should help me get through the rough times that I have experienced.

Her telling me this put a resolve in me that made me inconsolable. It wasn't that I didn't appreciate it, but it was very difficult after being unemployed and living in a shelter going on a two-year period. I didn't want to have to ask family members and friends to send a Christmas gift to my granddaughter and sign my name on a card. Going on Facebook I had to put up a front by posting pictures of myself mainly when I went to church, or to an infrequent interview looking like I was working at an office. I was embarrassed because of the fact that my degree that I earned wasn't worth the paper that it was printed on. I remained at New Tomorrow until the session was over for the day.

I would leave there and make my daily trek to the library to do my job searches online. Since I've move from Columbia, South Carolina, to Salisbury, North Carolina, I had applied for over four hundred positions for employment. Very few have led to an interview, some employers replied with a letter that is automated and most without a response. Whenever I'm at the library, I would post on my Facebook page that I was at my office away from the office. During the first week of attending the group sessions at New Tomorrows, I received a reply from United Rentals out of Charlotte. They contacted me back from an application that I had submitted from the Career Builders search engine. The position was for a management trainee, and it was starting out at forty thousand dollars a year with incentives that could take the pay as high as sixty five thousand a year.

When I received the e-mail, it told me to contact the person in human resources with a contact name and phone number. I was hopeful that this would finally be my ticket to moving up. I had given them a call to speak with a person from human resources about the position. They explained to me what the position detailed. I was excited about making this phone call, but I had to remember not to get too high from the previous disappointments that I had experienced.

It was an opportunity to move out of Rowan County and Salisbury. After talking to the person from human resources, going to attend New Tomorrows wasn't going to be a matter that I have to stress myself over. When I spoke to the gentleman from United Rentals, I heard a voice that appeared to have a genuine interest in me from what he was reading on my resume. After this experience, I was enthused still trying to remain calm just in case I was turned down for the position. I just have to remain focused so that if this opportunity presents itself that I'll be ready to step up to the plate. The man from United Rentals told me that I would receive an e-mail to give them a call for a date and time to be interviewed.

For the next couple of weeks, I didn't hear anything from United Rentals. I would attend the morning sessions at New Tomorrows being bored out of my mind until it was time to leave. One morning, Sheena told us that the group was going to be responsible for working in the soup kitchen. I questioned her as to why didn't they tell us this at the last minute. She told me that it wasn't up for discussion and that we should feel honored to do it. Sheena often talked down to the members of the group and most of the time without a reason behind it. I wasn't feeling her attitude that day, but I ignored it. I thought that this was a test that I was going through. So without further escalating the reason why I didn't want to do it, I did whatever duty that they asked me to perform.

I was still hoping that my contact with United Rentals was going to lead toward securing a job. I did what I would normally do when it came to get another chance to interview with the company. I continued to follow up by sending them e-mails, and making the necessary phone calls. This was so important to me because the location that they wanted me to work was in Charlotte. This was a perfect location for me to relocate to. I had my sister and brother that stay there. It would've been good for me, because I was just a little over an hour away to Columbia from Charlotte. This would be good access from the bus station to go there to visit my granddaughter. I never wanted anything this bad as an adult, because I felt that this is an opportunity that's presenting itself. I have to remain in the zone to be ready if an interview can come up.

Within a couple of days after my last e-mail, I received another e-mail from the human resources people at United Rentals. It stated that I was going to get the chance that I was hoping for. The letter told me that they wanted me to call them to schedule an appointment for a phone interview. The first thing that I did before I called their office was to drop to my knees at the work booth I was sitting at in the library to thank God. After I did that, I took a minute in an attempt to compose myself before I made the phone call. I got in contact and tried my best to conceal the excitement that I was feeling inside. We scheduled the interview for Wednesday the following week. This gave me plenty of time to prepare myself.

I made it a point of going to the career center to speak with one of the job coaches who were there on representing Rowan Cabarrus Community College. I spoke with the job coach and asked if I needed to make an appointment to practice a mock interview with her. She told me that we could do it that day, and about a half hour later, we commenced on practicing interviewing techniques. The techniques were a little different from what I was accustomed to, because I wasn't going to be exposed to seeing the person face-to-face. In some ways, when I thought about it, it was a little easier, because I didn't have the normal pressure of making eye contact with the interviewer. She reminded me that since she couldn't see me, she could hear certain inflections in my vocal tones, and I should make an effort to keep those tones as an even pitch. The job coach and I had practiced for almost an hour before the session ended. She instructed me to remain calm and to take my time when I have to answer a question that the interviewer will ask me. I asked her if we could meet the day before, and she agreed that it would be a good idea to do so. I thought that it would be a good idea just in case I had any other questions that she could help me with her professional suggestions.

I was anxious to get on with this interview. The days couldn't get here fast enough for me. It seemed like the clock on the wall didn't seem to move fast enough. Whenever I looked a clock it seemed that the time just stood still. The interview was made on a Tuesday at one twenty that afternoon, and was scheduled for a ten o'clock session the following week. I know that it was only in my mind, but every time I look at the clock, it was always one twenty.

My mornings were still being spent at New Tomorrows and trying to deal with the remedial work was getting on my nerves. Sheena would give us articles to read and listen to that were supposed to be inspirational, but my mindset was geared on doing things that could better prepare me for my interview. One morning, one of the group members came into New Tomorrows and turn on the VCR to finish watching the movie *The Passions of Christ*. He did that because a day earlier we were watching it, and we were told that we could watch the entirety of it on the next day. When she saw that the television was turned on, she went ballistic. Before the person admitted to turning on the TV, she went off on everyone in the group collectively. I told her that she didn't have to go about it the way that she did. She told me if I didn't be quiet that I was going to get written up for insubordination. I told her to go ahead and do that, because no one deserved to be talked down to. I had to remind her that I was not going to let some child talk to me that way especially when I didn't do anything to cause her to talk to me like that. The child I was referring to was Sheena. No, she wasn't a child, but she's not as old as me. She must've thought that she was talking to a person who wasn't equally yoked educationally with her.

Later during that writing session, one of the guest speakers who was scheduled come wasn't able to attend. At that point Sheena needed to fill out the time, because under the terms of agreement of the grant all of the group members were to remain in the facility until noon. So to fill out the remainder of the time, she had us to do an exercise in creative writing. She told the group that we could write about anything that we wanted to, but it had to be submitted as if you were writing something into a diary. She didn't put any parameters on the subject that we could write about. Okay, I wasn't feeling her today so I was going to be as expressive as possible, but do it with some couth.

The members of the group did the assignment and had to read their compositions. Some of them didn't want to do it because they struggled either reading or writing. Sheena pushed the issue and had those who couldn't do that well enough to do the assignment against their will. One person wrote two sentences, and Sheena was harsh with criticism. Another person did about four sentences, and again Sheena criticized people who didn't feel comfortable expressing themselves in writing. She wasn't unhappy with the majority of the group, just the two that didn't want to do the assignment because of the previously mentioned reasons. I was the last to do my presentation, and with the way that she acted, I wasn't holding back anything.

I read it to the groups and even given the assignment a title called "No Deal." I started it off like an old Rowan and Martin's Laugh-In skit. I said the title of my presentation is called "No Deal" by Leroy F. Bennett.

Dear Diary,

I have nothing to write about. This is an exercise about expressive writing, and I informed the program instructor that I wrote ninety-eight pages already in my journal. So I was forced to do something against my will. Here at Rowan Hating Ministries and this program at New Tomorrows, they don't give anyone that choice. I guess it's safe to say that the people who run these two places have a God's complex. They don't have any kind of networking skills to help the people acquire what they need most, which is employment or advancement opportunities. They want to be oppressors, and they'll talk to people in a condescending way with no regard to the other person's feelings. These places are a joke, and the people who run them are jokers with no jacks, no queens, no king, and no numbered cards. It's just the way that the deck is stacked. President Franklin D. Roosevelt gave the people a plan for success called the "New Deal." President Truman had the "Fair Deal" but here at Rowan Hating Ministries and this program at New Tomorrows, you have "No Deal"!

After I read the diary assignment, I was instructed to write for the class. The instructor told me that the content I presented was inappropriate. I told her that she's full of bull, and if she didn't want me to write anything, then she should've censored the topics from the beginning. She gave us autonomy to write on any topic we wanted to. This was a creative writing assignment that she gave the group to do, because the guest speaker for that afternoon didn't attend that day. One thing that I remembered that when I was teaching, if plan A wasn't available, then you better have a plan B ready. Do you think they'll give me free reign to write freely about anything that I want again?

That evening when I came in for the night, I made a point of letting my case manager Willie know what transpired at the group session. I didn't know if she was told him or David what happened, but I was going to assume the responsibility of my own actions for what I've done. When I explained to Willie, he didn't know anything about the incident that happened. I kept the assignment to let him and the intern Brian read it. Willie asked me what the assignment about? I told him that it was an assignment in creative writing. Willie said that unless she had put some parameters on the content, then I had every right to compose whatever I wanted. He also told me that I shouldn't have dissed the program. He knew the point that I was trying to make about my personal discuss with the shelter, the program and the fact that I was frustrated not having a job.

I was trying to find new ways of remaining calm, because during this time I'm focusing on trying to ace the interview so that I can secure this position with United Rentals. I was finding myself being more anxious in trying to be prepared for it. Nothing else mattered to me at this point as far as my personal surroundings. For once I was strictly thinking of myself and how getting this position could benefit me. I prayed more than I would normally do, and when I went to the library, I read more novels instead of looking through the job search engines on the internet. I was trying different ways of relaxing myself. I did this for several days before it was time for me to make the scheduled call for the phone interview.

As a final point of preparation, I went back to the career center for my follow-up mock interview. I had written down some things that I didn't think of before, and discussed them with the instructor from the career center about an interview. We went over the interview process for about a half hour. I asked her questions, and she gave me suggestions on what I should do if a certain situation should arise. By the end of the session, the instructor told me that I did a better job on the interview than I did the previous time I visited her.

She told me things to remember and try to remain calm. She had seen me in the career center over the year since the time she started working there and was hoping that I could ace the interview. This was one of the few times that someone must've wanted this position as much as I did. That touched me to the point that I started to cry when I left the building.

The next day came and it was approaching time for me to get ready for the interview. Now I've put my mindset geared on one thing, to get the employers at United Rentals interested to find enough positive qualities about myself so that they would want to hire me. I dressed in a suit as if I was going to meet the interviewer in person. Early in the morning, I asked JP if I could use his phone because it had unlimited minutes, and I didn't want to worry about a drop call. I went to use one of the study rooms at the library for privacy. I attempted to prepare for this interview as if I were applying for the position of an angel, and Jesus Christ himself was giving me the interview. I didn't need any distractions, and everything needed to be right. When the time came to make the call, I felt confident. I took a minute to meditate and ask God for favor just before I dialed the number. This was my moment of truth, and everything that I prepared for was weighing on this time that I was about to embark on.

I finally dialed the number and contacted the interviewer. I made the call about five minutes early so if there were any complications with the connection or the phone system, I could still contact them on time. When the interviewer answered the phone, I told him my name and that I was scheduled for an interview at this time. He acknowledged that I was scheduled and that I was a little early with the phone call. He sounded as if he was pleased that I called early when he told me that I must've been a Boy Scout because it appeared that I was prepared to do the interview. I told him that I was, and we had preceded with the interview. He told me about the job position in depth and what the requirements and responsibilities were. After he had given an overview of the position, the question-and-answer segment commenced. When he said, "Tell me about yourself," I felt comfortable, and all the nervous energy that I had built up inside of me was released. We continued to exchange dialogue until the interview as over. The interview session lasted about a good thirty to forty minutes. The one question that I asked before the interview was over was how soon were they going to fill this position. He told that they were going to hire the person then next week, and I will know something within the next few days. That was the last question that I had for him, and at that, I thank him for the opportunity to interview with the company. I sat in the room alone, and just kept silent and asked Jesus that he would find favor in me to receive the blessing of getting this job. I left the privacy room and immediately and went to the computer lab in the library to send them a thank you letter in the email address that I've received from them. I didn't know what to expect, but I honestly thought that the interview went well. Now I was only hoping that the interviewer and their company thought the same with me. Now I was feeling those same nerves that I had before the interview. They came back, but in a different way. I didn't know why, but I was hoping that having this feeling was going to be something that could be in my favor. I just knew that I needed to secure this job and hoped that this was going to be the beginning of a means of me moving on up.

For the next couple of days, I would reluctantly go back to the New Tomorrows program, but I did and then went to the library when the sessions there were over. Now when I thought about them contacting me, that time was going to be one of my biggest friends or my biggest foes. Now I was playing the waiting game. I was waiting to hear from them one way or the other if United Rentals was going to hire me. I was walking around town with knots in my stomach from having so much anxiety that I could hardly eat at any point during the day or evening. I figured that once I heard a good report from United Rentals, everything was going to be all right, and I'll regain my appetite.

By the second day after the interview, I returned to the library to check my e-mail. When I logged in to view the messages, I saw that I got an e-mail from United Rentals. When my eyes saw this, I closed them and meditated before opening up the e-mail to read it. What it was, was that I was afraid of receiving another message about their company going with another candidate. When I pulled up the nerve to read the message, my suspicions were confirmed. It was another e-mail just like hundreds of others that all read the same. I was shattered and whatever hope that I had for getting a job was gone. United Rentals decided to go with a candidate that they felt was better qualified for a position. This angered me. I had gone to the computer and wrote back to United Rentals. It wouldn't have bothered me so much if I had pursued them for a position. They found my resume from one of the many job search engines that I'm registered with, and they pursued me. I wrote them back and told them to take me out of their database system, and if they were to ever contacted me again that I'll find out who it was. When I do I would hang my foot so far up their ass that my toenails will be tickling the back of their tonsils from the bottom up.

I tried to stay at the library to read some sports, newspaper, or Facebook articles but I was too devastated to do that. I put all my hopes and aspirations into this interview for job. My devastation turned into frustration, and from there, I knew that I had to be alone. I went to a sitting area across the street from the Norvell Theatre and just cried so that I could get rid of the hurt. I sat out there on a very cool afternoon until four that afternoon. I made my way from there back to the shelter. I saw the case manager on duty, Keona, to ask her if I could get some things to take with me, because I was admitting myself into the mental ward of the Rowan Regional Medical Center's Lifeworks unit. Keona asked why I was going there. I told her that I had to get away from there before I killed somebody. Keona got her keys to the clothes closet that hold the belongings of the residents and allowed me to get a few things so that I could have a change of clothes when I arrived there. When I made that statement, the director of the shelter David overheard me from his office. I didn't make a direct threat to him or any of the staff members. I gathered some things and told Keona that I was going to Lifeworks. I didn't take a cab, and one wasn't offered to me from what the procedure to send someone who's sick out normally is.

I arrived at Lifeworks and told the nurses in admissions that I was feeling homicidal. I was given a brief physical and put into the observation holding facility until a room was available for me. While in there the professionals could examine me. I was in the observation facility for about twenty-four hours before they had a room available. I didn't come out of my room for the first day after I was admitted in the facility. I made out a food menu but didn't go out to the dining area to eat with the others. The following day I did eat with the rest of the people in the unit. I was prescribe an antidepressant and a sleeping pill when I came. Shortly after, I was given the first meal that I ate one of the nurses there told me that someone in the administration at Rowan Helping Ministries told me that I could not return to the shelter to reside there. I recalled the nurse telling me that, but I thought that she was joking. I remembered this nurse from the last time I was here. She and I would always play the dozens with each other so I didn't take what she said seriously.

I stayed at Lifeworks for a five-day period. I knew that if I had returned to the shelter, I would've put myself in some trouble the I really couldn't afford to try to get myself out of. Going there was the best thing that I could do for myself. When I was there, I was able to get the medications I needed to stop the depression and curb the violent tendency that I was wanting to release. Going to the group therapy sessions helped me understand that many of the things that were happening to me was because of things that I've done from the choices that I made. I put myself in this situation by moving to Salisbury in the first place. I had no one to blame for the circumstances that I'm experiencing, but myself. Once I was able to come to terms with that it was time for me to pick up the pieces to the puzzle and try to complete it. It was time for me to return, and to stop the insanity.

I was released from Lifeworks in the afternoon. While I was going through the building, I ran into my church pastor and the first lady. They were there to visit one of the parishioners of the church who had a relative that was ill. I spoke with them briefly, and proceeded to head my way out of the hospital. As I was walking back toward town, they saw me and gave me a ride. I told them that I was going to the library, and they were kind enough to drop me off there. Even though I know that they knew I was staying in the shelter I didn't want them to drop me off there. I wanted to go someplace that I felt comfortable, and since I've been living here, the library has always been that place of comfort for me. Being there I tried to gather my thoughts before I returned to the shelter. I wanted to be able to go back knowing that the world hasn't ended because I didn't get the job with United Rentals.

I stayed at the library until around seven that evening. I waited to arrive at the time when the line to enter in has been minimized during that time. When I arrived at the door, the shelter aide told me that I needed to see my case manager at the other entrance by the crisis assistance network. I went there and ranged the bell to alert them that I was outside waiting to see them. When my case manager Willie came to the door, he asked me why was I there. I told him that I was coming back into the shelter. Willie informed me that David had called up to the hospital and told them to inform me that I was persona non grata at the shelter. He told me to come inside to have a seat in his office. I asked Willie why I was kicked out. He told me that David said that I threatened to kill people there at the facility, and this was done as a measure of public safety. I was given a paper from them telling me that I've been dismissed as a guest from the shelter for threatening to take someone's life. I told them if that were the case, I wouldn't have admitted myself into the psyche ward of the hospital. Willie had given me a letter of dismissal that David authorized. It stated that I was not to be allowed to come to the shelter to receive any assistance from the shelter or the crisis assistance network. I could no longer come to get a meal from the soup kitchen and I could no longer be allowed on the property. If I were caught, I could be prosecuted to the fullest extent of the law. Willie allowed me to get some of my belongings from the shelter now, and will be allowed another ten days to get the remainder of my stuff. Before I left the shelter, Brian the intern gave me the number to a transitional house that was located in the next town over in Rockwell called Grateful Heart Community Services. He told me that JP who stayed at the shelter was living there now. Brian asked me not to tell anyone that he gave me the number to Grateful Heart probably fearing the repercussions of helping someone who just got kicked out of the shelter. I took the phone number and replied, "What number?" I called to see if they had a room there, but there was no answer.

I packed as much of my stuff that I could take with me. I didn't know where I was going to go or what I was going to do. The only thing that I knew from here was that I was going to have to find me some kind of shelter for the evenings. During the days I could spend the majority of my time in the library. I would go there when the doors opened and could stay there until the doors closed at nine in the evening on Mondays through Wednesday. On Thursday I could stay until six, and on Friday and Saturday, I could stay until five. Sundays were going to be a problem after church. I could go to attend church service at Shady Grove Baptist Church in Mt. Ulla. They would send out a van to the shelter and pick of people to come out there to worship. The pastor, Reverend Williamson, would have a morning service from ten in the morning that would end about two in the afternoon. Just before the congregation would return home for the evening the church would serve a Sunday afternoon dinner for its parishioners and homeless guest that attended the services.

My options for staying were limited, and I knew that I didn't have many choices. I tried to get back into the Lifeworks program, but they denied me access to return there. I couldn't ask my cousin, because that was the way that got me into this situation in the first place. My cousin and I had a great relationship prior to me moving in with her and her husband. When I was asked to leave, that relationship didn't sour, but the love that was there was never the same as it was before. Moving to my sister's place in Charlotte wasn't an option, because she was helping my oldest brother who moved there and there wasn't any more room in her place. Now I was truly on my own.

My friend Jean saw to it that I had something to eat in the mornings, and she would also get me something to eat for the evenings. I would go to the Wilco gas station when I woke up to take my washcloth, towel, soap, toothbrush, toothpaste, and deodorant to try to freshen up the best way that I could in the mornings. I would give Jean my belongings for her to stow away for me that included my army blanket, comforter, pillow, and overcoat. She would bring out a bowl of oatmeal and a cup of coffee for me to drink. I gave her my food stamp card to go grocery shopping to buy some beef bacon and turkey sausage for me, because I don't eat pork or food cooked in pork products. With the food stamp card, she would make me a couple breakfast sandwiches consisting of beef bacon, egg, and cheese on wheat bread. Since I had the oatmeal and coffee for the breakfast, I would eat one of the sandwiches, she made and take the other with me to eat later for my lunch. She would also give me a couple of bottled waters to go with some Hawaiian Punch drink mix packets. During the afternoon, other residents who knew me would sneak food out from the soup kitchen so that I could have something to eat. By the evenings, Jean who was living in their transitional housing program at the Eagle's Nest would either cook something for me or get a plate from the shelter and have me eat it. This was my only source of having something to eat until my food stamp card cleared for the following month.

I was out of the shelter for eight days before the first serious cold spell hit. During that time, I would stay out at the bus stop by the train depot. I could fall asleep there and stay overnight, but I would have to be up and have that area cleared by five in the morning before the buses started to make their way. When the coldest day hit, the weather forecast had a frost and freeze warning. I went to the police station when the library closed. It happened on a Friday, and I saw an officer going to his car. It was closed and I asked the officer if the station was open. He replied no and asked me how he could help me. I told him that I wanted him to take me to jail, because I was homeless and that I was barred from the shelter. He told that he couldn't do that because I didn't break any laws that would constitute him to arrest me. I asked him did he know that tonight was going to be the coldest day of the year. He told me that he did, and then asked me if I had any family or friends in the area who I could go stay with for the night. I replied and told him that if I did than I wouldn't have asked to spend the night in jail. He told me to go to the post office.

I took his suggestion and walked over there after Jean bought me something to eat. She was arguing with me about asking my cousin if she could put me up for the evening. I told her that I wasn't going to go that route again, and that sooner or later, something would come up. I continued to call Grateful Heart, but still hadn't received an answer from anyone who was associated with the program there. She had tears in her eyes and was crying on my shoulder just before I left. I waited for about an hour before I went into the post office so that I could try to attract as little attention as possible. Maybe it was because that the temperature outside was so cold that there wasn't hardly anyone on the street or driving through the town.

When I got to the post office, there wasn't anyone going to their mailboxes, and the few that did went to the mailboxes were on the other side from where I wasn't staying. Just a little after midnight, there was a man that came over to check on his mail on the same side where I set up my minicamp. It was just my luck that he happened to be a county sheriff deputy. He told me that me being there I was trespassing on federal property. I told him the same thing that I told the local police officer. I asked him to arrest me, because I wasn't allowed to go into the shelter and that I didn't have anywhere to go. I told him that it was inhumane to have someone who didn't have a place to require them to sleep outside in the elements. He told me that he wasn't going to arrest me, but that I needed to leave. He told me to walk around the area for about five minutes. When the five minutes were up, he would be gone, and I shouldn't sleep heavy because the next shift of postal employees will be coming to start their next shift about four thirty or five o'clock in the morning. I would have to be out of there by then or I would be facing federal charges of trespassing. I did as he said and returned after the five-minute period.

On the coldest of night, I would go to sleep in the post office, and on night that it wasn't too windy, I would be in Eastern Gateway Park that's adjacent to the bus stop. The one thing that I had to make sure that I had while I was sleeping in the elements was some hard candy. I had to keep that because if I didn't my mouth would get dry, and I could choke on the cold arid evening air. On extremely cold evenings I would return to sleep in the post office, and make my way back to the Wilco gas station in the morning to clean myself up. This was the routine that I had to do, but I had no one to blame for this situation but myself. These were the results of my consequences for making ill-advised decisions. All this time, while I had to endure what was happening, I had to stay prayerful. I had to do what many were told to do, and that was to pray without ceasing.

The days of being out of the shelter from the Rowan Helping Ministries didn't bother me as much as I thought that it would. The fact that I stopped going to the soup kitchen before I was dismissed from the shelter didn't bother me, because I stopped going there long before I was dismissed. The one thing that I can relate to about being out without a place to go is something that my friend Patrick had told me when he was kicked out for the six-month period. That if people see you out in the public knowing that you're homeless and penniless, they may not necessarily give you money, but they will see to it that you have something to eat. The only time that I was told to stay away from the shelter was at night. Some evenings when I went to take my usual place on the bus stop bench, there may be a church group passing by giving out blankets and a Styrofoam box hot meal. Another time there was a man who saw me from his pickup truck who stopped by after eating at the Thai restaurant and was kind enough to give me his take-out box and offer me a beer. I declined on the beer, but I did take the food, and the one time that I did receive money was when I was awakened by a couple walking back to their car from leaving a show that was at the Lee Street Theatre. The man asked me if I was all right. I told him that I was fine, but I asked him if he had a cigarette. He reached into his pocket and gave me two five-dollar bills.

Those were some of the rare incidents that people were genuinely concerned. They didn't care to know my name, but they displayed their compassion for someone who was less fortunate than themselves. It didn't matter to them what it was that caused me to be there, but while I was there that I should find a little comfort in whatever my situation was. When these acts of compassion occurred, I found comfort in crying, not because I felt sorry for myself. I would think back to what my granddaughter wrote when she said that maybe I saw someone who was down on their luck and I didn't go out of my way to display that kind of humanitarianism toward them. I reflected on that and I felt guilty because of it. She was right, and when a stranger who I didn't know would offer me something to help me, I just ate me up. When I reflected on those occasions, when strangers would go out of their way, it would eat me up in return.

By the twentieth day of being out of the shelter, the first major snowstorm of the year hit. Just a few days before that happened, I had slept on the bench and the temperature had dipped rapidly when I was able to catch a wink in the below-freezing temps. When I woke up, I couldn't feel my hands or feet. I could barely walk, but I made my way across the street from the bus stop to the pay phone to call 911 to get an ambulance to come there so that I could go to the hospital. I was experiencing frostbite, and if I didn't get there, things would've gotten worse for me. They came, got my information, and took me to the hospital. There I was treated, offered something to eat, and was released the same day. A few days later, the snowstorm came. Going to the post office wasn't a good idea at that time, because the few other homeless people who chose to sleep on the streets instead of the shelter started sleeping in the post office. This drew the attention of the police so the cops were making routine stops during the night.

I decided to make my trek from the bus stop to the hospital by the time the snow started falling. I went into the emergency room of Rowan Regional Medical Center carrying a garbage bag with my belongings in hand. When I arrived, there weren't very many people who were in the emergency room. There was a woman with a child and one other elderly couple. The elderly woman was someone who recognized me from the time when her church came to the shelter to volunteer their services there. We briefly exchanged greetings, and shortly after that, she was seen for treatment. I found a comfortable spot in the emergency room and opened up my laptop. They had Wi-Fi service so I connected and went to YouTube to watch the whole miniseries of Irwin Shaw television classic *Rich Man, Poor Man*. I was comfortable and warm from the elements of that snowstorm that was taking place outside.

One of the desk nurses who were on duty came from behind their station and asked if I was waiting for someone. I told her that I wasn't and thanked her for asking. I went back to looking at the video that was playing on my computer reminiscing about the first time that I saw that show on television. About thirty minutes later, the other person who was on duty came from behind the desk and asked me if I needed to be seen by a doctor or medical professional. I told them once again that I was fine. I continued to go back to viewing my program. I found comfort for the evening even if this was going to be a short stay. I didn't mind the concern by the employees at the hospital.

An hour had passed before the security guard on duty finally reached me. It was a female, and she too asked me if I needed to be seen by a professional. I told her that I didn't, but I knew in my mind that I couldn't politely try to dismiss her like I was able to do with the hospital nurses. The officer told me that unless I was there waiting on a patient or waiting to be seen by a doctor, I wasn't supposed to be waiting there. I explained to her that I was kicked out of the shelter and that I didn't have anywhere to go. I told her that I would understand if she had to cuff me and arrest me for trespassing and that I was willing to accept that. It was just inhumane for me to have to live outside in the snow. It would've been better for me to stay sometime in jail knowing that I could have a comfortable night to sleep. She didn't say anything at first, but when she opened her mouth, I could hear a New England accent. She inquired if I had anything to eat. I told her that I would be fine if I could just stay there until the storm passed. She asked me to follow her. I started to get my things, but she told me that I could leave them there and that they would be safe there since no other patients were in the hospital that evening. I followed her, and I just knew that she was taking me to a secure place to process me for an arrest. Instead, she escorted me to the cafeteria. She asked me what I wanted. I told her that I would be fine if I had a cup of coffee. She insisted that I get something off the hot menu to go along with that. I ordered some lasagna and a cup of coffee. She told me that she would allow me to bring the food back into the waiting area where my possessions were and allowed me to stay there until the storm passed.

I ate a very generous ration of food that this officer purchased with her own credit card and continued to watch the episodes of *Rich*

Man, Poor Man until it was watching me. By ten that morning, the snow had subsided, and I wasn't going to try to overstay my unexpected welcome, so I went into the routine of going into the men's room to groom myself before I went back out into the world. Before I left the hospital, I called my friend Jean to let her know that I was all right and that I slept in the emergency room overnight. I told her that I had something to eat and that I would be making my way to the library. Once I got my things together, I walked toward the library, but it was on a delayed opening and didn't open until eleven that morning instead of the usual nine o'clock time.

By now I was calling JP, the young guy who moved out of the shelter, to see if he could talk to the management at Grateful Heart to see if they had a bed open. I didn't know how many more days that I would be able to handle being out in the elements. I was able to get in touch with JP, and he told me that there would be a bed opening up soon. He told me that one of the guys who stayed there was about to move out and that he talked to the manager of the facility whose name was Alonzo. He gave me Alonzo's phone number and told me to keep trying to contact him. I called Alonzo but didn't get an answer, but I was able to leave him a message.

I didn't hear anything from Alonzo or anyone connected with Grateful Heart. Meanwhile I was really starting to feel the stress of trying to find a place for me to rest comfortably. During this time, after the storm, my usual digs of staying at the library during the daytime hours wasn't happening. There was another storm warning with the chance of snow or precipitation falling so the library was closing earlier than the normal hours. The day after the initial storm, the library closed at three that afternoon. Since it was a Saturday, the buses stopped running at four that afternoon. I wrapped myself in my blanket and comforter covering my head and face, so just in case anyone who knew me wouldn't be able to recognize me. I also made sure that I had plenty of hard candy so that the elements outside wouldn't choke me during the night.

My friend Jean met me at the bus stop to give me something to eat. She became more adamant about me going to my cousin's, but I was just as stubborn as she was and refused to go against what I knew wasn't going to be a good situation once I could get myself into the Grateful Heart Ministries. I went to the post office, but had to wait until it became dark because there were people who were going in there to check on their mail. Once it became dark, I went and found a spot at the post office and fell asleep until one of the employees came out from the sorting area to tell me and the others who were sleeping there that we had to go or the law was going to make a special guest appearance. I moved back to the bus stop area until the police told me to move from there at five that morning.

The next day was Sunday, and I met Jean that morning so that we attended church service that morning. We arrived at Shady Grove, and just before Sunday school started, I asked the first lady if I could meet with the pastor privately if it was possible. She told me that she would ask him and that she would let me know. The pastor agree to meet with me briefly, and I humbly thanked him for taking a minute to talk. I explained to him about my situation that I needed his help if he could direct me to another shelter or outreach ministry that would be able to help me secure a place to stay. He didn't know of any place, but opened up his wallet and wrote out a check for me to cash so that I could stay in a motel for the evening. He also asked the minister of music at Shady Grove if he could have me worked with him in his construction business. I met with the pastor and the minister of music after service so that we could mutually make arrangements to get shelter and some part time employment.

This was a welcomed break, and the first time that I slept comfortably since my unannounced stay at the hospital emergency room during the snowstorm. I checked myself into the motel the next evening after I helped out on the roofing job that the minister of music was working on. Anyone who knew me will have a good understanding that I'm not very mechanically inclined to do work that required labor. I'm more of a cerebral person that can do things that would require a pretty in-depth thought process. Although I didn't know a thing about roofing and less about construction, the minister of music was very patient by allowing me to work with him. I was blessed to work with him for the next three days, and I was paid under the table for each day of work that I did. The minister saw to it that I had lunch each day and was generous in giving me enough money to pay for the hotel room for the evening.

During the nights, I would continue to call over to Grateful Heart to make contact with the transition house, but still without success. I decided to call JP, and I was successful in making contact with him. He told me that Alonzo did receive my message, and he was going to contact me soon. JP told me that there was going to be a space that was about to open up, and that Alonzo would be calling me. This was the best news that I heard since I was dismissed from the shelter. I knew after hearing this news that my prayers were being answered. Having to spend this time living in the elements of the outdoors during the winter wasn't how I would have imagined that my life would turn out.

When I moved to Salisbury, it was with the aspirations that things would've been a benefit to me. When I asked my job I was working prior to moving into Salisbury for a transfer, they initially agreed. I would've been able to work out of the residents where I was staying with my cousin and come to the office in either Blythewood, South Carolina, or Charlotte. I was about to embark on another new frontier to begin a new chapter in my life. One that I had planned to make it better for me personally so that I could give my grand-daughter the things that I wasn't able to give her when I lived in Columbia. John Steinbach probably said it best from his bestselling book *Of Mice and Men*, "If you're not moving forward then where are you going?" My thing wasn't to try to remain stagnant but to move forward, and if this was going to be the start of something to get me off the street, then I'm ready.

Even when I was living as a homeless person in the shelter, there were still things that I took for granted. Having volunteers who got out of their beds as early as four in the morning just to prepare the breakfast meal for the residents who stayed there. Coming there in the afternoon so that I could get something to eat out of the soup kitchen, and coming in at night so that you can get a shower a hot meal. Being on the streets, I didn't have the liberty of eating in the morning or going to the soup kitchen. Getting a shower was non-existent and trying to remain fresh smelling was a job within itself.

Getting up during the same time as the volunteers who served the shelter guest was what I had to do. I would stop at the Wilco service station about that time to go in so that I could use the restroom. I would have my washcloth, soap, toothpaste, toothbrush, and deodorant so that I wouldn't be offensive being around people.

A few more days passed since the storms happened, and if going back to sleep on a bench was normal, then it was just that. I continued to call Alonzo at Grateful Heart Ministries on a daily basis, but it wasn't until later that week that I was finally able to contact him. I told him that I was living on the street for close to thirty days now, and that I wasn't allowed to come into the shelter. I explained to him about the circumstances that I put myself in that caused me to live on the streets. I asked if there was an open bed and told him that I would be willing to accept their rules because I desperately needed a place to stay. He told me that they did have a bed that would open up on the weekend, and if I wanted it, I could move in as early as Saturday. I told him that I would be happy to move into the place that day. Alonzo told me that he would pick me up that Saturday afternoon about three o'clock. This news happened on a late Thursday afternoon, early evening when I received it.

For once I was genuinely happy to be there, and to wait for a couple more days didn't make much of a difference to me. The first thing that I did was to drop to my knees to thank God for providing me this place to move into. As a believer in the father, it's true that the good Lord doesn't put more on you that you can't bear. During the time I was on the streets, I've been blessed that there wasn't any major illness that I had to endure, and most importantly, I wasn't in trouble with the law or physically harmed. As long as the weather report was favorable without gusting winds, snow, or rain, I could deal with it for a few more days. Even though I wasn't at Grateful Heart Ministries, I was thankful that God had delivered me from the ordeal of spending another week on the streets.

When people from the shelter or around saw me, they witnessed a difference in me. My walk to the library had a little more pep to it, and I was a lot more sociable than I was when I first became one of the many people in this country who had to live on the streets. Before

I knew I was going to Grateful Heart, I was reclusive, insecure, and lost whatever confidence that I had because I was ashamed of the situation that I had put myself in. I recalled the times when I knew of a person that I grew up with who was living as a homeless man. He asked me one time for a dollar to get something to eat. I knew him so I gave him a buck, but weeks later, I saw that he went to a parking lot in Newark and opened the doors to a late-model luxury car. For him this was a way that he preferred to make his living. He was good at it eventually, because he was driving a luxury car while I was struggling to take the bus to work from East Orange to downtown Newark. My attitude toward homeless people changed until I became homeless myself. I experienced the struggle of more than trying to get bus fare.

Being homeless wasn't a preferential lifestyle that I chose for myself to be in. I know what it's like to have to depend on a system that isn't very kind to the plight of your personal situation. I can't say that all agencies that are advocates for the homeless are as bad as the one that I've experienced with Rowan Helping Ministries. For me to do that is to say that all black people want to have the government support them so that they can live without supporting themselves.

It made me realize that the system that I experienced in Rowan County is one that resembles a hamster wheel. You enter the system looking for assistance, and what you receive is what they want you to get. I came into Rowan Helping Ministries with the thought that they would help get me, and others who needed the help, return back to mainstream society. What I witnessed was an agency that received grant funding and did little to assist the population of the homeless.

It was easy and more profitable for the administrators of the shelter to keep the homeless people there. Easy for them to house the veterans who were applying for their disability, because the Veterans Administration would pay the subsidies to the shelter at a higher than what the government programs would do for a civilian that was residing there. The longer the case managers didn't send you out to a job referral, the more secure the shelter administration and their board of directors were about receiving these subsidies.

Don't get me wrong. The crisis assistance network that helped the resident who lived outside of the shelter did more than their fair share. They were contributing to those who needed help keeping their lights on, help with their water bills and emergency rent or mortgage payments. I wouldn't doubt if they were operating in the red when the business was centered around the crisis assistance network. I had seen several people that I've been associated with, that have received help from the crisis assistance network. I have also witnessed the staff of the shelter selling supplies donated to them by the local drug stores that were allocated for the resident who stayed there, and others who were in need from going through the crisis assistance network. All that this did was display to me that the people in the administration had their hands in a cookie jar. Just like a child trying to get a snack before it was supper time. All of them were getting a little something out of it, but the real losers outside of the shelter residents were the employee who worked out of the shelter and crisis assistance network. I was sorry to see these actions, because it made me lose my faith in a system that I wanted to believe so bad that they're to help people who find themselves in destitute situations. It made me realize that the concentration that I had studied for wasn't respected in this part of the state of North Carolina. I wasn't going to concern myself with the way that this agency was being ran any longer.

I was genuinely concerned about the people who still resided there. When the shelter director would hold their monthly meeting, many of them wouldn't speak up about the improprieties that they witness themselves. Many of them were reluctant to do that for fear of being put out of the shelter without having the resources to go anyplace else. The one person that I was most concern was my friend Jean. She was a woman who fell into the system when her boyfriend kicked her out of his place. When she moved into the shelter, she and I were seeing each other. When she first moved in, she was attending school at the Rowan Cabarrus Community College to get her GED diploma. Jean left school at a young age, and if I'm not mistaken, she stopped attending school when her mother passed away in her senior year of high school.

When the 2014 started, David had made some changes. Jean would come to the crisis assistance network after her classes and would volunteer to work in the clothing department there. She was very thorough at doing what they needed her to do, and she would work like a mule that could plow you several acres of field in a day. The administration saw this good labor at the most affordable rate of her volunteering to do this and took advantage of her. The first thing that they did was to force her to attend the sessions at New Tomorrows. She would have to go there from eight in the morning to noon for the self-esteem classes, and in the afternoon, they asked her to work in the clothing department of the crisis network from one to three. That did nothing for a woman who was in the process of trying to get her GED. What the administration of the shelter did was a sin, and they did it as a self-serving purpose to help their own cause.

What they did was have Jean do a tradeoff. They moved her out of the shelter and into the transitional housing for her to stay in. They compensated her approximately seventy-five dollars a week for working at the crisis assistant network, but the price she had to pay was that working at the crisis assistant network and attending the mandatory self-esteem classes she was still going to be without achieving her GED. She told me that they were making it mandatory for her to go to the sessions for the self-esteem classes and to do the work in the crisis center. If she didn't attend the self-esteem sessions, then what the authoritative powers had informed her, her stay at the shelter was going to be a brief one. What they were doing in the process was violating her human right in order to get the best kind of work from her. At about five dollars an hour they were getting cheap labor out of her.

The day that I received the news that I was going to move to Grateful Heart, all hell broke loose. Jean and I have an item since she moved into the shelter. Before the administration had con her into doing their dirty work for them, she and I would meet in the early afternoons at the library. During the weeks when she was a student RCCC and not at New Tomorrows for the self-esteem classes, I would help her with study for some of her GED classes. On the weekends, we would reserve a private study room and check out some movies that she had, or the new ones that the library did. Being in there was like being in another world. We'd bring our popcorn and the library sold their own beverages so it was almost like having your own private movie date. We would be hugged up together, and one time, I received oral sex briefly. If either of us had some cash from a hustle job or from selling our food stamps, we would treat ourselves to one of the better eating restaurants in the area. It was either a Chinese joint or at Uncle Bucks. The one thing that I truly enjoyed about spending time with her was the fact that we mutually found a church that we both felt comfortable with in attending, Shady Grove AME Church. There, we both felt welcomed, but more importantly, we felt the spirit of the Lord there.

I was hoping that telling her would've made her happy that I was finally getting off the streets. Unfortunately it didn't go the way I hoped for. Going to the Grateful Heart Ministries meant that I was going to have to go into another town in the county. It is located three miles outside of the Salisbury border, and in order for me or anyone else to get there, it was going who didn't have a car. I explained to her that I was accepted to come into the program at Grateful Heart, and that Alonzo was going to pick me up in two days. I told her about the rules that were outlined in the program. That I was there on a two-week probationary program. I wasn't allowed to leave the facility unless I was doing work for their mission. I wasn't allowed to have any guest to visit me unless they were there to drop off something that I need like clothes, medication, or other supplies. No one could visit me inside the facility, only on the grounds of the facility. I would only be given two days out of the month to get a night out, and the straw that broke the camel's back. That and the fact I wasn't allowed to go back to my place of worship. I was only allowed to go to theirs since they were putting me up I had to be obligated to worship at their services only.

Jean wasn't happy about this at all, and she let me know her displeasure when she gave me my dinner that she made for the last time. I told her that everything was going to be all right, because the main point of emphasis was that I was finally going to get off the streets. She was very adamant about me asking my cousin if I could've moved in with her and her husband. There was no way that I was going to do that. Jean must've thought that I was going to take this opportunity to look for another relationship, but that was the furthest thing from my mind. Jean believed that I could've been able to do that because during the Thanksgiving holiday, my cousin and her husband went away for an extended holiday to visit both sets of in-laws in South Carolina and Virginia. Jean and I were allowed to stay in the house during the time that they were gone, but it came with an angle. They didn't want to take their pug dog named Jackpot (I always called him Jackass since the day I met the damn pooch). We made sure he got fed by the evening and that he didn't crap in the laundry area. We did that from that Tuesday evening of Thanksgiving week until they returned Sunday. That was a one-time good thing that was as convenient for them to have us to do that, but the bottom line is that they really didn't want us there. That's what I was trying to explain to Jean.

What I needed at that time was a bed to sleep in, a roof over my head, and place that I could say, even if I was reluctant to acknowledge, is a home. After I ate, Jean continued to express her displeasure with my decision about moving into the transitional house in Granite Quarry. We walked back to her place at the Eagle's Nest, and her displeasure turned into rage. As we were walking back, there we were passing behind the old Cheerwine soda factory. That was the quickest way to get back to the Eagle's Nest. Little to my knowledge the area that we were passing through was considered railroad property government land that was considered private, and if you're caught passing through there, you could be summoned for trespassing. There have been numerous time and countless days that people passed through there without ever being harassed by the law. It was just my misfortune that there was a Norfolk Southern railroad police nearby and he heard Jean screaming and cursing at the top of her voice. Passing through the railroad property was considered trespassing even if there weren't any activity on the dormant tracks that hadn't been used in decades.

The officer followed us as we passed by the railroad property and through the area that the shelter residents called the drugstore in order to get to her place. By the time that I was able to reach the corner, the officer had caught up with me and had called dispatch for a car that came shortly waiting for me. The only thing that I did to the best of my knowledge was trespassed on the property of Rowan Helping Ministries. I had no knowledge or idea that the property that everyone was using as a shortcut was property of the Norfolk Southern Railroad. The officer questioned Jean first because it was her voice that they heard screaming. They questioned her as to what was the reason that caused her to scream. To the best of my knowledge she must've told them that we were having a disagreement, but her rationalization and my own was that there wasn't a need for them to bring out the squad car. When I look back at the incident in hindsight, there was a need, because Jean freaked out about me wanting to move on.

After they interrogated her, two of the officers came to ask me what I was doing there. I told them that I was walking my girlfriend back to her place and waiting for her to give me my things. The shelter workers inside had called David and told him that the cops were talking to Jean and I outside of the shelter. The other officer was talking to one of the shelter aides to inquire if they knew Jean or myself. They told them that Jean was a resident of the Eagle's Nest, but I was a former resident that was kicked out of the property. The officer who was talking to me told me that I was going to receive a warning citation for trespassing. I told them that the next time that I was on the property of the shelter, I would be arrested and the administration would prosecute me to the fullest extent of the law. From there I was instructed to leave. I was standing in the middle of the three hundred block of Liberty Street on the corner of Liberty and Long, but the officer warned me that if I didn't leave, I would've been arrested then. I heard his instructions and left the area never to return again.

Not looking for any further trouble, I didn't want to stay so I went to a bench at Magnolia Park on West Innes St. I found a comfortable spot there for the evening. I still had the few things with me, enough to make myself a pallet there. Magnolia Park is a small non-secluded area that's in between the county building and next door to a group of row buildings that the downtown businesses use for their daily operations. Once I got myself into a pretty good place,

I noticed that I heard some gospel music coming from the upstairs of the photography studio. It felt that this was a sign of me passing through one season of my life into another. This was a signal to me that God was showing me favor, and his way of telling me that you need to remove yourself from this place.

I felt that this was a bullet that I had dodged, and along with what transpired, this move meant that I was going to have to make some changes in my life. The first thing that I needed to do was to separate myself from the current surroundings of being in Salisbury. I've been given a new lease on life when I spoke to Alonzo, and the people at Grateful Heart were allowing me to start fresh. Being at Rowan Helping Ministries had served its purpose for providing me shelter and sustenance that I needed while I resided there. Like all good things, they all have to come to an end. Another thing that I was going to have to do was to change my association with the people who I was around on a daily basis. That was going to be a pretty simple one for a couple of reasons. The first being the location of Grateful Heart. It's located three miles out from Salisbury. They have limited bus service that runs out to Granite Quarry to Salisbury. They only have thirteen beds that house only men, and the other was the majority of the people who I built relationships with in Salisbury I lost confidence in them. Letting go of those people was easy, because quite a few of them weren't looking for way to improve their own situation. Not to sound like I'm trying to put myself on a pedestal, but they weren't equally yoked as I. Some of them would hustle side jobs, and once they received their payment, they would request for a night or two out just to drink and get high.

The hardest person that I had to discontinue my association with was Jean. She was a very sweet person, but her displeasure about me moving to the transition house out of town was the last thing that I needed. Jean was a woman who needed to finish high school. She was still somewhat impressionable and very easy to influence when it came to volunteering her time for work that needed to be done at the shelter. When the administration asked her to volunteer her services, she was good at the sorting, cleaning, and setting up displays of the clothing articles for the crisis assistance network. Her talents didn't go unnoticed, because she was the first person that they requested if they needed help. In the process, the administration was slowly taking her away from school and placing her into their system of being a volunteer working shelter guest. The other thing was when it came down to me, she didn't like the fact that I knew and associated myself with women. The majority of the females that I knew were from working relationships.

Moving to Granite Quarry was easy, because of the situation that had taken place in Salisbury. My first night there at Grateful Heart, I was introduced to Sam by Alonzo. I was given the outline of the rules and had to sign a contract stating that I would adhere to them or be asked to leave. They must've known that I was a pasta lover, because that evening, we had spaghetti for dinner. I was shown where my bed and closet was for me to store my things. That evening after dinner, I took a long shower and went to bed quickly. It was the first time since being on the streets and at the shelter that I was allowed to sleep in a real bed and to take a hot shower. It was a twin bed, but it felt as if I was sleeping on a California king-size one. I went to sleep before nine that evening and didn't wake up until five o'clock that following morning. After living in the shelter for the past three years, you condition yourself to get up at or before five twenty in the morning.

When I woke up the following day, I went to my closet to get my clothes ready for church service. I took out a suit and pressed it off and made me something to eat before I got dressed. By the time nine o'clock arrived, Alonzo had come to the mission at Granite Quarry to pick up the guys so that we could attend church. He came to drive the church bus so that all the fellas would be in attendance for the service. We arrived at the church and had Sunday school at ten followed by worship service at eleven. When the Sunday school service was over, the service began being preached by the founder of the organization the Reverend Johnny Morgan. He owned a carpet and tile store and lived in the little town in the county called Rockwell. I was amazed when I got to the church that people would go to the altar to give thanks to God before the services commenced.

Reverend Morgan was a kind man, and when I first saw him, he reminded me of the Burl Ives character from the animated special Mr. Snowman from *Rudolph the Red-Nosed Reindeer*. He was a rotund white male bald with a white goatee that reminded me of the character that Burl Ives portrayed in the television special. I don't know but when he started his sermon, it struck a cord with me. It was entitled "By the Wayside." It felt like he was preaching to me specifically, because he was saying how society was judging people because of their past. It was a very powerful sermon that had me in tears, because everything that I had experienced to that point occurred to me since I moved into Rowan County. When the service was over, I always make an attempt to shake the hand of the person who delivered the message. I met Reverend Morgan and introduced myself to him. I wanted to thank him for accepting me to become part of the Grateful Heart family.

He accepted my thoughts and told me that God has some work for me to do. I told him that I was ready and that we're going to get this work done together. I can say that I felt welcomed from the moment that I arrived at Grateful Heart. I didn't know how long that I was going to be there, but I did know that I didn't want to become complacent with what was being offered to me while I was staying there. I was still wanting to become gainfully employed so that I can live independently. The goal hasn't changed since I left Columbia, South Carolina. My goal was the same for me to live on my own so that I could have my granddaughter come to visit and continue to spend some time with me here. Please don't get me wrong. I wasn't ungrateful for having to stay in the mission at Grateful Heart. Once again there's that proverb that I had to remember when living with others. Never overstay your welcome, because you may not be welcome to stay over.

CHAPTER 14

Maybe Change is Good

After that Sunday service, I had to get myself acclimated to the standard routine of the business that took place at Grateful Heart Community Services. On Monday, Wednesday, Thursday, and Friday evening at eight o'clock, there was a mandatory Bible study meeting for the residence to attend unless they were working. All the residents had to be inside the facility by that time and couldn't go out to smoke after the doors were closed. Tuesday morning at ten, there was another mandatory Bible study conducted by Pastor Johnny or another board member of Grateful Heart. On Monday, Wednesday, and Friday at noon, two of the residents would have to go to Wal-Mart to pick up grocery items as part of the Feed America Program that Grateful Heart had a contract with to feed the community of people who needed assistance with food. Once every other month, Grateful Heart would go to Charlotte, North Carolina, to the Second Harvest Food Bank to purchase food at a discount and also distribute that to the public.

All of the residents were required to be there unless they held jobs to assist with the distribution of food to the people who would call to make an appointment to receive food. Our job was to get the food and stock it when it arrived, then make up the boxes for the recipients and to clean up the leftover garbage. Recipients would receive meats, produce, non-alcoholic fluids, bakery, and dry goods. For a brief period at the end of the winter and the beginning of spring Pastor Johnny was also able to secure the distribution rights to give out the United State Department of Agriculture chicken to the public as well.

Early in my stay at the mission, I was approached by Alonzo and Pastor Johnny's wife, Brenda Morgan. Alonzo had informed her that I was good with working on the computer and that I could probably be able to account for the scheduling of people to whom the agency distributes the food goods to. Brenda took me and another person who came in shortly after I got in there and showed us how the intake process should be for new applicants. She told us that once a person has received their food, they would have to wait for a sixty-day period before they were eligible to receive another. Things seemed to be working out pretty good until I noticed that they had a horrible filing system for keeping records. I spoke with Brenda about creating a database with the computer, by creating spreadsheets of the monthly distribution of good on the Microsoft excel program. Also keeping the records of the client base on the computer through the Microsoft access program. Doing this made it easy for me for her to give the monthly account to the board members and stakeholders at the organizations that they were receiving their good from.

The first major task occurred for me at the end of March. I had to be accountable for the first quarterly report. Having to do this with a deadline caused me to work double time, because the records weren't very accurate. The people who were doing the intake and the accounting of recipients before I arrived had the records looking like a bunch of scrambled eggs. Fortunately for me, I had JP working with me, because he was the only other person who was computer literate enough to help Grateful Heart function properly in this area. The agency was able to dodge a bullet, and the Second Harvest was able to receive their quarterly report on time. With my display of being able to master those duties, I was asked to help the agency find funding sources by researching for grant opportunities.

Alonzo, Brenda, and Pastor Johnny were pleased with the work that was done. After the report was completed and submitted to the stakeholders, they decided that I should continue to provide the paperwork for their monthly and quarterly reports. This was pleasing in the eyes of the board members of Grateful Heart. They knew that they had someone in their facility who know how to account for their actions of the services that they were providing, and this gave them another outlet to look for other ways to help support their cause. For me, it gave me a feeling of being useful. It allowed me to channel my scholastic training and previous work experiences to do something that I had a passion for doing. Shortly after doing the intake and scheduling of the clients I was on YouTube to check out some videos because I had some down time. I noticed at that time that the people who made the five-hour energy drink had given away money to charitable causes to individuals and nonprofit organizations. It was a campaign that the company was doing called five-hour energy cares, and after seeing several of their videos, I figured that it wouldn't hurt for me to try to see what the criteria was to apply for the money that they were donating to this organization. This corporation was donating fifty thousand dollars if they believed that you were deserving of it.

I took the initiative to download a video program onto their computer, and I started taking pictures of the functions when we did the distribution of food on the days that it was scheduled. I took some pictures of the facility and the guys as they worked. I would continue to work on the paperwork and schedule the people to receive their goods while working on producing a video for the application for the five-hour energy cares campaign. Once I had enough pictures I started working on producing the video. I had to make sure that I had enough pictures to fill out the musical accompaniment to support it. Since Grateful Heart is a faith-based organization I chose to use the Clark Sisters "You Brought the Sunshine" as the song for the video. When the video was finished, I brought it to the attention of Brenda and Pastor Johnny by sending them an e-mail. I told them about the proposal that needed to be submitted to the five-hour energy drink people, and that one of the requirements was to submit a video of what the agency was doing.

On the following Sunday, when Alonzo picked the guys up for service, Pastor Johnny and Brenda met me in the vestibule of the church. They both expressed their pleasure about me finding a potential funding source to help them with the initiative of Grateful Heart. I explained to them that this wasn't a guarantee, but it was an opportunity to attempt to secure more funding. They understood it and agreed that we should meet during the week so that we can discuss other forms of researching grant funding. I told them that would be fine, because someone would have to pick me up to go out to their place of business. Brenda left soon after that to go sing with the church choir. Johnny stopped me just as I was about to take my seat to ask me what it was that I was passionate about. I was thinking to myself why on earth was this man wanting to know that it was that I wanted to do. I'm thinking that this is about to be some kind of a con. I didn't have to think about it for a minute, but not for the reason that I didn't know what I am passionate to do. Then it came to me in an epiphany. He wanted to know what I was passionate about because he didn't want me to leave this setup that he has. So I told him that my passion is to do live theatre. I wanted to write, direct, produce, and act in plays. Reverend Johnny asked me did I realize that the office I was working in was in an old school. I told him yes, and I knew about the auditorium inside of the building too, but I didn't trust the way that this was going. I couldn't put my finger on it, but it was something about it that just didn't sit too well with me. I was going to play along, because after all the ball is in their court.

The ground of where Grateful Heart Community Service was located at was an old school that was designated for African American who lived in Granite Quarry before integration took place. This was the old Shufford Elementary School that one of the residents Sam had attended when he was a child. The building is white granite that was constructed, and donated from the old quarry that the town is named after. In the main building was the office that we used to schedule clients for emergency food and clothing pick up, as well as researching for grants for the agency. The auditorium is housed in the main building, and before Reverend Johnny moved to the current church, he used to hold church services there. Also on the grounds is an adjacent building that held four other classrooms that were built later. There's a third building on the grounds that's connected by a breezeway. It's the old cafeteria, and this is used by the agency to stock the food that is received when they purchase it from the Second Harvest Food Bank.

The following week Pastor Johnny came over to the mission to pick me up to go to his business. I was to go there to meet with Brenda who was the administrative assistant for the agency so that we could work together on researching some grants. That afternoon, he dropped me off at his store to meet with his wife. Once I was there, Brenda took the rest of the afternoon off from the business to give me the document to download into my laptop that were related to their non profit so that I could have it when I started doing the research for some grants. This felt pretty good to me, because I was doing the work that I knew that I was capable of doing. For once I was starting to feel a certain amount of satisfaction knowing that I was helping others.

Just a couple of weeks after starting to look for other funding sources, I received an e-mail from the people responsible for donating grant money at the five-hour energy people. I spoke when their spokesperson who did the presentation on the telephone one after. The call was made while I was in the process of scheduling clients to receive their goods. She asked me about getting a contact number for Pastor Johnny, and why did I write to five-hour energy about the pastor and the organization. I explained to her what he's been doing in the community, and what he's started out with. I also explained to her that he's been a special person for taking myself off of the streets. We talked briefly before she left to contact the pastor.

The following Saturday, Pastor Johnny told me that he received the call from five-hour energy and that he believed Grateful Heart would become the recipient of the fifty thousand dollar grant. The next day after Sunday school service was over, he was more energetic than normal. He told the congregation about the call that he received from five-hour energy and told them that it was heaven sent. There wasn't any confirmation that the grant would be received, but like most Christians when we believe that something good is going to happen for our purpose, we claim it in the name of the Lord. Members of the church were excited, and many were please once the pastor told them that I was the person who was responsible for finding the potential funding source of the agency.

The following week, I was asked to be a greeter at the church, and I agreed and later asked to be the person who would greet the recipients who received the emergency assistance. It was a time that I felt validated in going back to college to earn my degree. I was helping the children and families receive the goods and services that they need. It had given me the satisfaction that others were benefiting from the resources of what Grateful Heart had to offer. During this time I was still taking some time to go into Salisbury to go to the library. Although I was doing the work that I was trained to do from the degree program, I wasn't receiving any compensation for the work. I understood that I wouldn't be getting anything in lieu of me living at the mission. Even when I went to meet with Brenda to see about researching and applying for grant, that if one was to be received by the agency that I would get a commission for doing it. There wasn't any mention as to how much the commissions would be. I wasn't counting on it being more than ten percent since this is a faith based organization. The funny thing about grants is that if you apply for them that there's no guarantee that you'll get it. To my best understanding, most philanthropists like to know that your agency has been audited before they disperse the funds to the grant applicants.

On one of my trips into Salisbury, I noticed that I received an inbox message on my Facebook page from a friend who used to rent out the upstairs space from my cousin when she had her shop A Little Sumthin' Sumthin'. He sent me a message asking me if I would be interested in helping him launch a local sports magazine. I told him that I would be interested in it and met with him at a local business that was adjacent to Magnolia Park. This was giving me the hope that my homelessness was about to end. I negotiated a deal with the magazine's publisher Brian that I would be interested in doing this with him as a writer and general manager of a publication called Victory Goals Magazine. My deal included; writing stories on the athletes, coaches and the programs, securing arrangements with the local school board for press credentials for the access to the sporting events and acquiring access to the sports information directors of Livingstone and Catawba colleges. There was also one other part of my deal with Brian, and it included that I had to receive a payment of twenty dollars a week, and fifty for the articles written. I knew that there wasn't a lot of money for a new start-up company, and I wasn't trying to break the bank.

I was feeling very inspired and wanted to see this part of my life to end. What this also allowed me to do was to take some time to work for a start-up company in town. Even though I hadn't received a living wage for working there, I didn't shuck any of the responsibilities that had been assigned to me by Grateful Heart. I would continue to do the work on scheduling the people who needed to receive the emergency assistance from the agency. I delegated that duty to JP since he was the only person who knew how to operate the computer. I made sure that I kept my obligation of getting the monthly reports together for the board members and the stakeholders when it was due. Also, I was there on the days that the emergency food and clothing supplies were to be distributed. Working at Victory Goals allowed me to pay my tithes when I attended the services at Grateful Heart. I started doing these duties between the two in April, and I was able to work a balance. In the evenings, when I arrived back from doing the work at Victory Goals allow gave me time to research the monies that were available from grants that were available for Grateful Heart.

One evening, when the group of guys was finishing up our evening Bible study session, I received a phone call from my granddaughter. The call surprised me, because she's a teenager now, and most of the time, she called me when she wanted me to help her with a problem with her homework or inquire about when I was coming to visit. I could hear from the sound of her voice that something was wrong. You always know when there's something wrong when your child talks to you, so I had to find out what it was that has this child so upset. I asked her what's wrong. She told me that she was staying at her grandmother's house for a week. That she arrived there the day before she called me, and the next day, she wasn't allowed to leave her bedroom or the area upstairs. She hadn't been able to go to the downstairs area to get something to eat, because my ex was downstairs with her friends, drinking and smoking weed. I felt so helpless in coming to the aid of my granddaughter. For once I wasn't able to truly be there for her when she called me and needed me the most. It took me a little longer than normal, because Shay'lee's mother was on vacation. When I finally contacted her, I explained to her what Shay'lee had told me about the events that occurred. She was going over the house to confirm what was happening with her daughter and her grandmother. I was waiting to receive a return call from Shay'lee's mother, letting me know that everything was fine with the child.

Knowing this was taking place with a child who I was instrumental in raising since she was four days old had really troubled me. Once I found out the circumstances, I made a point of bringing it to the attention of the people who were in charge of Grateful Heart. I spoke to Alonzo first and told him that I may need to go to Columbia to check on the welfare of my granddaughter. I explained to him what was happening and told him that I may have to go and stay longer than the two nights to secure her safety. He told me that I would have to speak with Pastor Johnny in the morning about it. Within the next couple of hours, my granddaughter's mother called to confirm that Shay'lee has gotten something to eat and that she's going to be all right. Before I hung up the phone with her, I spoke with my granddaughter and told her to call me back if anything like this happened that needed to be brought to my attention, and that I loved her.

The next morning, I made a point of calling Pastor Johnny to explain what has transpired with my granddaughter, and that I needed to go to Columbia to secure my child's welfare. I told him that she's over at my ex-wife's house and that the child was being neglected. I needed to go to the aid of my granddaughter, and that it may take a little longer than the days that were normally allotted by what has been mandated by Grateful Heart. I asked him because these were circumstances that I had no control if there could be an exception to the rule. The pastor asked me if I had anyone who could care for the child. I told him no, and if there was that, I wouldn't need to go through him in order to secure her safety. He granted me the opportunity to leave, but had reinforced the guidelines for being off the premises beyond the time allotted would cause me to lose the privilege of staying at Grateful Heart. I was appalled to know that the welfare and safety of my granddaughter didn't amount up to much from a person who professes to be a man of God. I found this to be very disturbing to me, because I had given everything that I had. I did whatever was asked of me to help the ministry grow at Grateful Heart. This was a family emergency that I told Reverend Johnny about, and for him to limit my access to handle this emergency was a slap in my face. This disappointed me to know that all of what has been asked of me to do in the name of the Lord didn't seem to be fair. I was slapped back into reality that I wasn't in control of my own life. I was at the mercy of the people who I was living off of.

I had to step back and take a better look at the big picture of what has developed, or hasn't developed at Grateful Heart Community Service. In the cafeteria, there was a stockpile of canned goods the public could benefit from. When the delivery truck from the Second Harvest food bank would come to drop off the food, the reverend would ask that the pallet of food be dropped off at the door of the cafeteria. This gave me the impression that he was doing some illegal stockpiling of food rations, and if the driver of the Second Harvest saw this, they would go back to their superiors to report the improprieties. I also started noticing that the growth of the congregation only happened when the good reverend took in the homeless people who were asking for the housing assistance. There wasn't a single person who had received any emergency assistance that came to the church to visit, let alone came to join as a member. Another peculiar thing happen when you were admitted into their program. You couldn't go to any other house of worship of your choice but theirs. The one thing that the Bible tells you is that God gives you free will. I questioned myself many times before, why we weren't giving this stuff to the people who need it the most. I knew that the respect that I held for this gentleman has gone by the wayside.

The one thing that bothered me the most was the fact that I allowed myself to believe that what was asked of me was being done in the name of God. Looking back at the things that have transpired since being there, this ministry gave off the appearance of being more of a cult than that of a non-denominational ministry. At that point, I knew that this wasn't going to be a good fit for me. There wasn't any promise of me becoming part of the organization, no mention of compensating me for the researching of the grants. I decided that I would do whatever I needed to do to try to stay, but I knew that I couldn't stay there. I had to find a way to get out from the control of Reverend Johnny and Grateful Heart. After being told that I couldn't go to care for my granddaughter, I wasn't going to go out of my way to do anything extra for them.

I began to spend more time in Salisbury than I did at the mission. Even though there wasn't much to do at the magazine, I decided to make it more of a commitment than it really was a cause for. What I did was to make my way into Salisbury in the morning with my laptop. I would get back into the routine of stopping at the library first to go through the job search engines. Finding a job has always been a priority, and I knew if I were to get one, I had to rededicate myself to staying focused on that. I would arrive at the library at nine in the morning and stay there until noon. I'd bring something with me to eat for lunch and would have that before I would head into the magazine. I enjoyed the time that I spent working on the magazine, but without any major sponsors, I knew that there wasn't much of a chance of me to make the kind of money I needed to help my situation. I needed to get myself into a comfortable living situation. This was something that I knew that *Victory Goals Magazine* couldn't afford for me, because it was a startup company. Most start-up companies are due to fail within the first five years. I knew that I didn't have that kind of time.

It was hard for me to accept the fact that I was going into the fourth year of living as a homeless person. I was accustomed to having a place that I could call home, my own car, and doing things on my own time as I wanted. Since being in North Carolina, I have only earned money from working as a program assistant from Gethsemane Missionary Baptist Church in their afterschool and summer enrichment program. I've done nothing else that was a money-earning venture. I've volunteered my time as an intern with Goodwill, office assistant with Grateful Heart Community Service, and the only stage production that I've produced didn't make a dime for Updaway Productions. It seemed that the only stage work that I've done was the only thing that people in Rowan County wanted me to do. My services to perform on stage were in demand. One of the artist who performed the art of the spoken word asked me if I would be interested in performing in a play that she has written. Before I went into the shelter, I would frequent the scene where artist would perform this art form. The woman who performed as the lead in my production *Sign of the Times*, Tyeisha, invited me to one of the recitals that she was performing. Once there, I had the chance to see the underground talent that was going on in Salisbury. I was introduced to an artist who went by the name of Charisma Flow. After the showcase of artist, Charisma and I spoke about probably getting together to work one day. What drew me to her was that the things that she was spitting in her poems were deep and very substantial. I could tell that she was the most conscious of the artist who had performed that evening. She told me that she had written a play called "9 Lives".

Performing is the one things that I could do that has always given me a sense of appreciation. I've accepted the realization that I'm not going to be the next Denzel Washington, but I know that I do have pretty thorough knowledge of the concepts of how to put on a stage production. When Charisma was telling me that her play focused on the issue of domestic violence and substance abuse, it was something that interested me a lot. This interested me because of the people who I spent time with when I was living at Rowan Helping Ministries. I saw some of the result of how people were living in that particular incident. I witnessed first-hand how some of the women who came to stay at the shelter had been victims of domestic violence. Most of them came there to live by themselves, but there were a few who had the misfortune of having to bring their children. To bring the consciousness of this topic to a stage production intrigued me even more that I felt compelled to do it. Doing this would give me a way to network with for a job.

By the time I was asked to perform in the *9 Lives* play, there were some other changes that were taking place at Grateful Heart.

I was asked to train a couple of choir member on the procedures of scheduling people to receive emergency assistance from the agency. I didn't mind doing that, because I didn't want to handle too many more responsibilities after being shunned when I needed to see about the welfare of my granddaughter. I showed them the process for scheduling clients and also how to produce the monthly and quarterly reports for the board members and stakeholders. The one thing that made me determined to leave Grateful Heart happened a couple of weeks later. Reverend Johnny introduced a new member who joined the church to the guys that were staying at the mission. He told us that she was coming on board to their organization as a case manager. That was the straw that broke the camel's back. Several months after I produced my resume to him and showed him that I had previous case management experience, it really pissed me off. A second epiphany came to me, that the work I was doing was no longer needed. I was being phased out. Before I allowed them to phase me out, I wasn't going to give them the satisfaction of letting them dictate to me what I can or cannot do.

More than being excited about doing the new play, I believed that this would've been the best opportunity to get out of Rowan County. I thought with the play being in Charlotte, that I may have the opportunity to find work while I was in town. Charlotte was the closest major city to Salisbury, and the opportunities for employment looked a lot more promising than anything that was where I was currently living. The rehearsal schedule was the thing that I was going to have to try to work out. They had rehearsals two evenings during the week and one on Saturday. The Saturday rehearsals I didn't have a problem to make, but rehearsing during the week was a problem. The weekday evening rehearsals took place on Tuesday and Thursdays at eight. In order for me to make rehearsal during the week, I had to ask to use my request for my nights out. I could only get two per month, and anything more than that would count against me as an unauthorized night. If I had three of them, then I would be requested to leave the mission. With the schedule being the way that it was, I had to think of what my options were. I had to notify Charisma who wrote the play and the director to let them know what my status was.

I never like coming out telling people that I was homeless. I didn't like it because it came with twenty questions and people feeling sorry for you. I appreciated the concerns of those that wonder how a situation like this could happen, but I was more interested in people who could help me find a solution so that I didn't remain homeless. There came a time when you're trying to do your best to conceal your anonymity, but there were times that you're no longer able to do it. I explained my current situation to the both of them. I told them that I could make the weekend rehearsals, but I would be limited on the ones that I could make during the week. I tried to extend that professional courtesy that comes along in the theatre. Most productions want to know what their actors work schedules are so that they can work the rehearsals around the actors and vice versa. They were very understanding and compassionate and allowed me to work my schedule around them. When I accepted this role, I knew that my time at Grateful Heart was winding down.

Grateful Heart was a place that provided me with a place to stay and let me do some of the work that I was trained to do after I graduated college, but there were restrictions that prohibited my personal and professional growth. The only way that I was going to be able to become gainfully employed wasn't going to occur in Rowan County. I knew that I was going to have to leave the small country town atmosphere and relocate into a larger city. Since I was staying in North Carolina, Charlotte was the obvious choice for me. The play that I was going to perform in for Charisma made that choice easier for me. Once I decided to make the move, I needed to find out about the public shelter. Every one of the shelters has their own set of rules, so researching it was the main thing that I needed to do to enter. Being that I had a government-issued telephone, having access to make contact had limited calls that I could make to the shelters. I had to rely on getting on the internet to research the information that the shelter posted. There wasn't very much about what were the requirements for entry into their facilities. The main point of emphasis spoke about their mission of providing shelter for people who were looking at trying to get off the streets. There wasn't any information on the guidelines for the qualifications of getting admitted into the shelter.

It was determined by the circumstances that I'll do this performance in Charlotte and would make it my new home. The rehearsals meant that I would go over my limit of days that were allotted for me to use during a month. Once it got closer to the date of the performance for *9 Lives*, I began to use my days. I used one day to go to the rehearsal during the weekday. I was able to catch the train that ran from Salisbury into Charlotte and made a stop in Kannapolis along the way. The rehearsal was conveniently located just across the street from the Charlotte Amtrak station. Doing this production was different from any other that I had done before. I did all the things that I normally did in preparing for the part, but when it was over, I had to stay in the train station for the evening. I made sure that when I purchased my ticket, I had a round trip that let me arrive in Charlotte on Thursday and return to Salisbury on the first thing smoking back there. The second time that I used my allotted day was during the week of the performance. I repeated the routine that I did the first time by staying in the Amtrak station and jetting back to Salisbury. The only thing that I had left was to do the performance on the weekend.

When I returned to Salisbury, I made a point to notify Reverend Johnny that I would have to leave Grateful Heart. I told him a couple of months prior to the show that I was going to be performing in Charlotte. I had invited him and the members of the congregation to attend if they could, but when I saw the reverend this time, it was to inform him that I had to move on. He expressed that he was sorry to see me leave and not have a defined place to go, but I think that was because I was a valuable asset to the Grateful Heart organization. Leaving Grateful Heart was somewhat bittersweet. I was grateful to them for allowing me to stay in their mission and having a chance to serve the people in the community. I had a very hard time coming to terms of needing to stay with my granddaughter when she was crying out for me to help her. If things would've been different, I could've seen myself being there to do the work that was asked of me. The one thing that the reverend wasn't willing to do was compromise. This was going to be a new excursion that I would have to take, another undertaking that I was hoping wouldn't happen but one that I knew was the only real option that I had to do.

I called my sister to ask if I could stay there for the weekend, and she was kind enough to let me stay for the day before the performance. I packed whatever I could take with me and asked the people at Grateful Heart if I could keep the rest of my stuff in storage until I was able to come back for them. Knowing that I left a good deal of my clothes, I figured that there was a pretty good chance that I wouldn't be coming back for them. I liked a lot of the clothes that I had, but I was at peace knowing that it was a very good possibility of losing them. I was ready to lose my possessions, but not the focus of becoming self-sufficient again. Charlotte was giving me a new outlook, and after being in a rural setting for the past four years, it was one that I welcomed. Growing up, I always thought that I would be living in a major metropolitan setting. I always imagine living in a nice high-rise apartment overlooking the city's skyline. It was time for me to make this dream a reality. Rowan County was just too country for a person who was used to growing up in a five-square-mile area that had a population of over fifty thousand people. When it was time to leave, I was more than ready to go. I needed to put myself in surroundings that I was accustomed to. New city, new outlook, and in the words of Patti LaBelle, a new attitude. This time I only hope that I was making the right choice. I was getting too old to keep making bad choices. Willing this be the turning point in my life where things will finally fall in my favor for a change.

CHAPTER 15

A New Room, A New Inn

I was able to stay with my sister for a couple of days before the show since she lived in Charlotte. I arrived in town that Friday evening as she and her son came to the train station to pick me up. She was gracious enough to allow me to stay there for a couple of days until the show started that Sunday evening. I had a couple of dollars in my pocket from hustling a couple of weeks prior to coming to Charlotte. I had received my pay from Brian for the articles of the *Victory Goals Magazine* that I had written. I had some money coming into town, so I wasn't totally flat broke. Plus having my food stamp, I wasn't worried about starving once I arrived in town. The only thing about coming into town with my current food stamp situation was that I was up for renewal of my benefits at the end of the month. I felt pretty comfortable coming into Charlotte even if I didn't have a place to stay once the show was over.

Asking my sister if I could stay there while I was looking for a job was out of the question. She and her son lived there, and my oldest brother was staying with her in her three-bedroom townhouse. The place was already crowded, and I was blessed enough to stay for the weekend while he was out of town visiting his fiancé who happened to be his childhood sweetheart. So for me to ask her if I could stay there, I didn't want to put her out of her way. My agenda for the weekend was simple. I had to go to the Hyatt Regency Hotel out by the airport for a symposium on domestic violence. Afterward, the cast was going to have a run through of the production from the beginning to the end at the house of the writer and producer, and then I wouldn't have to worry about another thing until the curtains were to go up at the Pease Auditorium on the campus of University of North Carolina-Charlotte. Most of my time when I was away from my fellow cast members was to get into my routine before I go on stage. I normally take the down time to continuously read over my lines to see how I can perfect them. Most of the other time is making sure that I had my outfits, makeup, and props ready before I go on stage. Just like in my personal life, when I go on stage, I know that I want to be fully prepared. I never liked going out in public looking half ass bad. I wasn't brought up that way, and it's just became second nature to me as an adult.

I made sure that all those things were in order by the time we finished the final rehearsal before the show. Once we finished that rehearsal, the director gave his final instructions for when he wanted the cast to meet at the venue. We needed to be there for a couple of hours earlier to do the sound and dress rehearsal for the final run through before the curtain call. When we were dismissed, I caught a ride with one of my co-stars who lived in the direction where my sister lived. She lived just about ten minutes from my sister's house. She exclaimed that it wasn't an inconvenience for her to drop me off. When I arrived at my sister's house, I rang the bell, but there wasn't an answer at the door at first. She asked me if I wanted her to wait until someone came home, but I informed her that I would be fine. I knew that my sister may have stepped out, because it was the month of October. From September to December, she did what my mother did by expanding her craft for profit. She would crochet hats, scarves, ponchos, bed quilts, and afghans among some of the things that she's done. I knew that she was out making a delivery of a product that she's finished making for a customer. I knew that my nephew shouldn't have been too far away, so I ranged the doorbell, waking him up in the process. My colleague saw that I was going inside and proceeded to drive to her destinations.

My sister arrived home not too long after that, and she told me that she wasn't going to do any cooking, because she was busy trying to get her orders together so that they could be delivered to her customers. This was why I was glad that I did have some money in my pocket, because my nephew was going to get some food from Firehouse Subs. I gave him my order as did his mother for hers. I told my sister that I had spoken with her son when I arrived if he would be able to take me to the venue. He agreed, and I wanted to inform her of the agreement. I also reminded her that I had two company tickets for her and a guest if they wanted to attend the show. She told me that it wasn't likely that she could attend. The show was going to take place on a Sunday, and her Carolina Panthers were playing against my brother's Cincinnati Bengals. She informed me that it was a pretty good chance that she wouldn't be able to attend with her deadlines steadily approaching. I totally understood that. Since being homeless, I've gained a better appreciation for the value of a dollar that I haven't had before. Several minutes after having this conversation with my sister, my nephew arrived back with the food. The order was taken correctly, and his timing couldn't have been any better, because I hadn't had anything to eat since earlier that day at the symposium so you could imagine me feeling famished.

When he arrived, he gave me my order and gave his mom back her change. Normally, if I were working, I would've told him to keep the change, but my order came down to a six dollar and forty nine cent sandwich. I couldn't afford to give him the change for making the run to get the food. I had to bring it to his attention that I gave him a ten, and I was to receive some change. He gave me two dollars back, so instead of me making a fuss over the dollar and change, I rolled with the punches. After all, I was staying in his mother's place, and I didn't need to get her upset over something like that. So I had to accept it. I didn't want anyone to get the wrong idea about me, because when I was working, I'd give a taxicab driver a ten-dollar tip to get me to my destination on time or early. I simply couldn't afford to give the little bit of money away that I had. After dinner, my sister asked me what time was the show, and when did, I needed to be at the theatre. She was asking me this because Duane was going out and wouldn't be back until early in the morning. There was going to be a pretty good chance that my sister was going to have to take me to the auditorium.

I didn't want to impose on her for much more because I knew that she was working in her busy season, and I didn't want to be the reason for any unnecessary stress on my behalf. So I was prepared just in case she had to take me into town to get to the theatre. After eating, I made sure that my stuff was packed and ready to go to the theater for the next day. I stayed in the room the rest of the evening, connecting with some friends on Facebook and doing the once-over of the lines for the production of the play tomorrow evening. I was looking forward to the play the next day because it was something new, a new production that dealt with a serious consciousness issue of domestic violence. This was a brilliantly written and thought-out production by the writer Charisma Flows. It was one of the only productions outside of the one that I wrote that cast me as a person of good character. I was doing the role of Reverend Wise. It included two scenes; both of them would take place in the church. One would be during the sermon, and the other would take place where I would have to perform a wedding. This was something that made me feel good about doing this performance. For once I wasn't being typecast as the bad guy. After going over the line for the last time and making sure that all my bags were packed, I decided to shut it down for the evening.

The next morning was a Sunday, and I wasn't used to getting up not going to a service on that day. After being at Grateful Heart, it was hard not to be conditioned to do anything else but attend a service on a Sunday morning. After I took the time to groom myself, I came downstairs to get a cup of coffee and started to get my outfits together for the performance. I asked my sister if her son came back from going out the night before. She told me that he was in, but he was sleeping. Then I asked her if she would be able to get me to the theatre a couple of hours before the show. She told me that she would, but this was an inconvenience because of the work that she was doing. Looking back in hindsight, I should've made arrangements with another cast member to see if they would've been able to pick me up. One other thing that I asked her was if I could use her iron. That statement was the straw that broke the camel's back on her. I don't know if it was the stress or what, but I was about to receive the riot act. She told me, "Why are you asking if you can use the freaking iron? Why don't you ask me where's the iron?" You're acting like you're staying at the freaking Holiday Inn." I don't know what gave her that idea, but I didn't do anything disrespectful to her or her house. For her to come out of her mouth to me like that truly hurt me. I don't know if it was the stress of her trying to meet her deadline to satisfy her customers, but I know that I didn't deserve to be talked to that way. I decided to get the iron, and get my clothes and anything else that I was going to take with me to the show. I had reluctantly asked her son if I could get a tie to wear for the show. He found one to accommodate me, and I was appreciative. As the time drew near for me to leave for the theatre, I became somewhat withdrawn from my sister. Growing up from childhood, I was taught to respect my older siblings, but I will give someone the respect that I expect in return. As she's driving me to the Pease Theatre in town, I knew just how I felt. I wasn't comfortable being around her, and if I'm not comfortable, I rather deal without you. I knew after I was dropped off that I will never go out of my way to communicate with her. I will text her for her birthday, Mother's Day, or Christmas. For me to go out to initiate a phone call or a visit, I wouldn't do it until I get an apology. If I didn't receive one, then I can live with my decision. If you continue to kick a dog, there's only so many times that the dog will not defend himself.

Now I was at the point that I knew that the only person that I could count on was me. The show was a success, but for some reason, I didn't have the same satisfaction that I had in past productions that I've done. Maybe because at this presentation, I didn't have anyone in the audience who came to see me. So there it was. I had to rely on the team of me. When the performance was over, my fellow cast members were in the lobby of the theatre taking pictures with each other and their family members. I felt like an outsider that participated in the production. While they were taking pictures, I was trying to find a way to get out of the theatre inconspicuously as I was going to take my possessions out from the area and try to find a way to the nearest shelter so that I can try to stay at their facility. I walked around the downtown Charlotte area until I found the shelter. I went to see if I could try to register for assistance, but was told that I would have to wait until the morning when the administrators came in.

That evening I walked from the shelter on North Tryon Street to the Mecklenburg County Public Library where I slept on a bench in the park across the street from the library. I made my public quarters there for the evening. I would use my suit bag and substitute it as a pillow and my pull-along tote bag I would have my feet on. I would pull my overcoat over the top of my head and breathe into it to help preserve the heat. The next morning, I woke up early so that I could go to see about registering to the North Tryon Street shelter. I went there to fill out the paperwork, but they didn't start doing the intake procedures until nine that morning. I had to wait outside until it was time for the employee to do their jobs.

I finally entered into the shelter so that the workers there could do their intake assessment to see if I was eligible. I've entered the facility and signed the list at nine that morning. I wasn't seen by a staff member before it was for them to get the facility ready to serve lunch. I, along with the others who were waiting to be processed for intake assessment, were asked to go outside of the facility to take lunch and come back to resume this process until after lunch was served. It wasn't until about three o'clock that afternoon when my name was finally called for the assessment. During this process, I was asked about my previous living arrangements. I told them that I had just moved there from Granite Quarry outside of Salisbury, but little to my knowledge, they were part of a network with the other homeless shelters throughout the Central Piedmont-North Carolina region. The person who was doing the assessment had cross-referenced me into their database, and it showed that I was a guest at the Rowan Helping Ministries. It showed my records of when I was dismissed from the shelter and any incidents that took place while I was living there. My former case manager, Willie, noted the record and it was documented for anyone who could access it to view. That part of the assessment didn't hurt my chances of me entering as a guest into the shelter. What did was when they asked me how long I had been living on the street when I told them that I was living on the street for seven days. That's what stopped them from allowing me to gain entrance into the shelter.

It is the policy of the Men's Shelter of Charlotte to admit people regardless of race, creed, sexual, or religious orientation. What I didn't know was that once I told them that I was on the streets for a total of seven days, I was seven days short of the minimal fourteen that's required to gain entrance into the shelter. I was stuck on the street for another seven. There was no reason for me to start crying over spilled milk since there was nothing that I could do about it. Once again, I was going to have to rely on my street knowledge to survive. I knew that I was going to have to spend the majority of my days at the Charlotte Mecklenburg County Library on the corner of Sixth Street and North Tryon. With still a little money on my food stamp card, I had to be resourceful when it came down to making sure that I was eating. At midday, I would have to carry all my possessions with me to go to the Urban Ministries that's located between the library and the men's shelter of Charlotte to have a bite at their soup kitchen, and then make another trek to the soup kitchen at the men's shelter. Once the library would close, I go to the Charlotte transit station where the local city buses and the light rail commuter trains would have their hub. Located there is the Epicenter. It hosts some restaurants, movie theaters, bowling alley, and other shops. Across the street from there is the Time Warner Arena. It's the home of the Charlotte Hornets, the minor league hockey team, the Charlotte Checkers, concerts, and was the place where the Democratic national convention was held in 2012.

These were the locations that I had to become familiar with, and I knew that this wasn't anything like being homeless in Salisbury. This was the major leagues of where the homeless populations existed in the Southeastern United States. There are approximately over two thousand people who made up the majority of the homeless population in the Charlotte Mecklenburg County area during 2014. According to the figures by the North Carolina Coalition to End Homelessness, children make up a quarter of the population, single men make up nearly half at forty-seven percent, single women are listed at seventeen, and veterans are the eleven percent.

It wasn't too hard not to see them especially when you were one in the number. Newbies, which is a term used to describe a new person entering into the community of people who have been there in the longer, when they enter into a new environment of the established homeless population, stick out. I myself really stuck out because most of the people who I ran across at the library and the Urban Ministries thought that I was an employee there. I didn't own a pair of jeans or khakis, and the only pair of sneakers that I did own, I left at the mission at Grateful Heart in Granite Quarry. Being in Charlotte was an eye-opening experience. Although I was raised in Essex County, in New Jersey, where the population practically mirrored that of Mecklenburg County, North Carolina, I knew I was a big fish coming from a small pond in Salisbury/Rowan County, but I was only a small fish in the big ocean of Charlotte/Mecklenburg County. Dealing with the days wasn't as bad as I thought it would've been. Once I entered the library, things were good.

I knew that for the next several days that I was going to have to get into a routine. I also knew that I had to find ways to try to stay warm in the evenings. My nights consisted of trying to find shelter from the elements. After the library closed, I would go to get something to eat from my food stamp card and normally stay in the transit center until one in the morning. I was there so much that I was humming the tunes that were being played on the Muzak system that was being piped throughout the center. I knew every highs, lows, and pauses of every song that came across the airwaves. Once one o'clock hit, the transit cops would clean out the area, and from there, that's when things started to become complicated. Trying to find a place that was, for lack of a better word, comfortable was hard to come by. Most of the good squatting spots were taken if you hadn't gotten there before dusk. Most of the regulars who lived on the streets for years would secure their spots shortly after sundown. I would find a bench along the strip of North or South Tryon Streets, and when they were taken, I would find a spot at the library to sleep.

The first three nights I was successful of sleeping on the property of the Charlotte Mecklenburg County Library grounds. On the fourth night, about four in the morning, one of the city cops who was on patrol told me and a couple of others to get up and keep it moving. When that happened, I made my way to the Urban Ministries to catch a shower. The "Urb," as it is known to the locals, was the place of resources for the homeless and disenfranchised people of Charlotte. If you didn't stay at one of the shelters and was living on the streets, it was the place to go to get a shower, get your clothes washed, and other services that were afforded to the less fortunate. The Urb was the place that you had medical service by doctors and nurses from the local hospital. The medical staff would come to the Urb twice a week to see clients who were on Medicaid or welfare and provide the medical attention that was needed. Also the Urb provided counselors and case managers that would assist people with their job readiness preparations, helping them register with the North Carolina Job Service so that people could go online to search for employment opportunities. Counselors would also assist the clients with resumes, cover letters, and application preparations. The staff also provided free toiletries, the midday soup kitchen, and emergency clothing. The one blessing that I was relegated to my time of living on the street was that the Urb was one place that I felt helped me the most. When I wasn't spending my time at the library, I was going to the Urb. The Urb was an oasis in the desert of disenchantment.

With only three days to go before I was to go back to the Men's Shelter of Charlotte, I had something happened that I was trying like hell to avoid. I ran into someone who knew me. The one thing that I was trying to do was to attempt to be inconspicuous as possible. I knew that while I had to do my time of living on the street, this was a good possibility. It's not like hiding in plain sight was an easy thing to do, especially when you're dressed in business attire and have to carry your possessions with you. I was leaving the Urb and the shelter after lunch on my way back to the library. I had my stuff with me in my rolling suitcase, and it drew the attention as I was coming toward the downtown area. One of the people who just did the show *9 Lives* with happened to see me as I was making my way back down to the library. I happened to hear what I thought was someone calling my name. I knew that I had some friends from school who lived in Charlotte, but I didn't announce it on my Facebook status that I relocated to the city so I ignored it. As I kept moving, acting as if I didn't hear them, they called out my name again. I knew that I couldn't ignore them, so I turned to look who it was. I didn't see them. I was wearing dark sunglasses as a part of me wanting to feel like I was part of the crowd, but without the glasses being prescription, I could barely see three feet in front of me. They called one last time, and I finally saw who it was. I politely waved to them and kept moving toward the library. I was embarrassed to have them see me while I wasn't looking my best.

The next two days were the same as the previous ones, but I was having a harder time trying to find a place to sleep. Only two more days before I had to go back to register at the Men's Shelter to see if I qualified to receive a bed. Through the grace of God, on the first night, I was able to find a bench across the street from the library. It happened to be on one of the busiest evenings of the weekend. There was some kind of festival that was taking place in the downtown area, but that didn't make a difference to me. For once I found comfort on a bench, and I had no problem with it. I was to the point that pride wasn't a factor in my life. I was broke, the southern weather was starting to change to the effects of the autumn, and the nights grew colder. I had pulled my snakeskin printed overcoat over my head so that no one could recognize me or see my face. I could hear people walking past me, and some of them were laughing. Others would say things that weren't very pleasing to the ear, but one person, who I didn't know must have seen my hand holding onto the coat, stuck a twenty-dollar bill into my hand. I pulled the coat from over my head and thanked him.

The streets and the crowds remained busy all evening long, but I didn't have any problem getting the rest that my body was telling me that I needed. It wasn't until about three that morning when I noticed that the crowd that was walking the streets that evening, as if they were trying to get to work like in the morning rush hour, was growing into the silence of the evening of a normal weeknight. By then I was able to rest without anyone disturbing me.

For about three hours I slept on the bench until a police officer pulled up in his squad car and told me that I had to move. I told him, "No disrespect, Officer, but I'm homeless and I have another day before I can see if I could qualify for a bed at the men's shelter. If you have to arrest me for loitering, then please do so." He told me that he wouldn't do that, but I couldn't stay there. He instructed me to go down to the underpass of I-77 straight down North Tryon Street. There I will find a church group who's providing breakfast and fellowship for the homeless. He told me that I should follow the small amount of homeless people who were walking down toward that direction. In my attempt to get arrested so that I know that I could have a place to rest comfortably and that the police department would secure my possessions, I didn't notice that there was a small alliance of homeless people walking in the direction that the officer told me about.

Every Sunday morning, a group from one of the local churches would have several of their parishioners come to the underpass to serve a hot breakfast that had fresh coffee, orange juice, eggs, grits, pancakes, and assorted breakfast meats—mostly pork, but being that, I didn't eat that. I was satisfied with what else that was being served. They would set up tables to serve the food and had other necessities that people would need such as sweaters, jackets, hats, socks, toiletries, and other clothing items. Most importantly, since this was their congregation was doing missionary work, they had spiritual literature and bibles. Once they had the majority of the people who were there to receive a meal, they held an open but brief church service. Members would sing spiritual songs while people were eating, and some of the recipients of the food would join in. Then the reverend who had his members serve the food would conduct a sermon. By the end of the sermon, the reverend asked the recipients if they would like to receive prayer. I was all in. Just because I wasn't in a place that was secure to lay my head down, I wasn't going to neglect the blessings that I know God will provide for me.

I did request for a prayer, but I went to the pastor himself to ask if he would pray for me and my situation. He politely obliged my request and prayed for my. At the end, he asked me if there was anything else that I needed, or did I want anything else to eat. I told him that I was very gracious for the hospitality that he and his members have extended to me, but I asked him if I could get a Bible. He went to the table and gave me one. He inquired if I was staying at the men's shelter, and I told him that I had one more day before I was going to be admitted into the shelter, and that I should be able to hold out one more day. The reverend told me that the First Presbyterian Church, going back up the street toward the library, would be serving breakfast there before their services for the public. I thanked him for the prayer and the Bible.

This was going to be a journey that I knew that I would never forget. The one thing that I noticed was that when you're homeless in North Carolina, Charlotte in particularly, you're not going to go hungry. During the weekends, you find people from religious and social groups that set up tables on the streets throughout the city just to feed the homeless population. It's done with the unmitigated selflessness by giving of themselves to their fellow human being. First Presbyterian Church does this act of kindness on a weekly basis, the Urb does it on a daily basis, and other organizations do it whenever they can gather enough volunteers. First Presbyterian serves a hotel-style continental breakfast every Sunday morning before they start their church services. They say a prayer before serving the food, and it's a gathering place where the normal homeless population meet. The members of the church serve the food and invite the homeless people to attend the service. Even though I was running out of my food stamp supply, going hungry wasn't going to be a major concern when I arrived in Charlotte.

It was my last night before I had my appointment to meet with the officials at the men's shelter to attempt to gain admissions into their facility. I couldn't sleep that night, so I spent the majority of the evening at the transit center until it was time to clear out. Once that happened, the bench that I slept on the night before was vacant again. This time it was a Monday morning, and there wasn't a single cop car that passed by me who told me that I had to keep it moving. I rested there for about four hours and then proceeded to make my way to the shelter. When I arrived there, it was just a little before seven in the morning. I was allowed to come in to get some breakfast, and then I had to wait until the staff arrived to process the new people who needed to register for the shelter. I was the first person to sign the list in the morning, but like many things that happen through a system of red tape, time was going to be a long thing in this process.

I had to play the waiting game, and I was in the waiting room until it was time to serve lunch. Everyone in the waiting room who wanted to get processed was asked to leave until the staff had finished serving lunch. I stayed for the lunch and returned to the waiting area when it was over. It was about one thirty in the afternoon before they reconvened for the intake process. The waiting had continued until eight that evening. At that time I was seen by someone to process me. They already had the documentation from my previous visit there, so it wasn't too long before they would assign me a bed, or so I thought. Before I could enter the shelter, there was a series of health-related questions that I had to answer. When I was finished doing that part of the process, a licensed social worker came to see how it would come that they would place me.

The men's shelter of Charlotte had two facilities. The one that I was at during the assessment process, on North Tryon Street, housed people who had job and were transitioning into independent living or were going through a substance abuse program so that they could learn how to live with their addictions. The other facility was located on Statesville Avenue about three miles from the downtown area. It was known to the homeless people of the area as the Dog Pound. People who didn't have a job and had no resources were housed there. After the assessment was completed, I was told that I would be given a mat to sleep on in the dining area, and my placement would be determined by the next day. I was given a mat with a sheet and instructed to go in that area for the evening. For the first time in seven days, I felt comfortable. I wasn't on the streets, and with the weather changing outside, it was a great feeling of warmth away from the elements. For all that it's worth, it was a feeling of security. I didn't have to worry about anyone telling me that I needed to get up and keep it moving in the early morning hour. For the next few hours, I could rest without interruptions.

Noticed that I said rest, and not sleep. *Rest* I define it as a verb for the homeless that means "to cease work or movement in order to relax, refresh oneself, or recover strength." *Sleep* I define as a noun that's "a condition of body and mind such as that which typically recurs for several hours every night, in which the nervous system is relatively inactive, the eyes closed, the postural muscles relaxed, and consciousness practically suspended." When you're given the circumstances of having your life's possessions with you and not a penny in your pocket, you're better off by not sleeping and resting to recover your strength from the stressful activity of trying to find a place to stay first, employment next, and attempting to become self-sufficient again. I knew people at the Rowan Helping Ministries where I stayed when people had something valuable of theirs stolen right in front of their faces when they were conscious. I wasn't going to take that chance with me. The only thing that I truly had of value was the computer that I owned, and I wasn't going to leave that out of my sight for very long. That evening, after I received my mat and sheet, I used my computer bag as my pillow to support my head. Once I found a spot, I can honestly say that I was able to get a comfortable night of rest.

The next day was almost a carbon copy of the previous one, but without the responsibility of having to register to become a guest in the shelter. Still I was waiting for a bed to be assigned to me, and I was hoping that I would've been assigned one at the North Tryon Street location. I was hoping that, because it's centrally located to the downtown area of Charlotte and the resources were very accessible to get to. Going to the Statesville Avenue location meant that I was going to have anywhere from a three- to five-mile walk back to that place every evening. I really wasn't looking forward to having to do that, but like I've always been told, you play with the hand that you've been dealt. When I woke up, I was given a towel, wash cloth, toothbrush, and other toiletries to get myself cleaned up before breakfast. Once I finished cleaning up, I had breakfast, and the rest of the day I had to wait at the shelter to find out what my fate was as far as being placed. I wasn't able to go to use the library, but the shelter did have a resource room where they had computers that the residents could use to look for jobs, housing, and veterans could view what kind of benefits that they qualified for.

Naturally, I threw myself into the computer resource center, because the focus for me was still trying to find something that would get me out of the shelter sooner rather than later. I went in there before lunch and returned there after lunch was over. About three thirty that afternoon, I stopped looking for jobs on the PC and heard the front desk call my name. I went over there with all my possessions in hand. I was asked to see the daytime social worker and to have a see in the waiting area again. She was with another person finalizing their paperwork just before she was to see me. Within the next ten minutes or so, I met her and was given where I would be staying. Her name was Christine, and she was a very nice lady to speak with. She asked me if I had a plan of action to get out of the shelter, and I replied that I needed to get help with the resources. She'd explained to me that if I was looking for resources, there were other agencies that had them. She gave me a list of these agencies and explained my stay at the shelter and told me that I would be place at the Statesville Avenue facility. It's a blessing that I was happy to get, but I know that the goal had to be to get out of being classified as a homeless person.

During the first week of staying at the facility on Statesville Avenue, there was a murder that took place over in the housing complex just across the other street. My bunk mate told me that it was a very good possibility that it could've been drug related. There were all kinds of police and emergency alarms and sirens going off all around including a police helicopter flying overhead with the searchlight looking for a possible suspect in the area. I remember the staff calling out to the guys that they could continue to take their smoke break on the hour at the half hour, and I was thinking to myself that I left a shelter that I thought was hell that suddenly seemed like heaven. I didn't have any minutes on my government-issued phone, but I did have plenty of text messaging left on it. I was so pissed off at my siblings and cousin with whom I lived with when I first moved in with when I came to North Carolina that I cursed each and every one of them out for knowing my situation and not caring enough to attempt to reach out to me. I told myself that I wasn't going to bother to contact them because, as far as I was concerned, the only family that I had was my granddaughter. She cared more about my welfare than any of them. I kept little contact with them from that one particular incident and didn't care if I could recover those bonds with them. Why should I care? They never cared to check on my welfare, knowing that I was doing all of the moves to try to better myself. Knowing this hurt me more than any physically violent act had ever did.

I didn't want to be at that particular location, but I was blessed just the same. I didn't know what was happening or how I was going to overcome this, but I was just praying that this hamster wheel that I was on would allow me to get off while I was here in Charlotte. I had to keep telling myself that this was finally going to be the stop for me, because I prayed to God that this was it.

CHAPTER 16

Here We Go Again

For my first two months in Charlotte, I used the list given to me by Christine to go to the agencies that were listed. The first thing that I had to do was to set up my priorities. I needed a mailing address to receive packages and letters, and I also had to get a new state-issued identification card. My driver's license was suspended although the dates on it were still valid for identification purposes. Also, my food stamps had run out at the end of the month when I was admitted into the shelter, and the place to do that was the Urb. The staff at the Urb allowed me to used their facility to receive personal mail and assisted me with the resource to get to the local Department of Social Services so that I can get my food stamps and also provided assistance for me to get a state ID without any out-of-pocket expense on my behalf since I didn't have the money to pay for it.

Christine was an angel who was a lot more apathetic as opposed to Pam Neal who was in the position of the shelter director. Pam was the person who I spoke to when I needed to secure a bed after I first arrived in Charlotte. When I first met her, she gave the appearance of being a cold-hearted individual. It was Pam who I saw on my initial time coming to the shelter, pleading with her if I could've been admitted into the shelter. Pam showed little, if any, compassion or any signs of understanding since she herself was once in the same situation. It wasn't that I didn't respect her in the position of authority, but she appeared to show that she didn't care about anyone's situation. This wasn't the first place that I've been that didn't deviate slightly from the rules, but it appeared to me that the women who were in the position of authority over the men weren't going to be the ones to do so.

I had to learn the lesson of acceptance that I didn't have the free will todo certain things that I wanted to do. Given the situation, there wasn't very much choice that I had. One of the choices that I did have when I arrived into Charlotte was where I was going to practice my faith. From one of the groups that came to serve their ministries was the church of Grace Memorial Baptist Church. They came with the members from their outreach ministry to serve the residents of the shelter. When they came, it looked like a little country church community that could've had the majority of their members that were there serving the residents. This wasn't like the ordinary group of people who would come in to serve. When the residents would enter into the dining area to eat, they would get into the serving line to receive their meals and have to wait for the staff to call for second servings. When the members of Grace would serve, they would have their missionaries come to the tables to serve the resident guests beverages and a second helping of dessert before the shelter staff would call for the second serving. That wasn't the amazing thing that caught my attention, but during the meal, their missionaries would sing gospel songs and sit down with the men to just talk with them.

I was impressed that they weren't there just to do a service to the community. From the members who I encountered, they were more interested in seeing how they can help. While the meal was being served, the television was on and a football game was playing. For once it felt to me like an afternoon church service that included the breaking of bread and some good old-fashion fellowship with the congregation members. The pastor of the church was Reverend Lawrence D. Mayes, and his congregation members made me feel compelled to own my desire to want to attend a service there so that I could fellowship with a church that I felt very comfortable worshiping with. One of the members made a homemade lemon Bundt cake. I asked one of the servers who made it, and they directed me to the elderly woman who did it. I went over to ask the elderly woman if she made it, and she said yes, she did. I asked her jokingly if she was single, and if so, did she wanted to get married. We both laughed after I said that, but she knew that was my way of saying thank you to her and the members for coming out to fellowship with us. Before the end of the dinner, I inquired about attending service to one of the people and was talking to the associate minister, Reverend Ivan Watts. He told me that they were up the road from the Statesvillle Avenue location and that they had a courtesy van that would pick up people who wanted to attend the services and would drop them back off to the shelter.

I appreciated this service that was provided by the church and made it a point to check them out. I saw the church one day when I was catching the bus. By the end of the year, on the final Sunday, I made sure that I was going to attend the service. I walked there from the shelter and was very pleased with the service that I attended. It reminded me of the church that I was happiest attending when I was a member of Second Nazareth Baptist in Columbia, South Carolina. The thing that impressed me the most was the fact that it was a small edifice that had a congregation who would pack the building. When the church announcements would come about, they had many different ministries that would perform missionary outreach services in their community. The welcome by the woman delivered was warm and engaging, and the word delivered by the associate pastor was another thing that had me feeling the spirit.

After service, I was invited to fellowship with the members and partake in some refreshment. It was a very welcoming environment that showed some love for me. They remembered me from the time that they came to serve the people at the shelter. They weren't judgmental about my status being homeless, and many of them were trying to see how they could help me. This was one of the rarest times that I could felt comfortable around people who knew about my situation and didn't feel as if I was being put under a microscope. I let them know that I truly enjoyed the service and the message that was delivered. The members told me that I should come back there next week because the pastor of that church would be preaching then and that he would be really bring the fire. Since I was looking for a church home, I decided to return there the following Sunday. By the end of the fellowship hour, they provided me with a ride back into town, and I knew in my mind if the service next week was anything like it was that day, I would be a member of the Grace Memorial Missionary Baptist Church. They asked me if they could pick me up from the main shelter on Tryon Street at ten o'clock for the following Sunday. I agreed to it and looked forward to attending another service.

The next weekend came, and once again, I was ready to worship in the house of the Lord. Living in this kind of situation, I wasn't very comfortable around people, but the one place that I was comfortable was being in church. In my search for a church home in Charlotte, I visited several churches. I found out that the Reverend John P. Kee had a church in Charlotte, and little to my surprise, it was only down the street from where I was staying at on the Statesville Avenue shelter. Naturally the music was slamming, and the message was good, but the spirit didn't move me. I'm not saying that it wasn't a spirit-filled environment. It wasn't filling me with the spirit. Another house of worship that I visited was the Victory Christian Center with the Reverend Robin Gool presiding. This was a big church with a national television audience, and one of the mega churches in the country. They said that former professional football player Randy Moss was a member of that church. I went to these and a few other churches who came out to serve the homeless community. They were extremely welcoming, but it was something special about the intimacy of the people of Grace Memorial that had me caught up in wanting to be part of something that I could help grow with spiritually.

When the service began, things were pretty much the same as they were last weekend. The program format was the same with the exception of the rotation of the ushers and the selection of songs that the choir sung. I still was feeling the spirit from the last week I visited there, but when it came time to hear the word from Reverend Lawrence D. Mayes, he did bring a very fiery sermon. Reverend Mayes was a retired public school administrator who had a church that was packed. As he would say, he was just a country man who grew up the son of a farmer, but you could hear in his speech that he was a well-educated man. The thing that drew me close to becoming a member of the church was the fact that the parishioners were a reflection of the pastor. Reverend Mayes had a genuine concern for the welfare of the people who weren't only the members of his church, but the community in general. Just before he began his sermon, he told the members of the congregation about a situation that took place earlier in the week. A woman who appeared to be distressed had her car break down and stopped in the church during the time he was in the church office. She didn't have much, but she was in need of food for herself and the young children in her family who needed the rations for the week. The pastor gladly obliged her and provided the lady with enough food and assisted her to get her car fixed so that she could make it back home. When I heard this story, I knew that I wanted to become a part of a ministry that serves like that. At the end of the service, when the doors of the church opened and the invitation to join was extended, I had no hesitation to do that. I immediately knew that this was going to be the place that I wanted to be a part of to worship and wait on the Lord. I joined when the call for church membership was announced at the end of the service. One of the members who I asked about when it came about visiting their church when their missionary group came to the shelter to serve came up there with me. I saw that she had a tear in her eyes displaying her happiness. I had one in my own knowing that this was what I wanted to do, and wishing that my parents were still alive to witness me joining a church that I know that the both of them would've been pleased to become members themselves.

As the following weeks were going along, I still hadn't secured any form of steady employment. One day, as I was making my way toward the library, I noticed that there were some of the people who resided at the shelter standing outside the building of the Charlotte Area Fund. For curiosity sake, I decided to go there to find out what was the big deal about this building. So I went inside to see what it was about. When I went in, I inquired to the receptionist about the details and what services do they offer. The Charlotte Area Fund is a private non-profit corporation and Mecklenburg County's designated community action agency. The purpose of the agency is to combat poverty by assisting low-income individuals and families with becoming self-sufficient. They provided job readiness skills and provided the community with emergency food and clothing assistance as well. I inquired to the receptionist about the program that was being offered there. I was told that in order to qualify for their program, I would have to take an entrance exam to see how I would be placed. They were using the same module for testing that I once used when I was the admissions director of the Urban League Ultra Center in Newark back in 1986. The test of adult basic education(-TABE) is the standard examination that agency's use for their clients who are entering into a basic computer and Word-processing classes. I felt comfortable knowing that they were still using the same basic test that had been used in the past thirty plus years.

Once I entered the doors of the agency and passed the entrance exam, I knew I was going to be prepared to go through the job readiness courses. The receptionist told me that the agency was networking with other local community-based organizations that would help with the job placement as well as internship training with other local business community partners. Before I would meet with an intake specialist and after testing, I saw that the agency had a PowerPoint presentation on their widescreen video monitor about the services that were provided. During one point in that presentation, they listed that there was a position that needed to be filled with their agency as a job developer. Just before the meeting with the intake person took place, I asked the receptionist if the position had been filled. I was told that it hadn't, but if I were interested in it, I should inquire about it with the intake specialist.

When the time came to meet with the intake specialist, she told me that my test scores were good enough to be accepted into the job readiness training program. The program was six weeks long, and once I complete it, I would receive a job readiness certificate and a stipend as the end. Also successful graduates of the program are eligible to receive an internship or apprenticeship program with some of the businesses in the Charlotte community. When I met with the intake specialist, she liked the majority of my scores. The test evaluated a candidate aptitude in spelling, language, mathematics computations, and applied mathematics. My language arts scores were pretty good, but the applied mathematics scores were at best marginal. The woman doing the intake told me that I would qualify to attend the job readiness classes, but the staff wanted me to attend the remedial math classes. I wasn't pleased about doing that, but I told her that I would attend.

She was sitting at the desk for the receptionist after I left her office speaking with her about my scores and the program. I inquired to her about the job posting for the job developer's position that was on the television monitor. She asked if I had a resume, and I informed her that I did. I was given a job application form to fill out about the position, so I took my time to do that. Naturally, I wanted to make sure that all the I's were dotted and the T's were crossed. I was starting to feel good about the having the potential of working at a non-profit organization, with the possibility of making a living at it again. I knew that working there in a non-profit there's not a lot of money to be made by assisting people, but it's that feeling of accomplishment knowing that you had a hand in helping another person advance themselves is what I find to be the most satisfying about working in that field. When I was finished filling out the application, I returned it to her. She looked at it, and I could see the expression on her face that she was pleased with the information that was on it. She had excused herself to find someone in the agency who could talk to me about the position.

Once again the adrenaline was starting to run throughout my body. In my mind I was saying to myself not to get too excited, because of the letdown factor that I've become accustomed to. After about five minutes of waiting on her, she returned only to tell me that I would have to come back to their office on Monday because the person who could talk to me was out of the office for the day. Since it was a Friday, I had to play the waiting game for another two days. That wasn't too bad, but still it's the anxiety that was hard to control. I also knew that it's easier to get a job once you have one. This was going on a five-year stint and I was doing things to try to help my chances of getting this position. When I left their office and arrived at the library, I immediately sent out a thank-you note to the intake specialist, and I went to their website to find the names of the people who could make the decision to hire me and sent them a cover letter with a copy of my resume. I was busy at work that morning also sending out e-mails and making phone calls to my friends and former colleagues who I knew if they would give a good word on my behalf could help push their decision in helping me get hired. Waiting is the worst part for me when it came to hearing back from the people who can hire you for a position. I only know that you have to remain patient because God will test your resolve when patience is involved.

When the weekend was over, I went back to the Charlotte Area Fund that morning to inquire about the position that I spoke with the intake specialist about. The receptionist told me that I was going to have to start working with the remedial math class. I was told that I could go into the computer classroom to use the resources of their system until the classroom teacher came in to give the instruction. While I was there, someone else was there using the computer for their job searches. One way or the other, we sparked up a conversation about the possibility of working with a non-profit agency. I found out from the conversation that she was told that she was going to be working for them in the capacity of the same position that I applied for. Once again, the disappointment hit me like a slow-motion punch, but I was looking at it the same way that a deer would look into the headlights of an approaching car. This was unavoidable, but instead of wanting to dodge this responsibility by running away and telling them to screw themselves, I took this disappointment with a grain of salt.

I only hoped that when I received the news by their new employee, I had my poker face in full effect. The math instructor was a retired teacher who was working with the agency to assist the trainees who were deficient in mathematics. I knew that I was a borderline student whose scores were just slightly below the average of what they were looking for. I went to the sessions reluctantly, but as I attended them, I didn't put forth the effort of really trying to master the mathematical computation. I didn't try to follow the rules, because I was still disappointed by the agency accepting another person for the job. I did just enough to get by until it was time for me to enter into the training classes at the Charlotte Area Fund. I knew that I was wrong in giving the instructor a hard time about mastering the math, but at that point, I really didn't care. It may seem to be somewhat of a childish behavior that I was displaying, but I was sick and tired of being turned down for positions that I knew that I was qualified for. I continued to attend the session on my own accord. I would only go for an hour and leave when that time limit was up. This continued until it was time to attend the job readiness classes.

The job readiness sessions were for four weeks. I had to attend them and do test daily at the end of the classes. The sessions started at nine in the morning and were dismissed in the afternoon by three o'clock. When I got there, the material that was being used was also something that I was familiar with. It was the JIST Works. This was another tool that I used when I was the admissions director at the Urban League of Essex County in Newark, New Jersey. The other part of my duties besides being the admissions director was conducting the business environment classes. It was the exact same concept, but with the materials that have been updated twenty-nine years later. The instructor was someone who I could relate to for a couple of reasons: he was an African American male from New Jersey a few years younger than myself, and he also wore his hair in the Jamaican sister locs style. Isaac Cochran was the sharpest knife in the draw who worked at the Charlotte Area Works. Not only was he a snazzy dresser, but spoke very intelligently. You could tell that he educated himself very well. He wasn't going to allow any of his trainees to fail on his watch because failure of the trainees reflected on him as the instructor.

Throughout the course, we were given lectures by professionals in the Charlotte area business community on financial planning, banking, and other agencies that included Charlotte Works another non-profit that was helpful in assisting in the placement of the course trainees with intern and apprenticeship positions. Mr. Cochran asked the class was there anyone who had their resume. I was happy to show him mine, and he destroyed it. I wasn't disappointed when he did that due to the fact that I didn't have any success with what I was doing. He gave the class a format that was a template in the Microsoft Word program. Gone was the objective, replaced by the pertinent information that would only help enhance my chances of getting interviews. The Charlotte Area Fund also provided the trainees with professional attire for those individuals who were in need of clothing for work and interviews, and trainees qualify for emergency food assistance once you completed the course. The financial planning and banking was extremely helpful, and I knew that I was going to have to use it later on once I got started working. There wasn't any need for clothes for me to use for an interview, because my locker and sleeping quarters were really overstocked. Meeting with the Charlotte Works people was my main concern. I wanted to get with someone who could possibly give me a hand getting my foot into someone's door. While doing the job readiness course, I knew that this could possibly be my best opportunity for getting there. I knew if I did that, there would be other barriers and hurdles to jump over. I didn't care. I only knew that I had to get into the inner circle of the Charlotte business community, and I would try to jump through all kinds of hoops to get there. The outlook was starting to look good again, but getting doors shut in your face was something that's always in the back of my mind. This time I was ready not to knock on the door, but to kick the damn thing in. "No" wasn't going to be accepted by me. It was no longer in my vocabulary.

CHAPTER 17

Moving Up or Moving Out!

A week before completing the course, one of the other trainees told me about a position with a temporary agency that was paying fourteen dollars an hour. It was a job that was at the worksite where there was the new Veterans Administration hospital. It was working with a clean-up crew at the construction site for the new building. This happened just a week before I was going to finish the course at the Charlotte Area Fund. My classmate JoAnn had been to the temporary agency just hours earlier during the day and secured a position with them as a payroll clerk. They had asked her if she knew of anyone who wanted to get paid to work at the VA. She in turned told me when I came into the Charlotte Area Fund later that day. I told Mr. Cochran about the opportunity, and he was very willing to try to assist me anyway that he could. He asked me what was it that I needed to work at the jobsite. I told him that I was going to need a pair of carpenter pants, a denim jacket, and a pair of size fourteen steel toe work boots. He told me that if the position led into a full-time position that would be good. I was told that if it didn't and if I needed to finish the course, I would have to start over again if the job continued through the end of the current class of trainees. If it ended earlier than that, I would have to come into the next class to make up the days and time that I missed. I agreed with him and chose to work with the temporary agency to assume the job at the VA.

Mr. Cochran asked me about my clothing and shoe sizes so that he could go to the Wal-Mart to purchase the items I needed to start work. After class that day, I went to the doctor's office as instructed by the temporary agency to give them a record of my urine to see if I would test positive for drugs or alcohol. I was never worried about that because I haven't really been drinking since I left my cousin's house in Salisbury, and smoking weed was something I hadn't done in about another eight years earlier. My classmate took me over there to the office, and needless to say, my result came up negative. We drove back to the agency to give them the results, and the person at the temporary agency told me to be there at six in the morning. This was a good start for me to put some money back into my pockets. The job started at seven in the morning until three that afternoon, with a half hour break for lunch.

I called back to the Charlotte Area Fund to let Mr. Cochran know that everything was secure with the temporary agency and that I was scheduled to start work in the morning. He asked me what was the address to the Statesville Avenue shelter, and that he would stop by there in the evening with the supplies that I needed to begin work in the morning. I thanked him and hung out with JoAnn until it was time for me to check into the shelter. She was kind enough to treat me and herself to something to eat. I told her that I owe her a great deal of gratitude for helping me get that position. She told me that she was going there to see about getting a position like that, but after the team at the temporary agency saw her resume, which had been restricted by Mr. Cochran, they inquired about her doing the payroll for them. When the staff asked her about finding laborers to do the work at the VA, the first people who came to mind were the guys in the class who were living in the shelter. After the running between the temporary agency, Charlotte Area Fund, their doctor's office back to the temporary agency and the Charlotte Area Fund, it was only time to get a quick bite and head into the shelter. It's amazing how time flies when you're keeping yourself occupied. I actually enjoyed the fact that doing this running around was actually good for my spirits.

I was dropped off at the shelter and made it back in time for the dinner break. I informed the front desk staff that my instructor from the Charlotte Area fund was going to be coming by the shelter to drop of some clothing for me so that I could start working at the VA in the morning. I needed to get them from him so that was prepared to work. I had to make sure that my case manager was informed of my status changing from being unemployed to working through a temporary service. Hope was the name of my case worker, and during the time that she was assigned to me, I found out that she was from the low country area of South Carolina. I would always tease her that we were family because I had some relatives from the same area as she was raised. I had to meet with my case manager once a month and we would discuss on the progress of my job searches and worked together on an exit plan to get out of the shelter once I became fully employed. When I met with her during the dinner hour, she was happy to hear that I was working. Even though it wasn't in my field of study, we both were happy with the accomplishment. She was informed and documented my progress for the record. About a half hour after dinner was served and the before it was time for the staff to alert the residents for their next smoke break, Mr. Cochran arrived with my work supplies. I let the staff know that my instructor had arrived and could I retrieve them. They allowed me to go out to his car to do so.

After getting them, I got my shower in, and I wanted to crash to my bed for the night. Normally, I don't request a wakeup call, but I wasn't going to take any chances of missing out on an opportunity to make this kind of money so I signed my name on the wakeup call list. The staff would come into the dorm and go to the bed assigned that requested to have a staff member wake the person up. I went to bed early that evening before nine thirty, and I never had a problem sleeping through snoring or loud noises. Even when I was a non-traditional student at Allen University, when I moved into the dorm, people would be playing their music loud into the early morning hours during the first month of school. I never let that noise distract me even back then. I learned how to tune it out. Good thing for me that I did, because when the semester was over, it was the only time

I accomplished reaching the president's list. Getting up I had that same kind of discipline to the point that I never really cared to hear the ringing or buzzing of an alarm clock. I probably was in my late twenties when I told myself that I would not use an alarm clock to wake myself up. I now have a system of checking the time whenever my biological clock tells me to go to the bathroom at night to check the time. After the first time I do that in the evening, I can never sleep hard unless I don't have to work the next day. Being at the shelters most of the time, you can have a wakeup call between the hour of five or six o'clock morning, times that you have to be out of your beds, eat a breakfast if you desire to do so, and be on your way out into the world.

I woke up the next morning at four o'clock. The time that I requested for the staff to wake me up was a half hour later. Even if they woke me up at four thirty, that allowed for plenty of time to get to the agency, which was a half a mile away from the shelter. The agency was only a little less than a mile from the shelter on Statesville Avenue where I had to walk over the I-85 bridge to get there. When I arrived there, it was packed with guys from the north side of town who had been regulars that had been going out on work tickets from months, probably even years. Most of the jobs that they were being sent out on the pay scale probably ranged from nine to twelve fifty an hour. The agency provided first-time workers with hard hat, fluorescent safety vest, goggles, gloves, transportation to and from the jobsite, and if you were fortunate enough to have your own transportation the other people who you transported to the jobsite would have six twenty-five added to their pay for the transportation. The agency was good, because if you wanted to, you could set it up where you could get paid for a completed day of work on that evening. You were issued a check card and given the option of collecting your pay that evening or at the end of the week. Like most of my colleagues, I chose to have some cash on hand just in case I needed it.

Everyone was waiting in the parking lot area of the agency, waiting to hear their name to be called for their work assignments and to receive their tickets. There was a storage facility that housed three picnic tables, two vending machines, one television, and a commode.

Being that this assignment was happening during the last week of the coldest month of the year, not too many people were hanging outside of the facility to smoke their cigarettes. The woman who was giving out the assignments started calling out the names of the individuals about six forty-five. My friend JoAnn arrived just before the names were being called, and shortly after the manager called the names, I heard her say mine. On the first day, there were six who rode in the company van, but there wasn't enough room for everyone to fit. The driver informed her that if someone had a car to take the other four people that he would need to do so. The manager got on the speaker, asking the people from the group if there was anyone who had a car that could take the rest of the members to work. One individual told her that he could do it so the manager authorize him to take the people and that he would be compensated for the gas when he got paid that evening.

I got into the work van that was taking the men to the site of the VA hospital, and five of them got into a car, including the driver who was taking them there. The driver of the work van asked the other driver who was taking the guys over if he knew where the site was. The other guy told him yeah, and that he'd be over there. Three of the other guys who were riding with the other driver must have been tight with him, and the other guy who was in the vehicle with them was like me, very green. The vehicle that I was in arrived there before the time we were told. Traffic was good going to the worksite, and there weren't any reports on the radio that there were any delays on I-85 or I-77. Once the workers got there, we were instructed by a foreman to go into a trailer to have a seat. I sat down, wondering what was going to be the next step. It was about a half hour later before the other workers met with the foreman. He had a list of names of people whose name he was calling out. All the guys were listed on the same ticket, but the irony of that was that the ticket wasn't there. It was still in the other car that the man who was driving the other employees hadn't arrived yet.

The foreman returned and still the other workers that left when we left the temp agency hadn't arrived. It was about ten minutes after the initial time that the foreman was inquiring as to who was there and who wasn't that the rest of the workers arrived. There was a complication after they arrived to the jobsite, but it wasn't because they were late. It was something that wasn't quite contractually correct between the agency and the construction contractors who hired us as employees to work there. The contractors had the workers look at a safety video and give instructions for being safe at the jobsite. Once we looked at the video, work didn't start after that until the contractors and the agency got into an agreement. Once we did start work, it was probably the hardest, most physically demanding position that I've ever worked—taking the leftover material out of the area from where the construction crew was working and disposing of the trash and recycling other materials that can be used again in another area of the building. After two hours of working, I found out that I had muscle that I never used before. I was starting to feel sore, and when lunchtime came, I was more than ready to take the break.

When lunch happened, there weren't any local restaurants or fast-food stores to get something to eat from. One of the guys with a car would go on the lunch run. He'd take your order and bring it back to you. I was blessed enough to have five dollars in my pocket to get three cheeseburgers from the dollar menu at McDonald's and an orange Hi-C with light ice. The one thing that I was grateful for was that the construction company supplies the workers with plenty of water. In order to perform a large-scale construction project, it's almost mandatory that you drink several times during the day so that you don't get dehydrated. Even if the weather was quite cold working in the elements, you still have the possibility of getting dehydrated. The guy who was riding with the crew members who came in late came over to me after the order was given to the gopher to talk to me. I asked him how was he doing, and he told me that he was doing all right and that he didn't think that he was going to come back to work on this particular job ticket. He told me that the reason was because he was riding in the car that was late. I told him not to worry about that. It wasn't his fault because they arrived late. I was thinking that he didn't have to sacrifice a good-paying job that allowed you to make fourteen dollars an hour. I was about to tell him that he could ask to catch a ride in the company van with me, but just before I was to let him know that, he explained to me that it wasn't a legitimate reason for the other driver to be late. I asked him why, and he told me that the rider and the other guys who were riding with him made a stop to get some weed. Not only did they pick some up, but got high before they reached the job. That left the guy uncomfortable, and he was ready to leave the job after that night. I made the recommendation of telling him to request to ride in the van and let the general manager of the temp agency know that he wanted to do that.

After lunch break was over, two of the guys who were riding with him decided that this kind of work wasn't worth getting a high-pay scale for, even if the scale was higher than anything that either one had worked for before. Another hour another person had left before the job was over, but the rest of us had toughened it out and completed the day. At the end of the day, the work van came to pick us up and took us back to the agency where we could submit the day's work ticket. Once the ticket was submitted to JoAnn, she would enter the information of the workers into the computer system and it would calculate the hours, taxes, and the deductions so that the workers could receive their payment that same evening once the figures were entered into the system. When our group ticket was given to her, the guys who left the work site were already there at the agency waiting to receive their pay. When our group work ticket was completed, JoAnn started calling out the names of the people who were working at the jobsite. Once everyone who completed out the day received their payment with their paystubs and new employees received their check cards, we were free to leave. The only people who didn't receive their pay stubs were the people who arrived late in the other car. The only person in the other car who did receive his pay stub was the guy who told me during the lunch break that he was thinking about quitting. The other driver and the four other people from the other vehicle didn't receive theirs. Even the other person who left early that didn't ride in the other car received his pay.

They asked JoAnn why weren't they able to receive their pay. She told them that she was instructed by the general manager that they have to see her in the morning before they could be paid. This act infuriated those men who wanted to get paid, and they were inconsolable to the point that JoAnn had asked them to leave or that the police would be called in. This wasn't a good scene in the twilight of nightfall. The place where the agency was was in between a U-Haul storage/rental and a gas station. It was a house that was converted into an office, where the workers would congregate in the rear of the house. Behind the rear of the house was the storage place where they would meet to wait to be called for the assignments in the morning and, in the evenings, to receive their pay stubs for the work that was completed for the day. During the dawn and twilight hours, the lighting in the rear wasn't very good, so if something violent that happened, it would've been the ideal place for an incident to occur. It was obvious to me that the guy who wanted to quit that was riding in the same car with them dropped a dime to the management that those brothers made a drug run before going to the job site. Good thing for him that his wife was waiting for him in the car when he got his pay stub and he jetted home. I could only imagine what could've happened to him if he had stuck around when those brothers didn't get their pay. Not sure of what was going to happen, but that was one of the few times since being homeless that I was scared of someone pulling out a firearm and getting trigger happy. Fortunately for me, there wasn't a need for JoAnn to call the cops, and they left disgruntled and unpaid for the evening.

The next morning, the general manager came into the waiting room where the employees gathered. She met with everyone who was getting ready to go out and asked some questions to the group. "How many of you are working for eight fifty an hour?" The majority of the room said they were. Then her next question was "How many of you would want to do a job that was paying fourteen dollars an hour?" And everyone said that they would. Then she told the group, "I had a job yesterday that I sent some people out that was paying fourteen dollars an hour. The driver who I sent out was late to the job, and he and his buddies decided to make a drug run just before going to the job site. "How many of you would make a drug run before taking a job that's going to pay you fourteen dollars an hour?" The guys and women in the room were calling the ones who did that act everything from stupid to jackasses. They made sure that they didn't call them a child of God. The general manager told them that she's going to replace the four people who didn't get paid from the job, and if she found out that they were doing any drugs, they wouldn't be able to work for that agency again.

It became obvious to the workers when they noticed the person who was riding in the car with the other people was there, and not the ones who were suspended from the job weren't on the premises. These guys who got suspended from the job and walked off had been with the agency for a good spell. So when they noticed that they weren't there and that the other person who told me that he wanted to quit was there, it became obvious to most that he was the one who dropped the dime on them. I was more scared for him at this point, after the general manager told the group that the driver and the people in the car made a drug run prior to going to the jobsite. I wasn't in the same vehicle as they were, so I didn't know if he engaged with them in getting high or what. I only knew once the general manager made that announcement, all the eyes of the employees were scanning the room. The other workers wanted to see who went out on the job with that driver. Some of their eyes started to stare at me, but I wasn't worried for myself because their stares were brief. Once they figured out who it was that dropped the dime to the general manager, the same stares that were looking at me later became whispers about the man who wanted to quit less than twenty-four hours earlier. After the announcement was made, the work day resumed with the manager calling out the names of the workers who needed to be assigned to the job site. What was really a crappy deal was that the general manager left the responsibility of getting the ticket signed from the construction site to the stool pigeon.

Since the incident, the agency was only assigned to send out the workers to that site to finish out the rest of the week. Originally this was supposed to be a four- to six-month assignment. The rest of the week was fine by me, because my body was as sore as it was when I used to have to go through conditioning drills like it was for basketball or football practices. I wasn't totally upset when the assignment ended, but I was kind of relieved because of the soreness that I had experienced. The best part about that was that I had a lot more money in my pocket than I did before. I had slightly less than three hundred dollars for working three days. This allowed me to get the kind of stuff that I needed. I didn't have to worry or bother another about bumming a cigarette and I could go to my church on Sunday and put something into the collection plate to pay on my tithes. It was one of the rare occasions that I felt somewhat normal even though I was still confined to living in the shelter. I was still working through the agency whenever there was an assignment.

I would catch the work van to the assignment that was out of town or in the county, and it would come to pick me up. There were only a couple other assignment that I worked for the agency, but they were in the afternoon and let me come back into the agency before eight in the evening. In order for me to do these assignments, I had to go through my caseworker, Hope, to get approval. That wasn't going to be an easy thing to do. All residents at the shelter were recently asked and required to check into the shelter no later than seven. Unless you were working a regular full- or part-time night job that wasn't involved through a temporary agency, then you too were also required to abide by this rule. This was a new rule that was recently instituted by the director Pam. I explained to Hope that I've been reassigned to a different job site and that it would require me to come into the shelter by eight. She told me that Pam and the board of directors said that working through a temporary agency wouldn't be looked at as a plan of action to get out of the shelter. She was good and understood that for many of the residents who were working through a temporary agency that this was their only way of making it out of the shelter. She didn't have a problem approving me to working as long as I was in by eight thirty. I was able to make it there at that time, because I explained to JoAnn that the authorities at the shelter gave me that ultimatum. JoAnn made sure that I was accommodated and went out of her way to see that I was at the shelter at the time I needed to be.

I worked in the afternoons during the next couple of weeks in Gastonia, North Carolina, at a local Rent Way store. The pay wasn't great as the previous job, but still it was pay that kept some change in my pockets. It was in the afternoon from one until seven thirty. I was still able to attend my job readiness training sessions at the Charlotte Area Fund. This meant that I was going to be able to finish the training that was required for me to receive the stipend for the course completion, and the assistance that I was seeking from the Charlotte Area Fund and the Charlotte Works agency for the internship or apprenticeship programs. Once the class was over in the mornings, I had to go into Superman mode. I would carry a change of clothes with me to use the restroom at the Charlotte works agency, change to do the job that was in Gastonia, do whatever needed to be done at the store, get picked up from there by JoAnn, and return to the shelter before eight thirty. I was feeling a little exhausted, but the good thing about that was that I was feeling like I was doing something that was working in my benefit for once. I could go down the street when I was working in Gastonia during my break and get a burger without using my food stamps to buy a frozen one that I had to use a microwave before I ate it, or stop at KFC to get a three-piece meal.

There are certain things that I've learned how to respect after becoming homeless. For instance, when I would go down the food line of the shelters to receive my evening dinner. I wouldn't eat anything that was put on my plate once the volunteers asked me if I wanted it. If I accepted it, I made sure that it was going to be eaten by me. It reminded me when I was a child and when my grandma Essie would come over in the mornings to prepare the food for the family since both Mom and Dad were working in the school system of Newark, New Jersey. She would always have dessert for us if we ate everything on our plates. If we didn't, she would say that "there are people in the world who would be glad to get what we don't want to eat." Being in this situation has humbled me and respect whatever I had was going to be devoured by me. I also learned to listen twice as much as I talked. Some things are worth listening to. Another example, if you listen for the understanding of what people are saying, you can receive as some good and bad information. Everything you hear out of other people's mouths isn't the gospel, but according to them it is. As a kid, I wasn't the kind of person who respected the authority figure. I respected the elders in my family, but when it came to school as a teenager, that wasn't always the case. As a freshman at Clifford J.

Scott High School in East Orange, I made the freshman basketball team. I didn't like going to Spanish class so I started cutting it. We had an away game one day, and unfortunately, my Spanish teacher saw me in the hallway and asked me if I was coming into her class today. I really had no plans of attending her class, but I told her that I had to tell the coach that I couldn't go to the game and I'd be right back to attend the session. Instead I went to meet with the coach and the rest of the team and went to play in the game anyway. The next night, my teacher called the house and spoke to my mother about the situation. Mom, being a teacher herself, hit the roof. She didn't tear me up like I thought that she would, but she kicked me off the team. Living in the shelter made me think about things like that in my life. I started questioning myself thinking what if, should have, would have, could have. When I was finally finished doing the soul searching, it was telling me that I couldn't look back. There's never been a person who had a time machine who went back and changed the destiny of their future. This wasn't a time to look back but to move forward.

When the assignment ended in Gastonia, it was time to finish up the classes for the job readiness certification. During the last week of the classes, Mr. Cochran had the trainees' fine-tuning their resumes, and the other part of the classes we were meeting with the people from Charlotte Works, nutritionist, financial planners, and bankers from credit unions and Wells Fargo who assist the group of trainees to open up checking accounts. By the time we finished our training, the staff at Charlotte Works made a luncheon for the group as part of a graduation ceremony. It was an intimate setting, and it was good that everyone enjoyed each other's company not just the trainees, but the staff as well finally let our hair down to chill without the concern of trying to perfect the skills that were taught to us. Most of the people I trained with, including JoAnn, had to come back to receive their stipends and meet with the staff members of the Charlotte Area Fund that following Monday. Other class members had to come back to meet with the people from the Charlotte Works agency. I had three days that I had to make up before I could receive my certificate and stipend. The students who were very computer literate were asked to comeback to take a class in Microsoft excel on working with spreadsheets. Students who lacked the computer literacy skills were asked to take the basic computer operations and word processing class. Some declined, but most of them had accepted me included.

In the interim, I would attend this class during the day, but the assignments that I was once getting weren't being given to me. Once again I had to rely on my wit and resources to look for a job. I remember once I went to a job fair that was held at the Urban League of the Central Carolinas in town. It was in town and within walking distance from the Charlotte Area Fund. I decided to try my luck to see if they had some openings there. Unfortunately, they didn't have any, but fortunately for me, I must've made a good impression with the job developer there, Mrs. Denise Moses. While I was there I happened to run into her, and I'd inquired about doing some volunteer work there. I reminded her that I worked at two other affiliates prior to coming to Charlotte. She told me to fill out the application, and she would introduce me to someone who was in charge of the volunteers. I was introduced to Jane Norman who was in charge of scheduling the volunteers for the volunteers for the job readiness classes. We met and spoke at length about what the agency was doing with their trainees to prepare them with their personal job searches. They had three different training sessions going on at the same time. There was a class for people who could do heating and air conditioning HVAC maintenance and repairs, another for fiber optic installation for high-speed cable and internet service and the on that I was interested in was the computer operations and job readiness training. I explained to Jane that I was interested in helping the trainees with the job readiness classes, because of the previous experiences that I used when I was working with the first affiliate of the Urban League that I was employed with in Newark, New Jersey. She explained to me that there were only about five to six weeks left. I was ready to accept the challenge.

We agreed to the terms of volunteering, and I was given a tour of the facility. I witnessed students and trainees receiving instructions from the professionals who were giving them the guidance in the

LEROY F. BENNETT

GED and job readiness programs class specifically. Once I entered into the job readiness class. They were holding a seminar with some officials from Johnson C. Smith University where some recruiters were talking to the students about admissions into their undergraduate program. Once they were doing that Jane introduced me to the classroom instructor for the program Mrs. Ella Scarborough.

Since I was new to the area I didn't have any idea who was as far as the right people to try to rub elbows with. Little to my own knowledge did I realize just how well connected that I was just about to become. Ella B. Scarborough is a Mecklenburg County Commissioner who served as one of the three County Commissioners elected At-Large to serve the Mecklenburg County community.

Commissioner Scarborough chairs the Economic Development Committee to encourage economic growth and prosperity for all people and businesses in the county. Because of her tireless efforts and results for the people of Mecklenburg County, in 2015. Beyond her duties as an elected official, Commissioner Scarborough is a former national board chair of the Election Committee; president of the North Carolina League of Municipalities; national chair of the Public Utilities Librarians; president of the Metrolina Librarians' Association; president of the Black Women's Caucus of Charlotte Mecklenburg legendary "Blackberry Bunch" to fund community programs and many more civil organizations. Prior to becoming a county commissioner Mrs. Scarborough she is a former five-term elected member of the Charlotte City-Council (three-terms in the district, two-terms at large) and in 2001, she won the Democratic Party's nomination as the mayoral candidate for the City of Charlotte, but lost to the future Governor of North Carolina Pat McCrory in the general election. Her name is respected and revered in the circles of the political and business community. She is the voice and advocate for the people of the community that she serves.

I didn't know just how well connected she was until I returned later that afternoon to the Charlotte Area Fund. I had spoken to Brian McCorkle the program director of the training program that I was a trainees there. I informed him that I was doing volunteer work with the Urban League agency, and was inquiring if they would be able to

342

help set me up with the apprentice or internship program with the Urban League. I was informed that they would make every effort to do so. Brian asked me what exactly was that I was doing with them. I informed him that I was assisting the new trainees in their job readiness program as a volunteer assistant, and that I was under the direction of Denise Moses, Jane Norman and Ella Scarborough. He told me that this was a good thing, because if the Charlotte Area Fund or the Charlotte Works agencies weren't able to accommodate me that I was working with people who could help me secure employment.

Not too sure of how things would evolve so I continued to volunteer at the Urban League in the mornings, make my daily vigil to the Charlotte Mecklenburg library and a brief stop at the Charlotte Area Fund just before heading back into the shelter for the evening. Going back there was the reality of doing communal living. Over the past months, there some of the guys staying there looked at me for advice about things that were related to education and employment. A few of them were part of a program provided by the shelter that allowed former inmates and substance abusers to attend job readiness classes for reentry into the workforce. Once they completed the courses, they would move out of the shelter and into a transitional apartment living. Like everything that deals with living in a communal setting there were restrictions that included being back at the facility no later than nine in the evening, no visitation in our apartment by members of the opposite sex, and any drugs that weren't prescribed by your doctor were not allowed along with consumption of alcoholic beverages. The participants would be able to stay there until they were gainfully employed. Once they would gain employment, then have to save up enough money so that their caseworkers would assist them to receive housing subsidies including section eight housing if they qualified for it. The guys who participated in the program would come to me for advice and recommendations mainly about their resumes. Most of the time they would see me in the library when they were finished with their day at the program, and they would ask me to critique their resume. If they agreed with my assessment of their resume they would throw me a few dollars my way to create or edit for them. It wasn't a lot of money, but enough to keep me in cigarettes.

The shelter in Charlotte wasn't as bad as the other places I stayed at in Rowan County, but the traffic was denser there. I could see people who would be there for only one day, and I wouldn't run across their paths again weeks later. The staff there was compassionate more so than the administrators that ran the place. Members of the working staff there who stood out from the others was my caseworker Hope Rivers, Michael Akbar, Vickie Craighead Davis and Randy Tapley. They were the most understanding and compassionate of the staff members who were employed there. Some of the other staff that worked there were friendly, but the one thing that I found disturbing was that the administration would empower women in the position of authority over the men who were living there. Now I'm not a chauvanist or a sexist for that matter, but you have to remember that we're looking at displaced veterans, people who have mental illness and others who suffer with substance abuse. One thing that I never lost sight of is that some of the people that live there suffer from mental illness, and you never know when an individual will go off without a warning. There would be time the director of the shelter that I resided would antagonize the resident guest who stayed there, and didn't appear to be aware of what the consequences of her own action could cause repercussions to her own circumstances.

Another thing that I've done ever since I had my Hotmail account I had signed up for alerts by the *New York Times*. I always had trusted that newspaper as a reputable source of accurate information. One day after hearing about numerous complaints about the treatment of the resident guest mainly by the Director Pam, I was reading an email alert from the *Times* about a homeless shelter director who was working out of a facility in the Bronx, New York. A former resident of a Bronx homeless shelter returned there Monday night, abducted its director, forced her to undress in her car, chased her as she tried to flee and then shot her in the street, killing her, police officials said on Tuesday. Witnesses told detectives that the victim, Ana Charle, 36, ran naked in the street from the suspect, West Spruill, 39, who was also naked as he chased her and opened fire."They hear nothing but the shots," a police official, who spoke on the condition of anonymity to discuss a continuing investigation, said of the accounts provided by witnesses, several of whom had dialed 911."It is fairly close range," the official said. "This is as bad a homicide as I've seen."

As Ms. Charle, of Queens, fell to the sidewalk on Bullard Avenue, near East 237th Street, the gunman returned to her car, put his clothes back on and walked away, clutching two bags, police officials said, citing the witnesses' accounts. Protruding from one of those bags was a gun, which the police said officers found when they took Mr. Spruill into custody. Detectives from the 47th Precinct also found three .40-caliber shell casings in the street, the officials said. Ms. Charle had bullet wounds to her temple, cheek and chest, the officials said. She was taken to Montefiore Medical Center, where she was pronounced dead.

Ironically when this story broke it coincidentally occurred on an evening when Pam was conducting a Town Hall meeting. This happens once a month when the administration wants to inform the residents of the shelter that there will be changes in policies for the shelter guest. On this particular meeting Pam had informed the residents at the Statesville Avenue shelter that they were going to do some structural renovations to the facility. Residents were informed that they would have to be eating their dinners on the outside underneath a tent that has been set up for them. Another condition about the renovations to the building meant that the residents would have to take their showers in a portable trailers specially equipped with five small shower stalls, and the administration also provided us with eight porta potties. Needless to say that this news made the natives unhappy. She informed the residents that they would have to make sure that all of their belongings were put into the lockers that were provided by the shelter, and if there was any extra clothing that wasn't in their lockers that they would have to be disposed of the articles of clothing. This had to be done in order to make the accommodations for the residents. Residents were getting rid of really nice barely used clothes that were donated to the shelter residents.

As Pam was about to conclude the town hall meeting she was fielding questions from the residents. One of the resident guests had asked her a question about what was he supposed to do about trying to keep his personal belongings under his bed and if there would be a problem with that. Pam abruptly came out of mouth disrespectfully to the man telling him that he doesn't matter, because the only thing he does is smoke weed all day every day in the parking lot of the North Tryon Street facility. Most of the guys at the meeting were laughing at the big time diss that she had just done to the brother, but when I heard that I was appalled to hear this come from someone in the management of the Men's Shelter of Charlotte. It wasn't fair of her to say that to anyone in that kind of forum in front of the other men who stayed there. Now if that person were to have came out and told her something about her past about being a homeless crack addict, and doing tricks to try to get her Jones on I'd be willing to bet you that he would've been dismissed from the shelter for insulting her about her personal past. Honestly I would've seen it as being justification on his action, because he didn't come out of his mouth toward her with any disrespect whatsoever. What she did was done out of malice, and an extremely poor way of exercising her authority.

Equally as bad as Pam was the morning shelter aide who was given control to supervise the staff and the men that stayed there was a woman by the name of Frankie. She didn't care for the men who stayed there, whether it was her own colleagues or the residents. Maybe it was due partially to the fact that she was a lesbian who portrayed the role of a Butch. always dressing in sweats or jeans with a sweatshirt. Never depicting any signs of femininity, and wouldn't mind getting to the point talking trash to you like she wanted you to take it to knuckle city if you dare to want to go there with her. Frankie had less respect for the men who stayed there more than Pam. If there was ever any slight infractions of someone breaking the rules, Frankie relished in her role of being the enforcer of the rules. There were a couple of times that some of the guys who stayed there who had grown up in the same neighborhood as her where they were wrong for breaking the rules for something that wasn't major, but she was the kind of person who wanted to talk down to you because of the circumstance that you were in. Frankie rarely bothered to give you a warning if you did break a rule. She figured that once you signed the contract on the back of the rule book that you were given by the shelter, your ignorance of those rules was not an excuse. She made it perfectly clear that her action for disciplining were going to be to the letter, severe and swift.

Once I saw that article, I made a point of bringing it to the attention of one of the shelter aides. It was ironic that this article about the shelter director came to be during the same week that the incident of our own shelter director was abusing her power over the men who were staying there. I asked one of the employees there if they had heard of an incident that had occurred in New York. They didn't hear of anything about it until I showed them a printout of the article. It was something that the support staff who worked there found to be disturbing also. I believe that they may have found it to be disturbing because if a regular shelter guest would take a chance to murder the top banana who was in charge of conducting the daily business of the shelter it could've been open season on the other staff members with little to no remorse. It was likely not to happen, but the possibility was there. After showing the article to the staff members the rumblings of discontent continued among the residents. I already knew that it stemmed from their discontentment with the constant changes, and the lack of not being able to secure long-term employment. The fact that they were being talked down to as if they were children by the management team of the shelter didn't make things any better. One of the guys were talking about how Pam show little if any sensitivity towards the people who stayed there. When he said that I took him to the side to show him the article from the *New York Times*. Once he read the article he echoed the same sentiments as the majority of the residents. I'm not a person who would discriminate another one because of their age, color, gender or sexual preference. If they're capable, competent and qualified to do the job than they should be there. Putting a female especially one who is totally insensitive in the position that they've put Pam in was a mistake that I believe in the long run will have big legal ramifications.

The one good thing that came out of the town hall meeting was that there was a two-week period to prepare ourselves for this transition. In the mornings Frankie was on her personal witch hunt to find people who were breaking the rules. In this process several people who were caught including myself were given a night out for not getting rid of the excess clothing that couldn't fit into their lockers. I was one of those people who was caught having the clothing that wasn't in my lockers. Many of the items that I wear are designer name brand items. I don't wear them to attempted to look like I'm part of a fashion show, but I haven't given up on my ambitions to return to working in the human services and non-profit field of helping people. Attire has always been important to my outlook and I always wanted to be prepared to look my best just in case I need to be somewhere that required me to look important. I tried to explain to Frankie that the jobs that I was applying for required me to look as close to professional as possible. I tried to explain to the management staff that dressing professionally would be to my advantage if I were to secure a career in the human services, or nonprofit field. They didn't want to consider that and decided to give me the night out. If I were to try to come back the next evening with my stuff in tow, I would've been asked to leave the shelter for a longer extended period.

Since I didn't have many options where to put away my clothes, I asked a high school friend of mine who was living in Charlotte. I found myself in the predicament that I needed someplace to stay for the night, and also to put my clothing articles in storage. I asked her if she would be able to help me store away some of my things in her garage. Like the angel that she has always been, she's blessed me and allowed me to keep my excess clothes there at her place, get a hot shower and to lay my head there for the evening.

Rochelle is a good friend of mine who used to sing on the Glee Club at Clifford J. Scott high school. Prior to moving to North Carolina some five years earlier, we both were on the committee for our high school class reunion. When I went to the thirtieth reunion there she was the person who sang the solo number of our class Alma Mater song at the reunion dinner. When I first moved to Charlotte we reconnected. I met with her for brunch at a diner a couple of miles down the road from the Statesville Avenue shelter. She was telling me of her plans for starting a nonprofit organization for youths ages seven to twenty-one in the Charlotte Area. She had a successful program when she lived up in Jersey called Positive Parents, and she wanted to do something similar here in Charlotte. The name of the program that she was wanting to do here would be called Empowering the Youth. The goal the program is to promote academics, non-conventional sports, entrepreneurship, and leadership. Rochelle was telling me that she wanted my assistance in developing part of the arts enrichment component of her program. I told her that I'd be happy to do whatever I could to help. She's saw some of the work that I've done through the pictures of previous productions that were posted on my Updaway Productions facebook page.

At that brunch with us was her colleague another woman who worked in the Charlotte Mecklenburg School System named Miss Jessie, and Rochelle's daughter Kaitlyn with her friend. I was asked if I would be willing to write and direct a play about the challenges that a seasoned teacher faces when they've been assigned as a mentor to a fresh college graduate who is in the classroom as a first year teacher. I also took the perspective of some teenagers as how the students viewpoint to include it into the storyline, so that it would have just the right amount of balance. When I finished writing the script for her I submitted a copy to her for viewing, and we agreed on the title for the script and named it "Teacher/Teacher."

After being a night in her house, I spent the better part of the day with her until the midafternoon. I asked her if I could be dropped off at the Statesville Avenue shelter, and granted my wish and dropped me off. I waited with the rest of the residents until the staff started to admit us in for the evening. The staff was told that if I could came back that I could be admitted only if all of my personals were able to fit into the locker. I bought back only the essentials that I needed. For a change it was good to be back into the shelter without being out on the streets. There was about a week before the renovations to the facility were about to take place, so I knew that I wanted to make sure that I had my bed to go to when I returned from being downtown all day. Being back there was a reminder that

I was grateful to have someplace to lay my head comfortably in the evenings. During my days of being at the Urban League, I would assist the trainees with their job readiness preparations in the morning. When the afternoon followed after they had completed their training I would use their computers to work on updating my own resume, fine-tune my cover letter, and do my daily pilgrimage to the Mecklenburg County Library.

Just before the trainees were about to complete their coursework, there was a job fair that was being held at the Masonic Temple where local banks, corporations, employment and nonprofit agencies were screening qualified candidates to work for them. The instructor of the class Mrs. Scarborough was getting the trainees putting on the finishing touches on their resumes so that they could attend the job fair. Just before the end of the daily sessions Mrs. Moses came to give the trainees the fine pointers of making a good first impression when meeting with the employers. Many of them were knew what was expected of them when they had to prepare themselves for the job fair. They knew that they had to be appropriately dress in business attire and knew that they had to give a pretty good sales pitch in order for the employers to be interested in them. When the trainees left I had copies of my resume in a folder and place them in my computer bag.

The next morning I got up early and naturally skipped breakfast. I took out my best suit that I was able to keep into the locker so that I could press it off with the iron. I wanted to make sure the trainees who I was assisting weren't going to be the only ones that needed to look sharp for their interviews. I wanted to look sharp enough that if anyone who was looking too hard, that I would cut their eyeballs. I saw a couple of the trainees arrive shortly thereafter. I arrived early at the Masonic Temple so that I could be prepared to start the networking and interviewing process. While waiting for the doors to open I saw that Mrs. Moses from the Urban League had arrived to set up a table that had been designated for them. Since I was a volunteer with the agency I was asked to assist her with the display materials and literature out for the people who would stop by their table for information. After completing the setup of the table for the Urban League, Mrs. Moses asked me if I wouldn't mind helping by giving out the literature and explaining about the agency and the services that they provide. I was more than ready to oblige to her request. Doing this favor for her wasn't hard because of the previous experiences that I had when I was employed at the other two Urban League affiliates. In fact for me it was a labor of love.

Much to my own surprise, when I worked the table for the Urban League, there were members of the Charlotte Area Fund who had a table set up for them also. I believed that they were more surprised to see me than I was to see them. When Mrs. Moses stepped away from the table people were coming there wanting to know about the training programs and other services that the League provided. Some of the employees from the Charlotte Area Fund stood just behind the people who I had the opportunity to explain about these services and were somewhat amazed that it appeared so natural for me to market the Urban League. The day was going better than I expected, because when I began I had their intentions of being another person who was there to network with the employers looking for a job with them. The next thing that I knew was that I was behind the table of one of the vendors at the job fair. Not to mention that it included lunch for the vendors who came to the job fair.

By the end of the day was able to meet with other vendors who appeared interested in my skills who wanted me to interview with them, and interview for the possibility of working for them. Days like that come few and far in between, but I'm thankful for them because it allows me to know that there is still hope for a middle-aged man who hasn't worked for a very extended time. Going back into the shelter at the end of the day, but I was more hopeful than I have been in a very long time. I made it a point of speaking to my counselor to let her know about the progress that I was trying to accomplish. Speaking with Hope was one of the few bright spots about living at the shelter. If there was truly anyone who was an advocate for the residents here, it was her. We discussed about what options I had for employment and always talked about an exit plan for leaving the shelter. It was at this time that I had my mind made up that if things weren't going to change that I was going to have to leave Charlotte and take my aunt up on her offer of moving to the Atlanta area. I wasn't certain if things were going to be the same way that they've been in the past, but I knew that I couldn't continue to allow this recurring cycle to continue. Someone told me that the definition of insanity is doing things the same way, and expecting different results. I wasn't going to continue to go insane by not being able to support myself by continuing to do things the same way over and over again.

Once the job fair was over, I had went on to the interviews with the vendors who were at the job fair things didn't seem to change much. I had interviews for another nonprofit agency for a job recruiters position, one with a call center and another with the Charlotte works agency that was trying to assist in placing me with a company. All of the interviewers liked what I was saying when I spoke, and I liked what they were saying but none of them were telling me the two words that I really wanted to hear the most by having one of them telling me that I'm hired. After the classes for the trainees had ended, I continued to go to the Urban League in Charlotte. There were still some of the trainees who were coming to the computer center to fine tune their resumes and cover letter who weren't placed into jobs. I was asked to help with another training class for people who needed to learn basic computer and word processing skill. Like the previous class I would continue to give my assistance to them. I figure that doing this would display that I had a value as a potential employee with the agency.

After a couple of week assisting in the creation of a curriculum that would engaged the trainees of the basic computer class, I was asking Jane if there was any way that I would be able to come onboard as an employee of the Urban League. Like the previous results, my request since I move to North Carolina, becoming an employee of the Urban League was one of the things that wasn't going to happen. That's when I knew the reality of me being able to work and live in the city of Charlotte wasn't possible. Unless I was biologically related to someone who was in the hiring authority, I knew that my chances of earning a living here wasn't going to happen. When I realized that this wasn't going to happen, my options of living in the city of Charlotte were coming to an end. How many hoops can you jump

WELCOME TO THE HOTEL CALIFORNIA

through, how many hurdles can you jump and how long will it take before people will realize that they have a lump of that's destined to become a diamond.

Even though I may have been disgusted by the Urban League's decision not to seriously consider me for a position, I didn't let that deter me from continuing looking for a position with someone that would take my skills and abilities seriously. I went back to the computer lab to get back onto my journey, and when I got settled looking for a different opportunity, I saw a position with the place that I've been housed at with the Men's Shelter of Charlotte. They posted a position for an employment specialist. I was thinking that this would've been the perfect opportunity for me to work in my field of study that I've received my degree in. I felt as if I fit the requirements that they were asking for. They were asking for a Bachelor's degree in social work, psychology, counseling or a related field and a minimum of two years' experience as a general case manager, employment case manager, or social worker; or any equivalent combination of education training and experience. The position didn't require transporting the residents to and from their jobsite, and it was doing something that I was very familiar with from my days of working at the other Urban League affiliates. I was feeling very positive that this would be the best opportunity for me to make an impact on the lives of my fellow homeless brethren. Once again, I contacted my friend and classmate Rochelle. I told her about the job opening and asked her if it were possible if I could reside at her place for a month if I got hired for the position. She agreed to let me do that if it came through.

When I returned to the shelter, I spoke with two of the shelter aides, Akbar and Michelle, who was the evening supervisor for the staff. Akbar would hold the Narcotics and Alcoholic Anonymous classes for the resident who deal with substance abuse. He took a minute to review my resume and cross-referenced it with the job description and qualifications. He thought that I was a good candidate for the position. The next staff person who I talked to about applying for the job was the evening shift supervisor, Michelle. She also agreed that my credentials were good, but she informed me that because I was a resident that I wouldn't qualify to work there. I placed my application with the shelter with the hopes that I would be an employee of the Men's Shelter of Charlotte. After dinner I went to see Hope to inform her about me applying for the job, and she thought that I should've been considered as a viable candidate for the job.

Hope was a good and fair case manager. Whenever I visited her, she was always inquired what steps I was taking to exit from the shelter, what appointments I was doing for job interviews, and really had a genuine concerned about the welfare of her clients. A good portion of her clients were young. So many of the younger clients that had to see her would attempt to try to pull the wool over her eyes, saying that they needed her help. They were going in there with an ulterior motive to spend a little extra time because she was a peer to their eyes more than a case manager. We were both hopeful that the hiring authorities would look at the content of the experience and not the fact that I had to resort to live in the shelter, which I was praying would be temporary. From her understanding, I believed that she thought that they were going to fill the position pretty quickly. I believed it also, because from the day that I filled out the application, I only had six days to submit it until the deadline.

As the time was passed, I would continue to go to my usual digs. More than anything, my stomach stayed in knots. I found myself losing sleep and because of the worry I was losing weight. I can't enjoy eating on a nervous stomach. Mentally, I wondered how I am holding up. As the days got closer to the application deadline, my stomach was like a pot of boiling water. By the time the deadline arrived that Friday, I was bundles of nerves, wound up like a tight spring that was being suppressed by tighter rubber band. If something were to have upset me, I would have exploded, like someone cutting the rubber band from the spring. Following the week of being nervous the weekend, I tried to find another avenue to calm me down. It was a couple of weeks later since I've place my application with the shelter before I found out that they had hired another person. Once I found out that they hired someone else, I took this as an act of discrimination. I went to the local Equal Employment Opportunity Commission to file a claim against the shelter. Just like

I would've done with a job interview, I made sure that I've dotted all the I's and crossed the T's by having all the proper paperwork together and available for the people at the EEOC. I was told that it would take several weeks for them to do an investigation and that I would be informed of the results. If the commission found that there were any improprieties, I would be informed about it and there would be a hearing.

At this point I was so frustrated with my experience of living in North Carolina that I had to make another life-changing choice. I knew that I didn't have any other choice but to take a minute and to look at what would be the best options for me. When it came down to looking at the facts, moving to Atlanta was the only logical choice. I called my aunt to see if her offer was still opened to me, and she told me that it was. I would have to make arrangements with my aunt and let my case manager, Hope, at the shelter know that I was going to need the assistance of the shelter to provide transportation to get to Atlanta. When I asked my aunt if her offer was still opened, she confirmed that it was, and that I would be staying with her daughter Olivia and her family.

When I told Hope about moving in with my family, she was truly happy for me, but I could hear the disappointment in her voice. Hope was one of the few people who believed in my skills, abilities, and experiences. She was disappointed by the fact that when I had applied for a position for the shelter to become a colleague, the hiring authorities had declined me. The reason that was given was that I was a resident guest and that had disqualified me from becoming a member of the staff. She expressed sympathy of my disappointment that the director of human resources and their board of directors turned me down on the basis of my living status, which was strictly biased. I made a point of telling her that I have made arrangements with my high school classmate to move in with her if I were to become employed. When my aunt told me that I was going to be living with my cousin Olivia, I would have to give Hope the contact number for her to talk with her and verify that I would be living with her family.

I spoke with my cousin and the first thing that she wanted to know was if I was doing okay. Her mother explained the situation to her, and Livie, as the family affectionately calls her, was more than willing to allow me to stay with her. I told her given the circumstances that I was doing well. Livie told me that she had a room for me, and that I would be welcomed to stay there. I told her that my case manager would be calling her to help finalize my travel and confirm that I'll be living with her. I told her that Hope would be giving her a call within the next couple of days. Hope was off on the weekends, and when she returned to work on the following Monday, she acknowledged that she would be available to speak with her that evening when I had to check into the Statesville Avenue facility for the night. With that being done, I had to let the people know who helped me the most that I was living on borrowed time for at least another week. I called my high school classmate Rochelle that I would need to come by her place to get the rest of my things to travel to my new temporary home in Atlanta. She told me that she would get them to me before I leave. I told my other classmate who lived in Charlotte, Michael Young, who had seen me walking several times from the shelter to downtown that I was going to move.

Before I was scheduled to leave, I would get into the word to have my spirit fed. I knew that I needed to keep myself grounded better in my study of the Bible, and because I had another opportunity, I could make one more visit to Grace Memorial Missionary Baptist Church. I was going to make sure that I visited there if I didn't do anything else major. The hardest part of leaving Charlotte was telling the pastor, Lawrence D. Mayes Sr., of Grace Memorial Missionary Baptist Church that I was leaving. Pastor Mayes and his congregation have truly been a blessing from heaven. During many of the times when the church had a fundraising event, they included me. Knowing that I didn't have any money to assist with the efforts, the pastor came out of his own pocket on my behalf to see that I had something to eat or an item that I could have used while I was staying at the shelter. I called him the night before I was going to attend my last service. I explained to him about my situation, and that I really felt like I found a church home for the first time since I left the last one I was with at Second Nazareth Baptist in Columbia, South

Carolina. Pastor Mayes understood and said if I was ever back in the area, I was always welcomed there.

The next day I went to the church to get my spirit fed. It was a great service, and as usual, the house was packed to the point that the ushers had to put folding chairs in the aisle. By the time that the service had ended, the pastor gathered the congregation in front of the pulpit. He turned to me and asked me if I wanted to tell them that I was moving to Atlanta. I didn't want to tell them and was somewhat reluctant to do so. After he asked, I felt obligated to do it since they've been really good to me. I knew that this would be the last time that I would be there to worship and fellowship with them. Before I acknowledged that this would be my last time being with them, I told the congregation that I had to take my glasses off to speak to them. I had to do that for two reasons—one, because if I were to look into their faces, I would be nervous; the other reason was that I didn't want to see anyone who may have been saddened by me leaving. I didn't want to cry, but I did. Leaving there was a bittersweet moment because of the friendships that I'd developed with the members. For the last time, when the service was over, I caught a ride down to the library downtown. It wasn't like the normal times that I spent there. I didn't look at my Facebook or any other social media pages like I normally would do. It was time for me to reflect on the times that I experienced in Charlotte and to try to set some new goals for moving to Atlanta. Taking the walk back from Tryon Street to Statesville Avenue was time for me to reflect on going to the churches in the area, thinking about how so many of them have opened up their doors to feed anyone who is homeless, extending the true love that they've been anointed to do with the spirit of God. I was thinking about how some of them would set up tables on North Tryon Street to feed people who wouldn't eat when the soup kitchens were closed. I was grateful knowing that I was taken care of when I didn't have a meal to eat or a place to stay. Charlotte was a place that I really wanted to try to live and prosper in. Before I would've been able to prosper, I needed to be able to work. Leaving there wasn't easy, because I found out that I made some pretty good association with the people who were exactly like myself.

When I first came to live at the Men's Shelter of Charlotte, I was more protective of myself, my possessions, and my surroundings. I knew that Charlotte was a bigger city than that of the rural surroundings that I had lived in before I moved there. Many of the residents didn't know how to take me and vice versa. When I took the time to allow myself to let them into my comfort zone, my eyes were opened. We were all in the same position trying to make it in this everyday thing that people call life. Trying to get through the daily things for the majority of people who live normal is a job for a homeless person. Things like going to a job and performing the duties of the position, coming home to relax, and having a good meal is something that most people who aren't homeless take for granted. Those who aren't homeless they will never be able to fully understand what the other things that are associated with the circumstances of being homeless.

A couple of days later, Hope called Livie and the process of me getting ready to move was in motion. I didn't know if I would be prosperous in Atlanta, but the one thing that I was looking forward to was the love of my family. My aunt wanted to see that my welfare and safety was secure. I was looking forward to being around family members. This was the first time that I felt a sense of being needed. Livie, Aunt Blonde, Yolanda, and the rest of the family gave me back my sense of dignity. I didn't know what the future held for me as far as employment, but I knew that I was going to take any job that could possibly be opened. Over the five years of being homeless, I have lost my vehicle and license for driving uninsured and admitted myself into a mental health facility twice. Some of my technical computer skills have eroded, because I haven't been working in an office environment to retain or gain any new computer concepts or applications. Still I know that I have to keep the faith of knowing that through everything that God has provided me with everything that I needed to still survive.

Living in the shelter had humbled me. Things that I've taken for granted I've learned to appreciate and be thankful for. Simple things that most people take for granted will be something that I will respect for the rest of my life. One of the main things that my aunt and cousins have given me is an opportunity to reconnect with my family. I knew that if they were going to give me a chance to resurrect my life with the love they have for me, I have to do the same with my own siblings. I'm blessed knowing that besides them, I have a brother who lives in the same vicinity. My relationship with my siblings didn't break down because of what they did, but it was due solely to the choices that I've made in my life during the past five years. I know that I would have to maintain my religious bond with God and, once I arrived in the new place, I would have to find a church home. If it wasn't for the grace and mercy of God providing for me, there's a very good chance that I could've been strung out on some drugs, getting involved with the wrong crowd with the possibility of going to jail or even finding myself in a grave before my granddaughter graduates from high school.

Most of the homeless people who I've encountered during this ordeal aren't homeless because they want to be. Some of them are there because of the dynamics of their circumstances have change dramatically. For myself, I wasn't doing drugs but I allowed my judgment and decision making to become clouded when my mother passed away. While I was homeless, I've been blessed to stay in touch with my granddaughter. She's been the biggest reason why I can't give up. One thing that she's done since I've been in this situation, Shay'lee volunteered to help feed the homeless, and if a homeless person were to ask her for some money, she will give it to them. I had to tell her not to give them money, but ask them if they were hungry. If they were and if she had a couple of dollars that she could spare, I told her to buy them a soda or a sandwich.

The one good thing that I know is that I'm loved and that I've been blessed to have come through this situation safely. Now I'm ready to check out of the Hotel California. In the shelter, there aren't any mirrors on the ceiling, pink champagne on ice. Some people are just visitors there of their own advice. There is a master table were you gather for a feast, eat the meal with a skinny knife, and the food taste like roast beast. One thing to remember when you're heading toward the door, you have to find the places back, to the place you were before. Relax from your nightmare; you are programmed to conceive. You can check out any time you like, and you can always leave. Time for me to hit the road. Check out time has been long overdue.

WORKS CITED

"Liner Notes - Hotel California (The Eagles)." *Liner Notes - Hotel California (The Eagles).* Web. 01 June 2014. <http://www.glennfreyonline.com/eagles/hotelcalifornia/linernotes.htm>.

"Salisbury Listed as No. 5 City with Soaring Poverty, but Some Say Study Doesn't Show Full Picture." *Salisbury Post.* Web. 29 June 2014. <http://www.salisburypost.com/article/20131219/SP01/131219626/>.

"The Rowan Free Press Plan to Lift Salisbury, NC Out of Poverty (Part I)." *Rowan Free Press.* Web. 29 June 2014. <http://rowanfreepress.com/2014/01/25/the-rowan-free-press-plan-to-lift-salisbury-nc-out-of-poverty-part-i/>.

"SBI Investigating Former Salisbury Acting Police Chief." *WBTV 3 News, Weather, Sports, and Traffic for Charlotte, NC.* Web. 01 June 2014. <http://www.wbtv.com/story/12227689/sbi-investigating-former-salisbury-acting-police-chief>.

"Lawsuit Filed against Police Chiefs, Officers." *Salisbury Post.* Web. 13 June 2014. <http://www.salisburypost.com/article/20120914/SP0106/309149954/>.

"Homeless Salisbury Man Charged with Killing Father a Decade Ago in Georgia." *Salisbury Post.*Web. 29 June 2014. <http://www. salisburypost.com/article/20130712/SP01/130719874/>.

"Violent Homicide Suspect Arrested by Task Force." *Violent Homicide Suspect Arrested by Task Force.*Web. 29 June 2014. <http://www. usmarshals.gov/news/chron/2013/071213.htm>.

"US Marshals: Violent Murder Suspect Arrested in Salisbury." *WCNC Wcnc.com.*Web. 29 June 2014. <http://www.wcnc.com/ news/crime/US-Marshals-Violent-murder-suspect-arrested-in-Salisbury-215260351.html>.

"Investigators: It's Unclear Why Parents Didn't Report Girl Missing." *Salisbury Post.* Web. 12 June 2014. <http://www. salisburypost.com/article/20130807/SP01/130809801/0/ SEARCH&slId=6>.

"Polygraph Expert: Sandy Parsons 'strongly Deceptive'." *Salisbury Post.*Web. 12 June 2014. <http://www.salisburypost.com/ article/20130821/SP01/130829933/0/SEARCH&slId=11>.

Mendell, Mark J., Anna G. Mirer, Kerry Cheung, My Tong, and JeroenDouwes. "Abstract." National Center for Biotechnology Information. U.S. National Library of Medicine, 26 Jan. 2011. Web. 14 June 2014. <http://www.ncbi.nlm.nih.gov/pmc/ articles/PMC3114807/>.

Baker, Al. "Former Resident Kills Director of Bronx Homeless Shelter, Police Say." *The New York Times. The New York Times,* 28 Apr. 2015. Web. 03 Sept. 2016.

"Ella B. Scarborough, At-Large." *Ella B. Scarborough, At-Large.* Web. 27 Aug. 2016.

"Home - Ella Scarborough." *Ella Scarborough*. Web. 27 Aug. 2016.

"Empower the Youth - About | Facebook." *Empower the Youth - About | Facebook*. Web. 17 Sept. 2016.

Leroy F. Bennett is a product of the East Orange School District in East Orange, New Jersey, where he graduated from Clifford J. Scott High School. He returned to college as a non-traditional student at Allen University where he was honored as an academic and collegiate all-American basketball player in 1996–97 by the United States Achievement Academy before he transferred to Benedict College. At Benedict College, he received his bachelor of science degree in child and family development and graduated cum laude. Leroy was a one-time long-term substitute and teaching assistant with the Richland County School District One in Columbia, South Carolina. He's also worked at two different Urban League affiliates. The first one was in Newark, New Jersey, and the other in Columbia, South Carolina, and he's also volunteered at a third one in Charlotte, North Carolina. He has also been known to be a basketball historian with a Facebook page dedicated to the American Basketball Association called the ABA Remembered. Leroy is an ardent lover of working with people who have been misplaced, disenfranchised to assist them in becoming self-empowered. Prior to writing this book, little did he suspect that he would become one of the many people who would rely on the services of others and who were in need of social assistance. This is the story of his five-year struggle to empower himself and become self-reliant again. Today he lives in Spartanburg, South Carolina, and is a document management specialist for a major financial institution.

CPSIA information can be obtained
at www.ICGtesting.com
Printed in the USA
LVOW07*0651281217
561067LV00019BA/342/P